Construction Arbitration

THE ADVOCATE'S PRACTICAL GUIDE

Andrew Ness and John Foust
EDITORS

ABA
AMERICAN BAR ASSOCIATION
Forum on Construction Law

Cover design by Sara Wadford/ABA Design

Printed in the United States of America.

27 26 25 24 23   5 4 3 2 1

A catalog record for this book is available from the Library of Congress.

Discounts are available for books ordered in bulk. Special consideration is given to state bars, CLE programs, and other bar-related organizations. Inquire at Book Publishing, ABA Publishing, American Bar Association, 321 N. Clark Street, Chicago, Illinois 60654-7598.

www.shopABA.org

CONTENTS

ABOUT THE EDITORS

Andrew D. Ness is a member of the JAMS panel of neutrals. He serves as an arbitrator in both domestic and international U.S. arbitrations, on dispute review boards, as Standing Neutral, as a mediator, and as a Neutral Evaluator, all in relation to complex construction and U.S. government contract disputes. Before becoming a full-time neutral, he was a practicing construction lawyer for 40 years, most recently as a partner in the Washington, D.C., office of Jones Day. A magna cum laude graduate of Harvard Law School, in his practice Andy assisted owners and contractors with troubled projects, resolving complex construction and design-related problems. He was lead counsel on a wide variety of large construction disputes heard in federal and state courts and via domestic and international arbitrations and participated as an advocate in over 70 mediations.

The projects Andy has been substantially involved in encompass a broad range, in terms of both geography and types of projects. In 2014–2018, in addition to his other responsibilities, Andy served as the leader of the Jones Day Middle East Construction practice, handling major disputes in Saudi Arabia and the UAE. Andy has been recognized by Chambers USA and Best Lawyers in America since each publication commenced coverage of Construction Law and while in law practice was consistently named one of the Global Most Highly Regarded Individuals by the International Who's Who of Construction Lawyers. He is a fellow of the American College of Construction Lawyers and is a past chair of the ABA Forum on Construction Law, the world's largest organization of construction lawyers.

John Foust is a construction lawyer based in San Francisco with over 20 years of experience in domestic and international arbitrations. He has participated in arbitrations in Dubai, Hong Kong, Ireland, New York, Minnesota, and California. In addition, he has substantial experience litigating the enforceability of arbitration agreements and arbitral awards in state and federal courts, including the enforceability of foreign awards under the New York Convention.

John served a three-year term as editor of *The Construction Lawyer*, the nation's preeminent scholarly journal dedicated to construction law, and a two-year term as chair of the International Division of the ABA Forum on Construction Law. He has been recognized as a leading construction lawyer by Chambers USA, SuperLawyers, US News & World Report, and the International Who's Who of Construction Lawyers.

ABOUT THE AUTHORS

Michael C. Loulakis is president of Capital Project Strategies, LLC. He provides procurement and contracting advice to owners on their capital projects, particularly those delivered through design-build, EPC, and P3. He frequently serves as an arbitrator, mediator, and dispute review board member, and he is a fellow in the Design-Build Institute of America and the American College of Construction Lawyers.

Robert J. MacPherson is a partner in Cokinos Young's New Jersey office. He has been practicing construction law for over 40 years and has been an arbitrator and mediator of construction disputes for over 30 years. Robbie is a fellow of the American College of Construction Lawyers and former chair of the ABA Forum on Construction Law.

Lisa Lombardo is a director in Gibbons P.C.'s Newark, New Jersey, office. She has been practicing construction law for over 20 years and has experience in both litigation and contract drafting and negotiation. Lisa is also on the American Arbitration Association (AAA) Panel of Construction Arbitrators and Mediators and on the New Jersey Superior Court Roster of Mediators.

Deborah Bovarnick Mastin is a full-time mediator and arbitrator based in Miami specializing in domestic and international disputes involving construction and infrastructure, real estate, government procurement, and energy. She is a fellow of the American College of Construction Lawyers, the College of Commercial Arbitrators, the Chartered Institute of Arbitrators, and the Dispute Board Federation. She is a Florida Bar Board Certified Construction Lawyer and a Florida Supreme Court certified circuit court mediator.

Deborah S. Ballati is a full-time neutral with JAMS in San Francisco, where she arbitrates and mediates construction disputes and other complex business disputes. Before becoming a full-time neutral, she was a partner at the San Francisco law firm Farella Braun + Martel, where she litigated a wide array of construction and insurance cases. She has been recognized as a leading California Construction Mediator in Chambers USA, 2020–2023, and she served as the first female president of the American College of Construction Lawyers. She is a past chair of the ABA Forum on Construction Law, as well as a recipient of the Forum's highest honor—the Cornerstone Award. She is recognized nationally for her expertise, and she lectures across the country on insurance, construction law, and dispute resolution.

Duffy O'Connor is a full-time neutral and the principal of O'C ADR, LLC, based in Minneapolis, Minnesota, where he practiced construction law for nearly 40 years, representing contractors, engineers, and project owners in connection with major commercial construction projects nationally. He is a AAA Construction Panelist and a member of its Construction Mega Project Specialty Panel. He is a former chair of the ABA Forum on Construction Law and a fellow of the American College of Construction Lawyers.

Wendy Kennedy Venoit is a partner with Cozen O'Connor in Boston, Massachusetts. She has extensive experience as both an advocate and arbitrator for complex construction disputes—domestic and international. Wendy is a former chair of the ABA Forum on Construction Law and a fellow of the American College of Construction Lawyers. She is a member of the AAA Council, Chartered Institute of Arbitrators, and a panelist on the AAA Construction, ICDR, and Mega Project Panels.

Albert Bates Jr., FCIArb, is a partner in the Construction Group of Troutman Pepper and leads the Group's International Construction Projects practice. In addition to serving as counsel, he is also a respected arbitrator and mediator. Among other honors, he is a fellow of the American College of Construction Lawyers, the International Academy of Construction Lawyers, the Chartered Institute of Arbitrators, and the College of Commercial Arbitrators.

R. Zachary Torres-Fowler is a partner in the Construction Group of Troutman Pepper Hamilton Sanders LLP based in the firm's Philadelphia and New York offices, where his practice focuses on complex U.S. domestic and international construction arbitration matters. He is also an adjunct professor and teaches courses on international arbitration.

Adrian L. Bastianelli, III, is Of Counsel in the Washington, D.C., office of Peckar & Abramson, where he performs mostly neutral work. He is a fellow of the American College of Construction Lawyers and a past chair of the ABA Forum on Construction Law, where he received its Cornerstone Award. He is a co-editor of *Construction ADR* and served as editor of *The Construction Lawyer* and *The Journal of the American College of Construction Lawyers.*

Kathleen Olden Barnes is a senior partner with Watt, Tieder, Hoffar & Fitzgerald, LLP. For over 30 years, Kathy has counseled clients at every stage of complex dispute resolution with expertise in heavy civil and underground construction and design issues. She serves as a neutral with the AAA and is an adjunct professor at the George Mason University Law School. She is a fellow of the American College of Construction Lawyers.

INTRODUCTION

Does it stand to reason that the highest function of the introduction to a practice guide such as this one is to help you figure out efficiently if this is a book you want to read? That is the goal of this one at least. Let us start by describing our target audience, the lawyer whom the editors (Andy Ness and John Foust) had in our head and imagined talking to when editing this book. That reader is a construction advocate who has some experience with construction disputes and court proceedings but who now needs (or will soon need) to take a complex construction dispute to arbitration for the first time. What do you need to know? Not just the basics about how arbitration differs from litigation, but what should you know about how the arbitration process works? How should you adjust your planning, your conduct as an advocate, your preparation of the case, and your presentation of the case at the hearing and afterward to fit this different mode of dispute resolution? This book is intended to provide the information you need to adjust your own personal style to a complex construction arbitration. It covers what you need to know but is not a step-by-step guide, since every case, and every lawyer, is different.

While that target reader provided the centerline for the book, we were careful to build a wider road. Meaning there is plenty to be learned here by attorneys with more litigation/arbitration experience or by those needing somewhat more information on the basics. Experts who testify in arbitration and want a better understanding of the process, as seen through the lawyer's eyes, should also find *Construction Arbitration* quite useful.

How did we approach this task? Very simply. We solicited the best, most qualified group of authors we could think of and asked them if they would participate. If they agreed, we asked them to pick the chapter they preferred from a brief outline (on the theory that they would contribute the most value when writing on a topic of particular interest to them). All of the candidate authors on our list were highly accomplished construction litigators, with numerous major arbitrations under their belts, most of whom have since shifted their primary focus to being construction arbitrators and neutrals. For ten chapters we had to ask only 11 candidates to participate. In other words, we got our first choices across the board, a true all-star team to share their expertise, insight, and experience. We asked them to be pithy and concise, and the result is a compact and readable 250 pages.

There is no place else where you can read the sage advice of Adrian Bastianelli (along with Jennifer Harris) on arbitration hearing strategy and tactics (Chapter 8) or hear from Albert Bates and Zachary Torres-Fowler on the ins and outs of the many options for structuring a construction arbitration hearing (Chapter 7). Mike Loulakis kicked us off with a great introductory summary of the advantages and disadvantages of arbitration, as compared to court litigation (Chapter 1). Robbie MacPherson and Lisa Lombardo took on arbitrator selection and added a very useful side-by-side comparison of the key provisions of the most-often-used procedural rules for construction arbitrations (Chapter 2). Two very experienced arbitrators (Deborah Ballati and Jim O'Connor) shared their perspectives on discovery issues in arbitration and related practice tips (Chapters 4 and 5).

Wendy Venoit very ably covered the waterfront on the various kinds of prehearing motions that can be advanced in arbitration, along with practical advice on when and how to use them (Chapter 6). Deborah Mastin thoughtfully covered structuring the arbitration process, including the key questions of adding additional parties (joinder) and consolidating two related arbitrations (Chapter 3), and Kathy Barnes addressed the limited options for appealing arbitration awards (Chapter 9). And finally, wearing a second hat as author as well as editor, Andy Ness contributed a thorough but concise guide to the differences between international construction arbitrations and those under U.S. procedures (Chapter 10).

We hope and believe that you will find in these pages many directly useful insights for the handling of a complex construction arbitration and will find yourself keeping this book close at hand when preparing for arbitrations years into the future.

ACKNOWLEDGMENTS

We first want to thank Asha Echeverria, chair of the Forum Publications Committee, and her predecessor, David Scotti, for their steadfast support for this book from the outset. Each of the authors, of course, put considerable time, effort, and, most important, thoughtful consideration into their respective chapters, for which we are everlastingly grateful. The book would be nothing without them. Finally, we want to thank Sarah Orwig, the Forum's long-standing and (thanks to the often-protracted book creation process) long-suffering connection to ABA Publications over many years, for her constant support, encouragement, and advice. It takes a sizable team to produce a book, and we were exceedingly lucky to have a great one.

Andrew Ness
John Foust

CHAPTER 1

Distinctive Features of Construction Arbitration

MICHAEL C. LOULAKIS

This chapter provides an orientation to the arbitration process as it applies to a significant construction case, especially focusing on how arbitration differs from litigation. As such, it is organized around the following questions:

- What is arbitration?
- What is the statutory basis for arbitration?
- What are some of the advantages of arbitration?
- What are some of the disadvantages of arbitration?
- Why is arbitration considered an effective way to resolve construction disputes?
- What are the important terms of an arbitration agreement?
- How does an arbitration unfold?
- What is the advocacy style in construction arbitration?
- How can a party enforce or overturn an arbitration award?

This chapter provides a high-level overview of arbitration. Subsequent chapters will provide more detail, insights, and many of the nuances associated with taking a complex construction dispute through arbitration.

I. What Is Arbitration?

The American Arbitration Association (AAA) defines arbitration as "the submission of a dispute to one or more impartial persons for a final and binding decision."[1] As an alternative to litigation, arbitration is a private and confidential process that, in construction cases, is based upon one or more agreements between contracting parties that they will arbitrate their disputes.[2] The agreement to arbitrate can take one of two forms: a predispute arbitration clause included as part of a contract or an agreement by disputing parties to take the matter to arbitration.

Because arbitration at its core is a consensual process that is contractually based, the parties have substantial flexibility in determining the process, so long as their agreements conform to notions of fundamental fairness. For example, the parties can restrict the powers of the arbitrators to only certain categories of disputes or only disputes less than a certain monetary value, or they can restrict the arbitrators from awarding punitive damages. The parties can condition the right to commence arbitration on a specific condition precedent, like mediation of the dispute or the issuance of a final administrative decision. The parties also frequently specify in their arbitration agreement process-related subjects such as (1) who will administer the arbitration; (2) where the arbitration will be held; (3) how many arbitrators will be appointed and the qualifications of those arbitrators; and (4) the extent, if any, of prehearing discovery that will be allowed.

Most arbitrations are administered by a private arbitral institution that provides administrative services like overseeing the appointment of arbitrators and collecting and disbursing the arbitrators' fees and expenses. Each arbitral institution has its own set of arbitration rules that govern the arbitrations it administers. The AAA is the market leader for this in the United States,

---

1. A Guide to Commercial Mediation and Arbitration for Business People, American Arbitration Association (Oct. 1, 2013).

2. In some instances, arbitration is mandatory by statute. An example is state statutes that require insurance companies to arbitrate disputes between them for the consequences of physical damage to automobiles (e.g., Va. Code § 38.2-2231). In other situations, the standard terms used by a particular industry require use of arbitration. Disputes relating to security transactions between customers and brokerage firms, for example, are required to be arbitrated through the Financial Industry Regulatory Authority (FINRA), a not-for-profit corporation that regulates brokerage firms and exchange markets and is supervised by the Securities and Exchange Commission.

but several other organizations, including JAMS, International Institute for Conflict Prevention & Resolution (CPR), Federal Arbitration, Inc. (FedArb), and National Arbitration and Mediation (NAM), are also frequently used to administer construction arbitrations.

However, the use of a third-party administrator is not a requirement, as the parties can decide to forego using an outside administrator and save the fees that it charges. Since this means that there is no administrator to oversee the appointment of arbitrators, it effectively requires that the parties agree on the arbitrator selection and additionally that the appointed arbitrator(s) be willing to handle invoicing, collection, and payments of fees and expenses themselves. Even when parties forego use of an administrator, they generally still agree to use a given set of arbitration rules to govern the process. For example, parties are free to agree that the AAA Construction Industry Arbitration Rules will be applied, even though the AAA has no administrative role.

Arbitration also encompasses processes that vary from the AAA's definition of arbitration. For example, the AAA's definition references "one or more impartial persons" as the arbitrators. When a panel of three is used, three impartial arbitrators are indeed the norm. But it is possible to allow parties to appoint nonneutral arbitrators ("party arbitrators"), with only the chair of the panel being neutral and impartial. The practical effect of this is to make the chair the ultimate decision-maker. The use of party arbitrators who are not neutral has substantially declined in recent years, but it remains an alternative form of arbitration. Likewise, the AAA definition envisions "a final and binding determination," but it is sometimes agreed that the arbitral award will be nonbinding or that the grounds for appeal will be broader than the default (discussed later).

That said, in the overwhelming majority of arbitrations involving U.S. construction projects, all arbitrators are impartial, and they issue a final and binding award at the end of the process. The "final and binding" feature is what makes arbitration a full substitute for litigation and differentiates arbitration from most other alternative dispute resolution processes, such as mediation (where the mediator helps facilitate the settlement of a dispute but does not have the power to impose a resolution or settlement) or a dispute review board (DRB) (typically a three-person panel that provides recommendations about how to resolve a particular dispute that are either nonbinding or temporarily binding until the end of the project).

In sum, the contractual flexibility of arbitration means that either party can seek agreement on whatever it feels is appropriate to make the arbitration process an acceptable alternative to litigation.

II. What Is the Statutory Basis for Arbitration?

The most important arbitration statute is the Federal Arbitration Act (FAA).[3] Enacted in 1925, the FAA provides the basic foundation for domestic arbitration. At the front end, the FAA makes it clear that if a lawsuit is filed where the dispute is subject to an arbitration agreement, the court is required, at the request of a party, to refer the parties to arbitration and otherwise enforce the agreement to arbitrate. At the back end, the FAA provides the standards and procedure for courts to confirm, modify, or vacate arbitration awards. The FAA also makes international arbitration awards arising from arbitral proceedings in other countries enforceable in U.S. courts.

Enactment of the FAA nearly 100 years ago turned public policy strongly in favor of arbitration. This is based on section 2 of the FAA, which states that arbitration agreements are "valid, irrevocable, and enforceable." When one party files a lawsuit against another notwithstanding an arbitration clause in the parties' contract, the party wishing to arbitrate can rely upon the FAA to get the trial court in short order to stay the litigation (per section 3) and compel the other party to arbitrate (per section 4).

Each state also has its own arbitration statute. The majority of these statutes are based on either the 1955 Uniform Arbitration Act (UAA) or its 2000 successor, the Revised Uniform Arbitration Act (RUAA). The UAA and RUAA address most of the same front-end and back-end arbitration issues covered by the FAA. Some state arbitration statutes also elaborate somewhat on how the actual arbitration process will work, such as clarifying the power of arbitrators to issue subpoenas to third parties.

The scope of the FAA is broad, in that it applies to an arbitration agreement in "a contract evidencing a transaction involving [interstate] commerce."[4] This formulation is broad enough to encompass most construction contracts with a value of a few million dollars or more. Several U.S. Supreme Court cases make clear that the FAA and its pro-arbitration stance preempt any state arbitration statute that attempts to nullify or limit contractual agreements to arbitrate, although provisions that simply supplement the FAA remain generally enforceable. The nuances of the relationship between the FAA and state arbitration statutes are complex and the subject of frequent litigation, although these issues only rarely affect construction contract arbitrations.

3. 9 U.S.C. §§ 1–16.
4. 9 U.S.C. § 2.

III. What Are Some of the Advantages of Arbitration?

While both arbitration and litigation result in binding outcomes, there are significant differences. The major reasons that parties often choose arbitration over litigation are summarized here.

A. Arbitrators as Decision-Makers

In litigation, the dispute will be decided by either a judge or a jury. The parties have virtually no influence on who the judge will be and relatively limited ability to influence the selection of a jury. Because arbitrators are selected directly or indirectly by the parties, there is a far greater opportunity to choose a decision-maker who the parties can be confident will be able to render a fair and informed decision of their dispute.

The "informed" element is particularly significant. Most judges are generalists and often have limited experience in an area such as construction law and problems encountered on construction projects. This is even more the case with a typical juror, who may not even have a remote understanding of the law or subject matter. On the other hand, it is highly likely (and the parties can even require in their arbitration agreement) that the arbitrators will have substantial expertise in construction issues. Many arbitrators will also have at least a reasonable (if not substantial) understanding of the applicable legal principles associated with the dispute. The chances are accordingly much greater that the result will be considered fair, well reasoned, and reasonable by the parties. Stated differently, win or lose, the parties are more likely to conclude that they were given a fair opportunity to convince knowledgeable industry people of their views on the dispute.

The fact that arbitrators are knowledgeable about the subject matter also helps to improve the efficiency of the process. They need not be educated about basic concepts—such as the change order process, what a differing site condition is, or the standard of care for design professionals. The expertise arbitrators bring to the dispute is generally seen as a primary advantage of arbitration.

B. Less Formal Than Litigation

Arbitration is much less formal than litigation. Arbitrators are not generally bound to follow the rules and procedures used in litigation, although they are required to respect the fundamental rights of the parties, such as providing a full and fair opportunity to present their evidence. The pretrial process in litigation includes extensive procedural rules governing the various discovery techniques and motions practice, and a significant portion of the cost of litigation is associated with these pretrial processes. The prehearing process in arbitration is not as formal, nor generally as robust, as that found in litigation. While arbitrations can certainly include discovery and prehearing motions, the process is generally more streamlined and simplified as compared to litigation. For example, discovery requests can be made verbally or through emails. Motions can be raised and presented for decision quickly, sometimes relying on emails and phone calls, and minimizing the necessity of having substantial written briefing.

Arbitration hearings are also generally less formal than courtroom trials. Exhibits can be admitted into evidence in bulk before the hearing begins, as opposed to having them introduced and moved into evidence one by one. The hearings frequently take place in a law firm or hotel conference room, where the environment is more casual and congenial. Many find that this lack of formality helps to minimize the hostility associated with litigation and makes witnesses and parties feel more comfortable with the process. Importantly, the rules of evidence that are the basis for keeping documents or hearsay testimony from being admitted in litigation are not generally applicable (other than attorney–client privilege and the work product doctrine). The arbitrators have the authority to use their discretion in determining whether to admit evidence and, because of the FAA, are generally liberal in admitting evidence. Knowing this, the number of objections by counsel at an arbitration hearing is generally much reduced.

C. Flexibility and Innovation

Because arbitration is based on agreement, the parties have substantial flexibility in crafting the details of procedure and process and can tailor the process to the dispute. This contrasts with the relatively rigid statutory and procedural rules in litigation. Some examples of arbitration flexibility include:

- Creating a discovery plan that is customized for the dispute.
- Selecting a convenient location for the arbitration hearing.
- Setting hearings according to the needs and availability of the parties and counsel, rather than the demands of a courtroom calendar. This can extend to the duration of the hearing day and setting hearing days on evenings and weekends when this meets the needs of the parties.
- Taking witnesses out of order to accommodate conflicting schedules.
- Choosing the form of award, where the parties decide the level of detail to be provided in the award. It can also extend to choosing alternative types of awards—such as bracketed (high-low) or baseball-style awards.

- Controlling the timing of the award. In a bench trial, the judge may hear the case and not render a decision until many months or even years later. Under most arbitration rules, the arbitrators are required to rule within 30 to 60 days after the hearing is closed.

Arbitration's flexibility also allows the parties and arbitrators to develop and use innovative techniques for efficiency and to generate cost and time savings. Some of the more creative approaches that have been used in arbitration include the use of (1) witness statements in lieu of direct examination, (2) chess clocks to allocate the available hearing time, (3) fact witness panels, and (4) joint testimony of expert witnesses. Witness testimony can also be reorganized to have all of the fact witnesses for all parties testify first and then follow that with all parties' expert witnesses. The respective subject matter experts can then testify "back to back" (e.g., first all delay experts, followed by all quantum experts). This can help the arbitrators contemporaneously assess the true differences between the experts.

D. Private, Confidential Setting

Litigation is a public process. Anyone can find out if someone has been sued. Anyone can look at the pleadings. Anyone can attend the trial and see the results. Needless to say, this can be a major problem for business reputations.

Arbitration, by contrast, is a private and confidential process, from the moment that a claim has been filed through the hearing and award. No case filings are public, nor is even the fact that an arbitration is pending made public. The parties control who is in attendance at the hearing, and outsiders and press representatives are excluded. Witnesses are examined in private, and documents disclosed or generated in the course of the arbitration are not in the public domain. This enables the parties to argue their dispute without fear of adverse publicity. It also helps avoid public exposure of sensitive information, such as trade secrets and business strategies, and disagreements with key business associates. While there are other advantages to arbitration, many entities view confidentiality as the single most important reason to use the process.

E. Speed and Cost Savings

Arbitration has a reputation for resolving disputes faster than litigation, and the statistics from the AAA, JAMS, and other organizations bear this out. Depending on what court you are comparing arbitration to, the difference can be stark, considering that some state and federal courts are notoriously slow, with cases on the trial docket for years awaiting a trial date. It is typically far easier to get a reasonably prompt, firm hearing date from an arbitration panel than from a busy judge, a situation that became even more evident during the COVID-19 pandemic. The availability of expedited arbitration rules is also a substantial factor. AAA and most other arbitral administrators offer fast-track procedures for smaller disputes (where no claim or counterclaim is over $100,000, under AAA rules). The AAA Fast-Track Rules require the arbitrator to close the hearing within 45 days of the initial scheduling conference and to issue a decision within 14 days thereafter. Litigation generally offers no such expedited alternatives. Moreover, the less formal and more flexible process helps arbitration to move faster than litigation.

Arbitration is also intended to be less expensive than litigation. Some of the prospective savings are the result of simplified rules of evidence and procedure that cut down the required hearing duration. Substantial savings generally flow also from reduced discovery and motions practice compared to litigation.

That said, there are plenty of examples of arbitrations costing as much as litigation and taking longer to conclude than the parties may have expected. The lawyers for the parties generally get the blame for this, although it is by no means always their fault. A very complex construction dispute involving very substantial amounts of money can sometimes reasonably require extensive discovery, including numerous fact and expert witness depositions and extensive production of electronically stored information (ESI), generally the most expensive aspects of discovery. The fees charged by the administering institutions are generally proportional to the amount in dispute (but always higher than court filing fees) and unlike in litigation, the parties must bear the fees charged by the arbitrators. The costs of arbitration multiply most significantly, however, when hearing dates need to be continued on multiple occasions, prolonging the dispute, and in particular when the hearing is not completed in one more or less continuous session, and additional hearing dates, often months later, must be found.

There are some examples of courts that arguably are more efficient than arbitration. In the Eastern District of Virginia's "rocket docket," you can expect a trial no later than nine months from the date the complaint was filed—even for complex cases. It is fairly unlikely that a complex construction arbitration will be heard within that same time period. But in general, a reasonably managed arbitration where discovery is confined to what is really necessary and the hearing is completed in one session will, on average, be less costly than the same case being heard in court.

Finally, in the international arena, U.S. companies that work internationally will almost always require that disputes relating to a project that is located in a host country outside the United States be resolved by arbitration (other than the rare case where the other party is willing to agree to litigate in U.S. courts). While the specific reasons for this vary, they generally revolve around the litigation process in the host country, such as concerns over (1) the integrity of the court system and judges of the host country, (2) whether the host country has clear and established legal principles in the relevant area, and (3) the ability to enforce a judicial award rendered by a foreign court.

IV. What Are Some of the Disadvantages of Arbitration?

As with any dispute resolution alternative, there are potential disadvantages to choosing arbitration that may apply in particular cases and situations. For example, (1) losing the right to a jury trial may be a particular concern to some parties; (2) some parties (most often public owners) may be concerned that arbitrators will be biased against them; and (3) the parties are required to pay fees of the arbitrators and administering institution which are typically far more substantial compared to the court costs of litigation. Another issue for some parties is the much-reduced ability to successfully appeal an arbitration award. Yet other parties may have sworn off arbitration because of one or two bad experiences in prior disputes.

Putting aside these issues, there are other factors to consider in assessing whether arbitration is preferable over litigation for your case. These include:

A. Difficulties in Managing Conflicts Involving Multiple Parties

With limited exceptions, arbitrations are limited to parties who have expressly agreed to resolve their disputes by arbitration. If a dispute involves a key party (such as the design professional) who has not agreed to arbitrate, that party cannot be included in the arbitration unless they consent. By contrast, subject to the limits of the court's jurisdiction, any party needed to completely resolve the dispute can be added to a litigation. Even if all needed parties have agreed to arbitrate with the other party to their contract, they may not have agreed to joinder in a multiparty arbitration along with other parties with whom they had no contract. In the construction context, these are issues best dealt with at the contracting stage, by making sure that all potential parties (design professionals and subcontractors as well as the owner and contractor) have agreed to arbitrate, under the same set of arbitration rules, and that the arbitration clause in each of their contracts includes an advance consent to be joined in a consolidated arbitration that includes all parties needed to provide complete relief and full resolution of the dispute.

If this is not the case, then some of the hurdles can be overcome, typically with added effort, as arbitration rules typically provide for joinder of additional parties and consolidation of multiple arbitrations where that makes sense. The hurdle that cannot be overcome is adding a needed party that has not agreed to arbitrate in any form. The risk when all needed parties cannot be joined in one arbitration is the potential for inconsistent results, plus the inefficiency of having to pursue parallel proceedings. Consider, for example, what happens when two subcontractors each blame the other for causing delays. Absent an ability to consolidate, the general contractor is forced to resolve the disputes in two separate proceedings, one with each subcontractor. This creates the risk that the general contractor could lose both cases and have no further recourse against either subcontractor.

B. Administering a Multiparty Arbitration

Even assuming that assembling all needed parties in one arbitration proceeding is accomplished, whether by agreement or use of the joinder and consolidation provisions in the applicable arbitration rules, administering a multiparty arbitration has more challenges than a two-party proceeding. For example, who has a say in selecting the arbitrators? Scheduling the hearing can also be a significant challenge, as it is harder for arbitrators to mandate hearing dates than it is for a judge. Courts are used to dealing with multiparty litigation, have more robust procedures for doing so, and often have more ability to control the proceedings, including setting pretrial deadlines over the objections of some parties.

C. Limited Availability of Summary Judgment

Primarily because the failure of the arbitrators to consider relevant evidence can be a basis for later overturning the award, obtaining summary determination of an issue in advance of the merits hearing is a significant challenge in arbitration. Summary determination is not precluded and does occur in arbitration under the right circumstances. But it is relatively rare compared to the frequency with which summary judgments are entered in litigation.

D. Limitations on Discovery

Most arbitration rules provide for document discovery as a matter of course but attempt to limit depositions and make no provision for interrogatories or requests for admission. The AAA Construction Industry Arbitration Rules, for example, provide for depositions only in large, complex cases and only "in exceptional cases," at the discretion of the arbitrators. That said, broader discovery is often agreed by the parties (potentially with some pushback by the arbitrators if it seems disproportionate to the needs of the case). But for those who really want to assure the availability of broad, litigation-style discovery, this is more reliably available in litigation.

E. Concerns That Arbitrators Will Disregard the Contract Terms and the Law

Because the ability to successfully appeal an arbitration award is quite limited, there is a view that arbitrators can do what they want, without regard to the contract or the law. Parties who are hoping for a strict application of contract requirements, such as notice of claim requirements, might feel that they will fare better before a judge, whose decisions are subject to a full review on appeal. Arbitrators certainly have discretion in how they arrive at their awards and, on balance, it is probably a fair point that arbitrators consider overall fairness more often than at least some judges. The arbitrator selection process is an opportunity to control this to an extent if it is a concern, however. Nevertheless, those who see this as too big a gamble are likely to prefer to have a judge hear the case, on the theory that a judge will be more likely to follow the contract and law—given that the decision is subject to the supervision of an appellate court.

F. Making the Decision to Arbitrate

There is one more aspect of arbitration that can be seen as a disadvantage—the decision about whether to use arbitration essentially has to be made at the time the parties enter into the contract, before either party knows the specific nature of the actual dispute. As noted earlier, once an arbitration agreement is made, it is enforceable and cannot be unilaterally rescinded. It is certainly possible that the parties can agree upon a different dispute resolution process than what is set forth in the contract, after an actual dispute arises. They may mutually agree to arbitrate in lieu of litigation, or vice versa. They also can agree to modify the requirements of the contract's arbitration clause in any way that they both decide makes sense. But once a dispute arises, changes to the contractual dispute resolution process are relatively infrequent, because one party or the other will often perceive that the contractually specified process gives it a tactical or strategic advantage.

V. Why Is Arbitration Considered an Effective Way to Resolve Construction Disputes?

Arbitration is a popular way to resolve construction disputes. Arbitration is either specified or the default option in most standard form design and construction contracts, including those published by the American Institute of Architects (AIA), ConsensusDocs, Design-Build Institute of America (DBIA), and the Engineers Joint Contract Documents Committee (EJCDC). In addition to the general advantages of arbitration, there are several reasons why arbitration is an effective method of dispute resolution for construction disputes.

- *Construction disputes are document and fact intensive.* The procedural informality and flexibility of the arbitration process often make it much easier to bring out the facts, whether from witnesses or documents, than would be the case in litigation, including through the use of summaries and demonstrative exhibits. Experienced construction industry arbitrators both readily grasp the issues and are adept at sorting out the many details involved in a typical construction dispute, whereas both judges and juries can become quickly swamped by such details.
- *Site visits.* Site visits can materially assist the trier of fact in visualizing the issues and providing context for the dispute. While site visits are possible to arrange in litigation, this is logistically challenging at best and generally impossible when the court is in a different jurisdiction than the project. Arbitrations have far fewer challenges in arranging site visits, even multiple visits, and for that matter it is even possible when appropriate to hold the hearing at or near the site.
- *Strong pool of potential arbitrators.* There is an abundance of excellent construction arbitrators around the country, greatly aiding the ease of use and utility of arbitration. Even when the case is centered on a particular subset of construction projects and issues—such as a design-build contract, a project using modular construction, issues relating to BIM (Building Information Modeling), or a power plant dispute—there is a reasonable pool of qualified potential arbitrators available with that specific experience.

Finally, while the construction industry ranks as the largest industry in the United States, most construction entities, whether owners, contractors, or subcontractors, operate in a relatively small world, with lots of points of interconnection between the participants in their specific corner of the construction market. As a result, there is likely little to be gained, and potentially much to lose, from becoming engaged in a public court fight with another industry player in their market. The confidentiality of arbitration is accordingly of real value.

Even with all of the compelling reasons to use arbitration for a construction dispute, there remains one potentially major disadvantage to construction arbitration. The challenge of dealing with multiple parties in arbitration, discussed previously, is the one significant potential disadvantage of arbitrating construction disputes. Construction disputes are prone to involving multiple parties, given that there are many entities involved on every significant project. While several techniques exist to mitigate these challenges, they still add complexity and cost to the arbitration process when it involves multiple parties.

VI. What Are the Terms of a Typical Arbitration Agreement?

The organizations that administer arbitrations, such as AAA and JAMS, have simple, standard arbitration clauses that they recommend. Standard form contracts that provide for arbitration also include model arbitration clauses. The arbitration clause in one of the industry's most well-recognized standard form contracts, AIA Document A201-2017 (General Conditions of the Contract for Construction), reads as follows:

> § 15.4.1 If the parties have selected arbitration as the method for binding dispute resolution in the Agreement, any Claim subject to, but not resolved by, mediation shall be subject to arbitration which, unless the parties mutually agree otherwise, shall be administered by the American Arbitration Association in accordance with its Construction Industry Arbitration Rules in effect on the date of the Agreement. The Arbitration shall be conducted in the place where the Project is located, unless another location is mutually agreed upon. A demand for arbitration shall be made in writing, delivered to the other party to the Contract, and filed with the person or entity administering the arbitration. The party filing a notice of demand for arbitration must assert in the demand all Claims then known to that party on which arbitration is permitted to be demanded.
>
> § 15.4.1.1 A demand for arbitration shall be made no earlier than concurrently with the filing of a request for mediation, but in no event

> shall it be made after the date when the institution of legal or equitable proceedings based on the Claim would be barred by the applicable statute of limitations. For statute of limitations purposes, receipt of a written demand for arbitration by the person or entity administering the arbitration shall constitute the institution of legal or equitable proceedings based on the Claim.
>
> § 15.4.2 The award rendered by the arbitrator or arbitrators shall be final, and judgment may be entered upon it in accordance with applicable law in any court having jurisdiction thereof.
>
> § 15.4.3 The foregoing agreement to arbitrate and other agreements to arbitrate with an additional person or entity duly consented to by parties to the Agreement, shall be specifically enforceable under applicable law in any court having jurisdiction thereof.

An effective arbitration clause need not be this detailed but should establish the agreement of the parties on the following key issues: (1) the administrator of the arbitration (here the AAA); (2) the arbitration rules (here the AAA Construction Industry Arbitration Rules); (3) the location of the arbitration (here the place where Project is located); (4) any conditions precedent to arbitration (here no earlier than the mediation request, as mediation is a required preliminary step in the dispute resolution process set out in AIA Document A201, and no later than the statute of limitations bar date); and very importantly (5) the award of the arbitrators is final and may be enforced by a court.

Two other key subjects that should be covered by the arbitration provision are the scope of the arbitration (i.e., what disputes are arbitrable?) and the selection process for arbitrators, if something different from the default process in the selected arbitration rules is desired.

The AIA's arbitration provision contemplates that "Claims" will be subject to arbitration, with Claim defined as

> a demand or assertion by one of the parties seeking, as a matter of right, payment of money, a change in the Contract Time, or other relief with respect to the terms of the Contract. The term "Claim" also includes other disputes and matters in question between the Owner and Contractor arising out of or relating to the Contract.

This broad definition, and particularly the phrase "arising out of or relating to the Contract," ensures that any dispute between the Owner and Contractor relating in any respect to the contract will be subject to arbitration. This is the most common formulation, and the one that best avoids the potential for disputes over what is arbitrable and what is not. That said, it is not unusual for the scope of arbitration to be narrowed, in particular to impose a dollar limitation on disputes that are arbitrable, requiring that disputes over that amount be litigated instead. Such a limit is often adopted when the parties agree that the benefits of arbitration better fit smaller disputes (however defined) but that the formality of litigation is preferred for larger disputes. Other limitations that are sometimes seen are limits precluding arbitrators from awarding injunctive relief, or damages for bad faith or punitive damages.

A default selection process for arbitrators, including the number of arbitrators, is included in every set of arbitration rules. The AIA's arbitration provision defers to the AAA Rules by remaining silent on this topic. Many rules leave the choice of appointing one arbitrator or a panel of three to the administering authority, in the absence of an agreement of the parties. To provide greater certainty on this, many arbitration clauses explicitly identify what the parties want, including not only the number of arbitrators but also the minimum qualifications of arbitrators and the process of selecting them. If you have specific preferences with respect to the arbitrator selection, make sure that they are set forth in the arbitration agreement. The important issue of arbitrator selection is the subject of Chapter 2.

VII. How Does the Arbitration Process Unfold?

The arbitration process as it functions for a significant construction case is addressed in detail in the following chapters. But the basic features of the process are outlined here, based on the AAA Rules, which are generally similar to those of other administering organizations.

An arbitration commences when the initiating party (the Claimant) submits a Demand for Arbitration (Demand) to the AAA. The Demand identifies the counterparty (the Respondent), location of the arbitration, and expected number of days of hearing. The Demand will also describe the dispute and relief sought, although this description is often quite brief, and the Claimant serves the Demand on the Respondent. Once the AAA receives the Demand and the appropriate filing fee from the Claimant, it sets a deadline for the Respondent to answer or file a counterclaim.

If the arbitration agreement is silent as to arbitrator selection, the AAA will identify a list of potential arbitrators, and the parties then strike unacceptable names and rank the reminder in order of preference. More commonly, when three arbitrators are to be appointed, the parties agree that each party will appoint one arbitrator, and the two party-appointed arbitrators will select the third person, to serve as chair of the panel. Many other variations are possible.

Once the arbitrator(s) have been duly appointed, the first step is a preliminary hearing to discuss the management of the case, most particularly scheduling of the prehearing events and hearing dates. Following the preliminary hearing (which is typically done by phone or video meeting), the dates established for prehearing events, such as discovery steps and disclosure of witnesses and exhibits, will be set out in a Case Management or Scheduling Order. In more complex cases, there may be several interim preliminary hearings/status conferences scheduled as checkpoints where the arbitrators can confirm that the case is moving ahead smoothly to hearing. The complexity of the prehearing timetable will depend on how extensive the agreed prehearing process and allowed discovery will be.

At the arbitration hearing, each party will have a full opportunity to present whatever evidence and arguments it has to support its positions, first Claimant and then Respondent. All witnesses will be subject to cross-examination. Generally, there will be an opportunity either to submit a prehearing brief or to make an opening statement, and sometimes both are permitted. Transcription of the hearing is not required but is frequently requested for substantial cases. At the conclusion of the evidence, there will be an opportunity for either final argument or submission of posthearing briefs. Many times, the choice between final arguments and posthearing briefing is not made until the hearing, in consultation with the arbitrators.

Once all the evidence has been presented, and any agreed posthearing submissions are received, the arbitrators close the record. The AAA Rules require the award to be rendered no later than 30 days from the close of the record, although this can be extended by agreement. The AAA Rules provide for different forms of award with different levels of detail, including a reasoned opinion, an abbreviated opinion, or findings of fact and conclusions of law, but at a minimum the award must include a concise written financial breakdown of any monetary amounts awarded.

VIII. What Is the Advocacy Style in Construction Arbitration?

The advocacy style in arbitration is generally more informal than when appearing in court. Beyond that, here are five general points that you might want to consider:

- *Explain to the arbitrators the essentials of your case early on.* Counsel used to a litigation-style approach may be inclined to provide relatively little information in their initial submissions—such as generally denying liability or stating that "damages will be in an amount to be determined later." This is not the optimal approach in arbitration. Most construction arbitrators are interested from the outset in understanding the nature of the dispute and the key issues, and some want to know this even before they agree to serve as an arbitrator. The initial submissions (Demand for Arbitration and Answering Statement) do not need to be overly detailed, but they should describe enough of the facts and reasons for the dispute to give the arbitrators a reasonable understanding of what the case is about.
- *Arbitrators may want to know the answers to questions you don't ask.* Most judges are unlikely to fill in the gaps of a witness examination by asking questions that might help explain an issue—such as "Why did you do it that way?," "Why didn't you notify the owner that you disagreed?," or "Did you ever consider doing X?" Arbitrators in general are more active questioners than judges. Arbitrators with a deep technical background are frequently prone to ask tough technical questions that were not addressed in either direct or cross-examination. Counsel need to understand this as they prepare their witnesses and should think about asking the obvious questions before the arbitrators do so.
- *Take advantage of arbitration's informality.* Advocates who treat the arbitration process in the same manner as litigation are generally less effective than those who appreciate and use arbitration's informality. Arbitrators can get frustrated with excessive evidentiary objections, motions that have little chance of success, and an unwillingness of parties to streamline the process. Informality is one of the key benefits of arbitration—take advantage of it.
- *Keep in mind the backgrounds of your arbitrators.* If you have experienced and knowledgeable construction arbitrators, conduct the arbitration accordingly. You probably do not need to explain to them what a CPM schedule is and how critical path activities differ from those with float. Instead, focus on what is unique about your contract or project. Avoid taking legal or contractual positions that strain credulity or are theoretical and impractical. Experienced arbitrators can quickly assess a counsel's construction competence by the reasonableness and practicality of the positions being advocated.

- *Be both professional and nice.* Judges deal with conflict full time and, while they expect counsel to be professional and courteous, they are used to conflicts between counsel and have the power to address them. Judges nevertheless dislike hearing counsel bicker over minor issues. But construction arbitrators dislike this even more. Poor behavior, from berating or denigrating witnesses to snide remarks to failing to give small courtesies, is not well received and does not help your client's cause. Being professional and nice does not guarantee winning. But helping make the hearing run smoothly and make the process more enjoyable for everyone involved will both be appreciated by the arbitrators and reflect well on you and, by extension, your client.

IX. How Can a Party Enforce or Overturn an Arbitration Award?

The litigation process culminates in the entry of a judgment that is legally binding and sufficient to proceed to execution, via attachment or other means of collection when needed. Arbitration culminates in an award that a contract makes final and binding between the parties to the contract but that does not have the equivalent legal effect of a judgment. If the award is not voluntarily paid, it must be converted into a judgment entered by a court in order to access the legal tools for collection. Both the FAA and state arbitration statutes set out abbreviated processes to confirm an arbitration award and enter a judgment that incorporates its monetary award. While an abbreviated process, there are nevertheless associated attorneys' fees and court costs.

If the losing party wants to fight the award, it has the right to do so through a process formally called "vacatur"—that is, having the award vacated. This process is also set out in the FAA and state arbitration acts. Under the FAA, a request to confirm the award and a request to vacate it are generally heard in the same proceeding.

The grounds for vacating a duly entered arbitration award are narrow and limited. The grounds for overturning the award focus mainly on the conduct of the arbitrators and, as stated in section 10 of the FAA, are:

> (1) Where the award was procured by corruption, fraud, or undue means.
>
> (2) Where there was evident partiality or corruption in the arbitrators, or either of them.

(3) Where the arbitrators were guilty of misconduct in refusing to postpone the hearing, upon sufficient cause shown, or in refusing to hear evidence pertinent and material to the controversy; or of any other misbehavior by which the rights of any party have been prejudiced.

(4) Where the arbitrators exceeded their powers, or so imperfectly executed them that a mutual, final, and definite award upon the subject matter submitted was not made.

As discussed in Chapter 9, there is substantial case law regarding each of these grounds, but in general terms it is safe to say they are not interpreted broadly. Overturning an arbitration award is a challenging task, at best. Note also that arguing that the award is simply erroneous, not supported by the facts or the law, is not a ground for vacating it. There are, however, quite limited circumstances where the award may qualify as demonstrating "a manifest disregard of the law," which, in the federal appellate courts where this ground is recognized, is considered a form of the arbitrators "exceeding their powers."

In short, an arbitration award brings finality to the dispute in many respects more quickly than a judgment, due to the limited ability to overturn it. Many see this finality as an advantage of arbitration, while others view the lack of full appeal rights as a significant disadvantage.

CHAPTER 2

Arbitral Forum and Selecting Arbitrators

ROBERT J. MACPHERSON
LISA LOMBARDO

The ability to select your arbitrator is a key feature of private commercial arbitration, and attorneys and the parties should take full advantage of the opportunity. This chapter discusses specific issues that come up when deciding on an arbitrator, whether it be a sole arbitrator or a panel, as well as issues that are unique to selecting a panel, including the selection of party-appointed arbitrators and a panel chair.

To begin with, one should always thoroughly research the background and experience of the available arbitrator pool. In the case of a party-appointed arbitrator, a preselection interview is not only permissible; it is highly advisable. Asking those candidates for samples of awards they have written, redacted to remove confidential information, is also a good practice. When selecting arbitrators off a list, don't rely solely on the arbitrator's bio or CV. Ask others who have personal experience with the candidates if they would be willing to share their views.

Before an arbitrator is selected, it is critical to have full and comprehensive disclosures of his or her past business, professional, and personal relationships among the parties, the attorneys, and the witnesses (both fact and expert) who may have a role in the arbitration. An undisclosed relationship could lead to a finding of arbitrator partiality, which is one of the few grounds for vacating an award.[1] Normally, it is the prospective arbitrator who makes the disclosure,

1. 9 U.S.C. § 10(a)(2); Uniform Arbitration Act § 23(a)(2)(A) (2000).

which a party can then use as the basis for an objection to the arbitrator's service. However, if the parties know of a disclosure that perhaps should have been but has not been made, they should not hesitate to raise it. Likewise, if an arbitrator's disclosure raises questions or concerns, those should be addressed before the appointment is made final. Unresolved disclosure issues that do not surface until an unfavorable award is issued can lead to litigation and uncertainty over what was intended to be a final and binding decision.[2]

You cannot spend too much time on investigating a potential arbitrator. It will be time well spent because once an arbitrator is selected, you will be stuck with him or her, for better or worse.

I. The Role of the Arbitral Body and the Arbitral Rules

The ability of the parties and their counsel to select an arbitrator or panel of arbitrators is one of the key advantages—and distinctions—of arbitration. However, parties should not underestimate the important role the arbitral institution or body plays in administering the arbitration and must be mindful of its rules in determining what body is best suited to oversee their dispute.

An arbitral body is a formal institution or organization whose role is to administer the arbitration process. Each arbitral body has its own set of rules that provide a framework for the arbitration and its own form of administration to assist in the process. As such, arbitral bodies are often referred to as the "gatekeepers" to the arbitration.

Often the governing contract between the parties to the dispute contains an arbitration clause that designates a particular arbitral body to administer the arbitration. If not, the parties must agree upon the arbitral body that will oversee the arbitration at the time a claim arises or agree instead to proceed on an ad hoc basis. An ad hoc arbitration is one that is not administered by an arbitral body such that the parties, and their counsel, will have to handle the administrative aspects of the arbitration themselves—for example, the appointment of the arbitrators, the infrastructure and technology needed for the hearing, the collection of fees, and so on. While multiple articles have been devoted to the respective advantages and disadvantages of an ad hoc arbitration versus arbitrations administered by an arbitral body, where cost is not the driving factor, administered arbitrations are typically preferred over ad hoc arbitrations. Placing the administrative burdens on the parties risks them being unable to

2. A good example is *Vollers Excavating v. Watchung Associates*, unpublished decision, N.J. Super. Ct. App. Div., Docket No. A 3242-07T3 (2009).

reach consensus, and on the arbitrator is counterproductive as their time is better spent focusing on the merits.

The larger domestic arbitral bodies such as the American Arbitration Association (AAA), JAMS, and National Arbitration and Mediation (NAM) have case managers assigned to arbitration matters that act as intermediaries between the parties and the arbitrator. The same is true for the better-known international arbitral bodies, such as the International Chamber of Commerce (ICC) and the International Center for Dispute Resolution (ICDR). The case managers help facilitate scheduling and coordination, oversee case management issues, and ensure deadlines are met and fees are timely paid. One notable exception to the use of case managers is the International Institute for Conflict Prevention & Resolution (CPR), which offers an option for nonadministered arbitrations where the parties can request the assistance of CPR only for discrete functions.

So exactly what does it mean to "administer" an arbitration, and how is that accomplished? Typically, the administration is through an oftentimes complex and detailed set of rules governing the arbitration process from its inception through the award and sometimes even beyond. The rules that govern a dispute are typically based on the nature of the dispute—commercial, construction, employment, and so on—and the amount in controversy, taking into account all claims and counterclaims.

All of the larger domestic arbitral bodies publish various sets of arbitral rules, some of which were specifically designed for construction arbitrations. The AAA Construction Rules and Mediation Procedures were developed with input from the National Construction Dispute Resolution Committee, an advisory group founded in 1966 by the AAA in cooperation with the American Institute of Architects and other industry, trade, and professional associations.[3] The AAA's Fast Track Construction Rules limit the cost and time of a hearing and apply to all two-party cases where no party's disclosed claim or counterclaim exceeds $100,000. If the claim or counterclaim exceeds $1,000,000, the Procedures for Large, Complex Construction Disputes (LCC) will apply. The Fast Track and LCC Rules amend the Regular Track Rules. In most cases, regardless of the particular rules that apply, the AAA rules provide for a preliminary hearing with the arbitrator, or panel, to organize the proceedings. The AAA rules provide a lengthy checklist of what to discuss during the hearing.

---

3. *Construction, Real Estate and Environmental*, AM. ARB. ASS'N, https://www.adr.org/construction (last visited Apr. 11, 2023).

JAMS offers multiple sets of rules for construction arbitration, including Engineering and Construction Arbitration Rules and Procedures (JAMS Construction Rules), Engineering and Construction Arbitration Rules and Procedures for Expedited Arbitration (JAMS Expedited Construction Rules), and Surety Adjudication Dispute Resolution Rules (JAMS Surety Rules). Most recently, JAMS issued its Optional Expedited Arbitration Procedures, which are designed for a more efficient arbitration by limiting depositions, document requests, and e-discovery.

NAM offers three types of arbitrations: (1) "Open Arbitration: a hearing in which the arbitrator hears a case and renders a final decision"; (2) "High-Low Arbitration: a process in which the parties, by agreement, restrict the range of an arbitrator's decision by establishing 'high' and 'low' parameters"; and (3) "Baseball Arbitration," which typically involves the submission by each party of his or her last best figure and the reason why it should be accepted, with the arbitrator's determination being restricted to either one figure or the other.[4] Like most arbitral bodies, NAM offers several sets of arbitration rules, including a set of Standard Rules and Procedures which it recommends for cases where there is "no pre-existing contractual arbitration provision," and a set of Comprehensive Rules and Procedures, which it recommends "[f]or cases referred to NAM as a result of an existing contractual provision."[5]

Like the AAA, JAMS, and NAM, CPR Rules are organized by the subject area of the dispute and whether the dispute is domestic or international. CPR also has a separate set of rules for nonadministered arbitrations, which are designed for use without the oversight of an administering entity. Under this rubric, the arbitrator and the parties administer the proceedings themselves. If for some reason the parties are unable to select an arbitrator, an ADR provider entity may assist with the selection. The selected arbitrator manages all aspects of the proceedings that are not governed by the parties under their agreement. One of the primary advantages of an ad hoc (i.e., self-administered) arbitration is cost savings, as it typically costs less than an administered arbitration where the parties pay a filing fee to the arbitral body that is separate from the fees charged by the arbitrator.

(At the end of this chapter is a table that summarizes the key variations in the rules promulgated by the AAA, CPR, JAMS, and NAM.)

---

4. *Arbitration*, NAT'L ARB. & MEDIATION, https://www.namadr.com/services/arbitration/ (last visited Apr. 11, 2023).

5. *Rules, Forms, & Fees*, NAT'L ARB. & MEDIATION, https://www.namadr.com/resources/rules-fees-forms/ (last visited Apr. 11, 2023).

II. Arbitrator Selection Options

A. Selection Procedures as Prescribed under Applicable Rules

Barring an agreement where the parties have preselected their arbitrator, the arbitral body facilitates the arbitrator selection process. NAM's website contains biographies of select neutrals, and rosters for up to three states can be obtained by filling out a request online. JAMS publishes its list of arbitrators on its website where a search can be run by location, practice area, language, and background. CPR allows only individuals or companies who are CPR members to access the CPR list. In contrast, the AAA treats its list of neutrals as proprietary and does not make that list publicly available.

The arbitral bodies also differ in the way in which the tribunal is selected once a dispute arises. If the parties to a dispute before the AAA have not appointed an arbitrator and have not provided another method of appointment, then generally the case manager submits a list of potential arbitrators to the parties, who then may strike a specified number of names and rank the remaining names in order of preference. The highest-ranked arbitrator will be invited to serve. Unless the parties have agreed otherwise, if the parties are unable to select an arbitrator through this method, the case manager may administratively appoint the arbitrator. In accordance with the AAA rules, unless the parties have agreed otherwise, the case manager will appoint the chair of a three-member panel.

With regard to NAM, if the claim amount is $10,000 or less, the NAM administrator will appoint the arbitrator. For in-person/oral arbitration hearings, unless both parties agree otherwise or NAM determines in its discretion that another method for the selection of the arbitrator is appropriate for the case, the parties shall select the arbitrator from identical lists containing at least five names, if a sole arbitrator is to be appointed, and eight names, if three arbitrators are to be appointed. Each party may strike two names from the list and number the remaining names on the list in the order of its preference.

Under the CPR Rules, arbitrators may be selected by the parties (1) through direct designation for appointment, (2) through CPR's screened selection procedure, or (3) through CPR's list procedure where not less than five candidates will be provided, if one arbitrator is to be selected, and no less than seven candidates, if two or three arbitrators are to be selected. The "screened selection" procedure is unique in that two of the arbitrators are selected by the parties without knowing which party selected them.

JAMS also provides a list of arbitrators if the parties do not agree on an arbitrator. JAMS sends the parties a list of at least five arbitrator candidates in the case of a sole arbitrator and at least ten arbitrator candidates in the case of a three-arbitrator panel. Each party may strike two names, in the case of a sole arbitrator, or three names, in the case of a three-person panel, and then rank the remaining arbitrator candidates in order of preference. The remaining arbitrator candidate with the highest composite ranking shall be appointed the arbitrator. The parties are to agree on the chair, and if they cannot, then JAMS designates the chair.

B. Sole Arbitrator versus a Panel of Three

Parties to an arbitration agreement are generally free to structure the arbitration as they see fit, including the number of arbitrators who will hear the dispute. Assuming you have the ability to choose the size of the panel, what factors should go into your decision?

We start with the fact that a three-person panel costs more than a single arbitrator. It may not be three times the cost of a single arbitrator (depending on the panelists' respective hourly rates), but the increase will be significant. The fact that the rates of the arbitrators may vary and, secondly, that the arbitrators will most likely divide up certain responsibilities, such as hearing and deciding discovery disputes or other procedural matters,[6] will keep the costs of a panel down to something less than three times the cost of a single arbitrator. But you will be paying three arbitrators to attend each day of hearings and for each day of panel deliberations. Assume an hourly rate of $500 per hour per arbitrator and five days of eight-hour hearings, and the cost can quickly add up.

Perhaps a more important consideration when deciding between a single arbitrator and a panel is scheduling. It is difficult enough for the opposing lawyers to find a string of days when both are available for hearings. You then need to factor in the availability of the client, witnesses, and experts. Layer in the need to coordinate the schedules of three busy arbitrators, and finding enough available hearing days in the near future can become next to impossible.

But if cost and scheduling were not factors, it is hard to imagine why anyone would choose to have a dispute submitted to a single arbitrator. If, for whatever reason, you lose the ear of that single arbitrator, you may well find yourself snatching defeat from the jaws of victory. If that single arbitrator does not have the background or experience to fully understand and correctly decide the issues presented, the result will be certainly disappointing for one party and maybe both. Most of us make better decisions when we are able to

---

6. *E.g.*, American Arbitration Association Construction Industry Arbitration Rules (July 1, 2015) [hereinafter AAA Construction Rules], Rule R-45(b).

discuss the issue with others and allow our decisions to be informed by the observations and analysis of others we trust and respect. Most arbitrators will tell you the decisions rendered by panels they have been on were better reasoned, more comprehensive, and easier to reach than when they had to make the decision themselves.

All this leads to a truism we all know—two heads are better than one. But can you possibly have a panel of two? As Harry Nilsson observed: "Two can be as bad as one. It's the loneliest number since the number one."

This is where the simple, elegant solution of Adrian Bastianelli[7] comes into play.

The experience of most arbitrators is that, in the vast majority of cases, the panel comes to a consensus on the award and dissents are rare.[8] However, it would be dangerous to use a panel of two without accounting for the possibility of an impasse and having a way around a hung panel, tied one to one on the outcome. The Bastianelli Solution is to have one member of the two-person panel be designated as the tiebreaker in the event the two selected arbitrators cannot agree on the award. The tiebreaker is chosen at the time the panel is selected and can be agreed to by the parties, selected by chance (e.g., picking a name out of a hat), or designated by a third party. The name of the tiebreaker is then placed in a sealed envelope and given to the two panel members, who are instructed to open the envelope only in the event an impasse is reached.

Using a two-person panel along with the Bastianelli Solution can result in a significant cost savings, make scheduling easier, and still result in quality awards. Experience tells us that in most cases the envelope will never be opened.

C. Other Panel Selection Methods

The processes set out previously for selecting arbitrators used by AAA, JAMS, and NAM are simply the default methods specified in their respective rules. In many if not most cases, the parties and counsel vary from those default methods when selecting arbitrators, which is entirely permissible.

The simplest and perhaps best arbitrator selection method is for the parties to agree on the arbitrator or arbitrators. While the parties do not see eye to eye

---

7. Adrian Bastianelli is a construction lawyer, mediator, and arbitrator who practices in Washington, D.C. He is a co-author of Chapter 8.

8. Dean Thomson & Jesse Orman, *Inside the Black Box: The Preferences, Practices and Rule Interpretations of Construction Arbitrators*, 12:2 J. Am. Coll. Constr. Law. 13 (Summer 2018).

on the dispute that got them to the arbitration in the first place, they should at least try to mutually select the arbitrators. And if the parties themselves are too estranged by the dispute to agree on anything, their counsel should try. Lots of time and energy will go into arbitrating the dispute. Spending time and money fighting over an arbitrator would not seem to be a good use of resources.

But human nature being what it is, there is a good chance the parties will not be able to agree, in which case the Federal Arbitration Act and the Uniform Arbitration Act (the latter adopted in one form or another by many states) offer some guidance.[9] Under those laws, where the arbitration agreement does not provide for a method of appointment of the arbitrator, or where the agreed method (such as the default method specified by the arbitral body's rules) fails for any reason, a party can petition a court to appoint an arbitrator.

In between agreeing on an arbitrator and having the court appoint one, there are a number of ways to go about selecting arbitrators.

Arbitrator selection need not wait for a dispute to arise. Just as construction contracts frequently designate a set of arbitral rules and/or an arbitral body to administer a potential arbitration, there is no reason why the agreement cannot also designate specific arbitrators. If you choose to go this route, be sure to do the following. Reach out to the prospective candidates, ask them if they are available and are willing to serve, and ask that they clear conflicts. You should provide alternates to account for the possibility that one or more of the selected arbitrators may not be available when a dispute arises, which may be several years after the contract naming them is signed. You should also consider whether the selected arbitrators should be kept up to speed on the progress of the project by way of periodic reports and/or on-site meetings with the parties. This involves an additional cost but has been used successfully under the dispute review board model.

Perhaps the most commonly used method where there will be three arbitrators is to have each party select one arbitrator and then have those two select the third. The party-selected arbitrators can be left to their own devices to identify candidates for the third position, or the parties can identify candidates for the two selected arbitrators to consider. The selection of the third arbitrator can alternatively be left to the arbitral body, such as the AAA, under the applicable rules.

Flipping a coin, playing a game of darts, or picking names out of a hat can also be employed, but at the end of the day the best method is one that results in a panel that all parties have confidence in.

---

9. *See* 9 U.S.C. § 5; Uniform Arbitration Act § 11.

D. Considerations in Selecting Party-Appointed Arbitrators

The first thing you need to know when selecting a party-appointed arbitrator is whether the party-appointed arbitrators are to be neutral or partisan. In this context, neutral means that the party-selected arbitrators shall not act as advocates for the parties that appointed them and shall not have ex parte communications with them, while partisan means the opposite. Ordinarily, the question of whether the party-appointed arbitrators are to be neutral or partisan will be determined by the arbitration agreement or by the applicable rules. If you have an agreement that calls for party-appointed arbitrators to be partisan, be sure to discuss that with your arbitrator candidates, as there are some arbitrators who will not accept assignment as a partisan arbitrator.

Who would make a good partisan arbitrator? Obviously one who is a good advocate, but also one who is persuasive, since he or she is only one vote and will need the support of at least one other arbitrator to carry the day. Much of what is discussed next regarding arbitrator experience and personality also applies to the partisan arbitrator. You should also raise with your partisan arbitrator the need to be mindful of a shift in the sentiment of the other panel members toward neutrality. If the other appointed arbitrator acts in a more impartial manner, it is likely that the other arbitrator and the jointly selected neutral will form an alliance that negates the vote of your partisan appointee, unless your appointee can temper his or her partiality and work in a more cooperative mode to reach a consensus award.

If the arbitration clause allows for partisan arbitrators, and if the other party does not want to change that, you may have no choice but to appoint an arbitrator who will take on that role. But the better course would be to work hard to convince the other party to abandon the partisan arbitrator model.

The modern trend, and best practice, is that party-appointed arbitrators must be neutral unless the arbitration agreement expressly states otherwise. For example, Rule R-15(b) of the AAA Construction Rules provides:

> Where the parties have agreed that each party is to name one arbitrator, the arbitrators so named must meet the standards of R-20 with respect to impartiality and independence unless the parties have specifically agreed pursuant to R-20(a) that the party-appointed arbitrators are to be non-neutral and need not meet those standards.[10]

---

10. AAA Construction Rules, *supra* note 6, Rule R-15(b). *See also* JAMS Engineering and Construction Arbitration Rules and Procedures (June 1, 2021) [hereinafter JAMS Construction Rules], Rule 7(c) ("Where the Parties have agreed that each Party

There are practical reasons for avoiding the use of arbitrators who will be partial to the party that appointed them. The partisan arbitrator duplicates the role of the parties' lawyers. In the way of advocacy, what will the partisan arbitrator add? What the parties should want is a panel that will work together to call balls and strikes, not one where one partisan arbitrator tries to interfere with the batter, while the other tries to interfere with the pitcher, all while the neutral member tries to make sense of it all.

Other than neutrality, what you should look for is an arbitrator with both subject matter and process experience. For a construction dispute, that means a construction lawyer, design professional, contractor, or other person involved in the construction industry. If, as is more often the case in construction disputes, the matter will involve expert testimony, consider someone who has the relevant experience, be it in engineering, scheduling, or whatever is at issue. If the issues are legal in nature, a construction lawyer may be more appropriate. A word of caution, however, is to avoid looking for another advocate for your arguments. What you want is someone who can help the other arbitrators understand and apply the technical and legal principles at issue to the facts. That is where process experience comes in.

You may know lawyers or engineers with experience in the subject matter of your dispute who you think would be ideal arbitrators. They also check the neutrality box. They may have even handled arbitrations for others or been a witness in arbitration proceedings. However, if they have never sat on an arbitration panel, they may not be good choices.

The role of arbitrator requires a unique skill set, only some of which may be acquired through education or training. Lawyers may have a leg up on other construction industry people, as they have been trained in adjudication and more likely than not have some experience with those processes, including arbitration. But unless they have sat as an arbitrator, you will be throwing them into a role they may be uncomfortable filling. At a minimum, you will want your party-selected arbitrator to have at least some arbitrator training but preferably actual experience as an arbitrator. With that kind of background, he or she will understand what is expected of him or her as an arbitrator, including mundane things, such as the need to commit to hearing dates well in advance, as discussed later. And that brings us to personality, which is a critical consideration when selecting a panel member.

Arbitrators, almost by definition, need to make difficult choices. Both sides can't be right. There will be winners and losers. As a panel member your

---

is to name one Arbitrator, the Arbitrators so named shall be neutral and independent of the appointing Party unless the Parties have agreed that they shall be non-neutral.").

candidate must be able to work cooperatively with the other panel members. We have discussed how a partisan arbitrator's vote can sometimes be effectively disregarded by the other panel members. The same is true of the vote of a panel member who does not understand how to reach a consensus. A take-charge person who may be fine as a sole arbitrator could be the wrong choice for a panel member. Likewise, a person who is easily persuaded and tends to go along to get along may not be the best choice. The ideal personality for a panel member is one who works well with others but who is also unafraid of diplomatically expressing opinions different from others on matters of importance.

Availability is a key consideration for arbitrator candidates. Be sure to confer with your candidate and confirm he or she is available to devote the time necessary to hear the case during the anticipated time frame. Perhaps more importantly, make sure your candidate understands he or she will be expected to commit to several days or even weeks of hearings well into the future. He or she also needs to understand that those hearing dates may be adjourned or even cancelled if there is a settlement, leaving a hole in his or her schedule that may be hard to fill. Unless the candidate is willing to make such a commitment, consider someone else.

Arbitrators tend to charge by the hour, although some charge by the day or half day. For those who are attorneys, the hourly rates will be close to what they and other attorneys in the area charge. Experience and (for those in a law firm) firm size will impact rates. Should cost be a consideration? It should, as fees for multiday hearings can quickly add up. Some arbitrators may also charge cancellation fees if scheduled hearings are cancelled on short notice. First, find an arbitrator that meets your qualifications. If the rate or cancellation fees seems high, seek to negotiate a lower rate. Arbitrator fees are not the place to look for savings, but on occasion there is some room for negotiation.

In summary, the ideal party-appointed panel member should be neutral, have experience in the issues likely to be raised, and have actual experience sitting on a three-person panel.

E. Considerations for Selecting the Panel Chair

The title "panel chair" would seem to identify an important person in the arbitration process. But if you search the rules of either AAA or JAMS, you will find scant references to the role of the chair. In fact, the only specific role of the chair under those rules is to make procedural rulings.[11]

11. AAA Construction Rules, *supra* note 6, Rule 45(a) ("[I]n a multi-arbitrator case, if all parties and all arbitrators agree, the chair of the panel may make procedural decisions."). *See also* JAMS Construction Rules, *supra* note 10, Rule 7(b).

Why then is it important to think about the qualities to look for in a chair? For the most part, interactions between the parties and the panel will be through the chair. During the preliminary stages, the chair may handle most prehearing calls and conferences with only limited or even no participation by the other arbitrators. Thus, the first impression the other arbitrators will get about the case, the parties, and the attorneys may be from the chair. While a chair, like the other two arbitrators, has only one vote when it comes to the award, the chair does act as presiding officer and sets the tone and pace for the entire process. The chair is also typically given the authority to rule on evidentiary objections during the hearings. While by tradition the chair is often given the task of writing the first draft of an award, that is by no means certain. If the award turns on an issue within the expertise of another panel member, he or she may do the first draft, or the tasks could be divided up among all three.

The role of chair comes down to managing the arbitration process, and managing the attorneys and the parties, such that the hearings are conducted effectively and efficiently. If that happens, the panel can spend most of its time and effort listening to the evidence and arguments and deliberating over the award. So, first and foremost, the chair needs to be a good manager of people and time.

Prior experience as a chair is preferable, but an arbitrator who has extensive experience as a panel member would be a safe choice and may well bring new ideas on how to conduct proceedings based on past experience, good and bad.

An important thing to keep in mind when it comes to selecting a chair is that the parties may or may not have a direct role in selecting the chair. If the arbitration agreement spells out the method of selecting a chair, whether expressly or by referencing a particular set of rules, that method will govern, absent agreement of the parties to change it. In many cases, it is the other two panel members who jointly select the chair. For those reasons, when selecting any arbitrator, it is a good practice to select only candidates who could fulfill the role of chair if necessary.

III. Key Variations in Potentially Applicable Rules (AAA, JAMS, CPR, NAM)

The following table summarizes the key variations in the rules promulgated by the AAA, JAMS, CPR, and NAM:

Rules	AAA Construction Industry Arbitration Rules, Standard Track (effective July 1, 2015)	JAMS Construction Rules & Procedures (effective June 1, 2021)	CPR Administered Arbitration Rules (effective March 1, 2019)	NAM Comprehensive Dispute Resolution Rules and Procedures (effective April 18, 2022)
Initiation of a Case	File with the AAA a demand for arbitration, pay the administrative filing fee, and provide a copy of the demand and the applicable arbitration agreement to the opposing party.	The Arbitration is deemed commenced when JAMS issues a Commencement Letter based upon the existence of one of the following: a post-dispute Arbitration Agreement fully executed by all Parties and that specifies JAMS administration or use of JAMS Rules; or a pre-dispute written contractual provision requiring the Parties to arbitrate the dispute or claim and specifying JAMS administration or use of any JAMS Rules or accompanied by the Parties' agreement that the Arbitration shall be administered by JAMS; or a written confirmation of an oral agreement of all Parties to participate in an Arbitration administered by JAMS or conducted pursuant to JAMS Rules; or a copy of a court order compelling Arbitration at JAMS.	Simultaneously deliver to the Respondent a notice of arbitration and an electronic copy to CPR.	A case may be initiated one of two ways: the parties may send a jointly executed submission form to NAM's headquarters, or one party files a Demand for Arbitration by forwarding the fully executed Demand for Arbitration to the respondent.
Deadline for Filing Answer/ Counterclaim	Within 14 days after respondent receives notice of claim.	Within 14 calendar days of service of the notice of claim.	Within 20 days of CPR's receipt of the notice of arbitration and filing fee.	Within 30 days of service of the Demand for Arbitration.

Rules	AAA Construction Industry Arbitration Rules, Standard Track (effective July 1, 2015)	JAMS Construction Rules & Procedures (effective June 1, 2021)	CPR Administered Arbitration Rules (effective March 1, 2019)	NAM Comprehensive Dispute Resolution Rules and Procedures (effective April 18, 2022)
Consolidation or Joinder	If the parties are unable to agree to consolidate related arbitrations or to the joinder of parties to an ongoing arbitration, the AAA shall directly appoint a single arbitrator, known as the R-7 arbitrator, for the limited purpose of deciding whether related arbitrations should be consolidated or parties joined.	JAMS may decide that the new case or cases shall be consolidated into one or more of the pending proceedings and referred to one of the Arbitrators or panels of Arbitrators already appointed. When rendering its decision, JAMS will take into account all circumstances, including the links between the cases and the progress already made in the existing Arbitrations. Unless applicable law provides otherwise, where JAMS decides to consolidate a proceeding into a pending Arbitration, the Parties to the consolidated case or cases will be deemed to have waived their right to designate an Arbitrator as well as any contractual provision with respect to the site of the Arbitration. Where a third party seeks to participate in an Arbitration already pending under these Rules or where a Party to an Arbitration under these Rules seeks to compel a third party to participate in a pending Arbitration, the Arbitrator shall determine such request, taking into account all circumstances he or she deems relevant and applicable.	CPR may consolidate where (1) the parties have agreed to consolidation; or (2) all of the claims in the arbitrations are made under the same arbitration agreement; or (3) the claims in the arbitrations are made under more than one arbitration agreement, the arbitrations are between the same parties, the disputes in the arbitrations arise in connection with the same legal relationship, and CPR finds the arbitration agreements to be compatible. Prior to the appointment of an arbitrator, CPR may, at the request of any party, allow third parties to be joined in the arbitration as a party, unless, after giving all parties an opportunity to be heard, CPR finds that joinder should not be permitted. No additional party may be joined after the appointment of an arbitrator unless all parties, including the additional party, agree.	The arbitrator may hear additional claims that were not mentioned in the Arbitration Request Form, provided the Party adding the claims notifies the other Party at least 30 calendar days prior to a scheduled Arbitration, the additional claims are timely as of the date on which they were added, and the other party is not prejudiced in its defense by such addition. The arbitrator shall not consolidate claims of different parties unless the claim is a Class Action claim and then only where the underlying Arbitration agreement allows for the submission of class actions to Arbitration.

Rules	**AAA Construction Industry Arbitration Rules, Standard Track (effective July 1, 2015)**	**JAMS Construction Rules & Procedures (effective June 1, 2021)**	**CPR Administered Arbitration Rules (effective March 1, 2019)**	**NAM Comprehensive Dispute Resolution Rules and Procedures (effective April 18, 2022)**
Mediation Required	Required in all cases where a claim or counterclaim exceeds $100,000, but unless the parties' agreement includes a requirement for mandatory mediation, any party may unilaterally opt out of mediation.	Not required; however, the parties ***may*** agree at any stage of the Arbitration to submit the case to JAMS for mediation.	Not required, but the arbitrator may request CPR to arrange for mediation or CPR may invite the parties to mediate.	Not directly addressed.
Modification of Rules	The parties may modify any period of time by mutual agreement, provided that any such modification that adversely affects the efficient resolution of the dispute is subject to review and approval by the arbitrator.	The parties may agree on any procedures not specified herein or in lieu of these Rules that are consistent with the applicable law and JAMS policies (including, without limitation, Rules 15(i), 30 and 31). The parties shall promptly notify JAMS of any such Party-agreed procedures and shall confirm such procedures in writing. The Party-agreed procedures shall be enforceable as if contained in these Rules.	The parties may agree in writing, or on the record during the course of the proceedings, to modify the Rules, with the exception of Rule 22—providing that neither CPR nor any arbitrator shall be liable to any party for any act or omission in connection with any arbitration conducted under the Rules—which cannot be modified without CPR's written consent.	NAM reserves the right to modify its Rules at any time without prior written notice to the parties. The parties are free at any time to enter into a written agreement to amend or modify any of NAM's Rules. However, NAM's Fee Schedule is not subject to such modification except in the sole discretion of the NAM Administrator.

Rules	**AAA Construction Industry Arbitration Rules, Standard Track (effective July 1, 2015)**	**JAMS Construction Rules & Procedures (effective June 1, 2021)**	**CPR Administered Arbitration Rules (effective March 1, 2019)**	**NAM Comprehensive Dispute Resolution Rules and Procedures (effective April 18, 2022)**
Jurisdiction	The arbitrator has the power to rule on his or her own jurisdiction, including any objections with respect to the existence, scope, or validity of the arbitration agreement.	Jurisdictional and arbitrability disputes, including disputes over the formation, existence, validity, interpretation, or scope of the Agreement under which Arbitration is sought, and who are proper Parties to the Arbitration, shall be submitted to and ruled on by the Arbitrator. The Arbitrator has the authority to determine jurisdiction and arbitrability issues as a preliminary matter.	The tribunal has the power to hear and determine challenges to its jurisdiction, including any objections with respect to the existence, scope, or validity of the arbitration agreement.	Not directly addressed.
Number of Arbitrators (if not set forth in underlying arbitration agreement or otherwise agreed to by parties)	One arbitrator unless the AAA, in its discretion, directs that three arbitrators be appointed. A party may request three arbitrators in the demand or answer, which request the AAA will consider in its discretion.	The Arbitration shall be conducted by one neutral Arbitrator with respect to any disputes arising from residential construction or with respect to any disputes, whether arising from residential or commercial construction, where the collective claims and counterclaims, in the aggregate, are less than two million dollars, unless all Parties agree otherwise. The Arbitration shall be conducted by three neutral Arbitrators in all other disputes, unless the Parties agree otherwise.	One arbitrator where the claim or counterclaim does not exceed $3 million, unless CPR, in its discretion, decides that three arbitrators be appointed due to the complexity of the case or other considerations. In all other cases, a tribunal shall consist of three arbitrators.	One arbitrator where the Claimant seeks $1 million or less. In all other matters, the NAM Administrator has the sole discretion to determine whether a matter should be heard by one or three arbitrator(s).

Rules	AAA Construction Industry Arbitration Rules, Standard Track (effective July 1, 2015)	JAMS Construction Rules & Procedures (effective June 1, 2021)	CPR Administered Arbitration Rules (effective March 1, 2019)	NAM Comprehensive Dispute Resolution Rules and Procedures (effective April 18, 2022)
Discovery	The arbitrator shall manage any necessary exchange of information among the parties with a view to achieving an efficient and economical resolution of the dispute, while at the same time promoting equality of treatment and safeguarding each party's opportunity to fairly present its claims and defenses. The Rules clearly signal that interrogatories, open-ended demands for production, and depositions are considered inappropriate in arbitration. Generally, the parties will be required to produce documents that they will rely upon in the hearings, or that are in their possession, not otherwise available to the other party, and "relevant and material."	The Parties shall cooperate in good faith in the voluntary and informal exchange of all non-privileged documents and other information (including electronically stored information ("ESI")) relevant to the dispute or claim immediately after commencement of the Arbitration. They shall complete an initial exchange of all relevant, non-privileged documents, including, without limitation, copies of all documents in their possession or control on which they rely in support of their positions; names of individuals who may have relevant knowledge or who may be called as witnesses at the Arbitration Hearing; and names of experts who have been retained or who may be called to provide expert testimony at the Arbitration Hearing, within 21 calendar days after all pleadings or notice of claims have been received. Final expert reports of testifying experts will be exchanged as scheduled in the Preliminary Conference or within 14 calendar days after the close of discovery. The Arbitrator may modify these obligations at or following the Preliminary Conference.	The tribunal may require and facilitate such discovery as it shall determine is appropriate in the circumstances, taking into account the needs of the parties, efficiency and minimizing costs.	The parties shall conduct discovery on a voluntary basis, the procedure of which shall be agreed to by the parties. Failing such agreement, the arbitrator(s) shall have the power to order such discovery it considers necessary. Factors considered by the arbitrator(s) include the nature of the claim and counter-claim; the expedited nature of the Arbitration process; and relevance of the discovery sought by a party. The cost of discovery must be commensurate with the amount of the claim, and the request must not be unduly burdensome.

Rules	AAA Construction Industry Arbitration Rules, Standard Track (effective July 1, 2015)	JAMS Construction Rules & Procedures (effective June 1, 2021)	CPR Administered Arbitration Rules (effective March 1, 2019)	NAM Comprehensive Dispute Resolution Rules and Procedures (effective April 18, 2022)
Discovery *(cont.)*		Each Party may take two depositions of either an opposing Party or individuals under the control of the opposing Party. The Parties shall attempt to agree on the time, location, and duration of the deposition, and if the Parties do not agree, these issues shall be determined by the Arbitrator. The necessity of additional depositions shall be determined by the Arbitrator based upon the reasonable need for the requested information, the availability of other discovery options and the burdensomeness of the request on the opposing Parties and the witness.		
Dispositive Motions	Upon prior written application, the arbitrator may permit motions that dispose of all or part of a claim, or narrow the issues in a case.	The Arbitrator may permit any Party to file a Motion for Summary Disposition of a particular claim or issue, either by agreement of all interested Parties or at the request of one Party, provided other interested Parties have reasonable notice to respond to the request. The Request may be granted only if the Arbitrator determines that the requesting Party has shown that the proposed motion is likely to succeed and dispose of or narrow the issues in the case.	The parties may discuss dispositive motions at the initial pre-hearing conference. A party may make a preliminary application to the tribunal to file a motion for early disposition of issues.	No rules in particular, but generally the arbitrator(s) shall have the authority to make rulings on motions.

Rules	AAA Construction Industry Arbitration Rules, Standard Track (effective July 1, 2015)	JAMS Construction Rules & Procedures (effective June 1, 2021)	CPR Administered Arbitration Rules (effective March 1, 2019)	NAM Comprehensive Dispute Resolution Rules and Procedures (effective April 18, 2022)
Evidence	The parties may offer such evidence as is relevant and material to the dispute and shall produce such evidence as the arbitrator may deem necessary to an understanding and determination of the dispute. While conformity to legal rules of evidence is not necessary, the arbitrator shall take into account applicable principles of legal privilege, such as attorney-client confidentiality. The arbitrator shall determine the admissibility, relevance, and materiality of the evidence offered.	Strict conformity to the rules of evidence is not required, except that the Arbitrator shall apply applicable law relating to privileges and work product. The Arbitrator shall consider evidence that he or she finds relevant and material to the dispute, giving the evidence such weight as is appropriate. The Arbitrator may be guided in that determination by principles contained in the Federal Rules of Evidence or any other applicable rules of evidence. The Arbitrator may limit testimony to exclude evidence that would be immaterial, cumulative, or unduly repetitive, without infringing the opportunity of all Parties to present material and relevant evidence.	The tribunal is not required to apply the rules of evidence but shall apply any lawyer-client privilege and work product immunity. The tribunal shall determine the applicability of any privilege or immunity and the admissibility, relevance, materiality, and weight of the evidence offered.	The arbitrator will be guided by the Federal Rules of Evidence but strict conformity to the Rules is not required. The arbitrator(s) will consider evidence that the arbitrator(s) deems relevant and material to the dispute and will accord such weight to the evidence as the arbitrator(s) deems appropriate.

Rules	AAA Construction Industry Arbitration Rules, Standard Track (effective July 1, 2015)	JAMS Construction Rules & Procedures (effective June 1, 2021)	CPR Administered Arbitration Rules (effective March 1, 2019)	NAM Comprehensive Dispute Resolution Rules and Procedures (effective April 18, 2022)
Emergency Relief and Interim Protection	Before an arbitration is initiated, a party may seek emergency relief and an emergency arbitrator will be appointed within one business day, and a schedule established within two business days. After an arbitration is initiated, the arbitrator may take whatever interim measures he or she deems necessary including injunctive relief and measures for the protection or conservation of property and disposition of perishable goods.	The Arbitrator may grant whatever interim measures are deemed necessary, including injunctive relief and measures for the protection or conservation of property and disposition of disposable goods. Such interim measures may take the form of an interim or Partial Final Award, and the Arbitrator may require security for the costs of such measures. Any recourse by a Party to a court for interim or provisional relief shall not be deemed incompatible with the agreement to arbitrate or a waiver of the right to arbitrate.	Before the tribunal is constituted, any party can request that an interim/emergency measure of protection be granted by a special arbitrator. The arbitrator will be appointed within one business day and shall conduct the proceedings "as expeditiously as possible." The (regular) panel may take any interim measures as the tribunal deems necessary to preserve assets or property.	An emergency arbitrator may be appointed before the appointment of an arbitrator for a matter. NAM will attempt to appoint the Emergency arbitrator within one business day of receipt of the request. The Emergency arbitrator shall, within two business days after appointment, or as soon thereafter as possible, establish a schedule for consideration of the request. After an arbitrator(s) is appointed, he or she may issue an Interim Order regarding the subject matter of the dispute.

Rules	AAA Construction Industry Arbitration Rules, Standard Track (effective July 1, 2015)	JAMS Construction Rules & Procedures (effective June 1, 2021)	CPR Administered Arbitration Rules (effective March 1, 2019)	NAM Comprehensive Dispute Resolution Rules and Procedures (effective April 18, 2022)
Closing of Hearing	The arbitrator shall specifically inquire of all parties whether they have any further proofs to offer or witnesses to be heard. Upon receiving negative replies or if satisfied that the record is complete, the arbitrator shall declare the hearing closed. The time limit in which the arbitrator is required to make the award shall commence, in the absence of other agreements by the parties, upon the closing of the hearing. The AAA may extend the time limit for the rendering of the award only in unusual and extreme circumstances.	When the Arbitrator determines that all relevant and material evidence and arguments have been presented, and any interim or partial Awards have been issued, the Arbitrator shall declare the Hearing closed. The Arbitrator may defer the closing of the Hearing until a date determined by the Arbitrator in order to permit the Parties to submit post-Hearing briefs, which may be in the form of a letter, and/or to make closing arguments. If post-Hearing briefs are to be submitted, or closing arguments are to be made, the Hearing shall be deemed closed upon receipt by the Arbitrator of such briefs or at the conclusion of such closing arguments, whichever is later.	The dispute should in most circumstances be heard and submitted to the tribunal for a decision within six months after the initial pre-hearing conference.	No particular rule, but the implication is that the arbitrator(s) must declare the hearings closed.

Rules	AAA Construction Industry Arbitration Rules, Standard Track (effective July 1, 2015)	JAMS Construction Rules & Procedures (effective June 1, 2021)	CPR Administered Arbitration Rules (effective March 1, 2019)	NAM Comprehensive Dispute Resolution Rules and Procedures (effective April 18, 2022)
Reopening of Hearing	The hearing may be reopened on the arbitrator's initiative, or by direction of the arbitrator upon application of a party, at any time before the award is made.	At any time before the Award is rendered, the Arbitrator may, ***sua sponte*** or on application of a Party for good cause shown, reopen the Hearing.	No procedure for reopening per se, but within 20 days after receipt of the award, either party may request the tribunal to clarify the award; to correct any clerical, typographical, or computation errors, or any errors of a similar nature in the award; or to make an additional award as to claims or counterclaims presented in the arbitration but not determined in the award.	No explicit procedure for reopening, but within 15 days after the receipt of the Award, either party, with notice to the other party, may request a correction of the Award regarding any clerical, typographical, or mathematical error in the computation of the Award.
Time for Award	Within 30 days from the date of closing the hearing, or if oral hearings have been waived, from the due date set for receipt of the parties' final statements and proofs.	The Arbitrator shall render a Final Award or a Partial Final Award within 30 calendar days after the date of the close of the Hearing as defined in Rule 22(h) or (i), or, if a Hearing has been waived, within 30 calendar days after the receipt by the Arbitrator of all materials specified by the Parties, except (1) by the agreement of the Parties; (2) upon good cause for an extension of time to render the Award; or (3) as provided in Rule 22(i).	The final award should in most circumstances be submitted by the tribunal to CPR within two months after the close of the proceedings.	The arbitrator(s) will attempt to render the final Award within 30 days from the date the Arbitration is declared closed.

CHAPTER 3

Shaping the Complex or Several-Party Arbitration

DEBORAH BOVARNICK MASTIN

Construction arbitrations, by their very nature, tend to be complex on many levels. Construction projects are structured by multiple tiers of contractual relationships, and generally those contracts contain indemnity and other risk-transfer provisions. Those risk-transfer exposures are frequently protected with insurance coverage and excess insurance coverage. As a result, arbitrations arising from disputes on a construction project often involve numerous parties, potentially including the owner, the owner's representative or construction manager, the design professional, the design professional's subconsultants in a variety of architectural and engineering disciplines, the construction contractor, the contractor's subcontractors and vendors, and an insurance carrier or two for each of these entities. Yet the obligation to arbitrate generally flows from arbitration agreements that are contained in contracts between only two of these parties. If the two parties to an arbitration that is premised on a particular contractual arbitration agreement do not agree to join additional parties to that arbitration proceeding, the following questions arise: whether to allow the joinder of additional proposed parties to the arbitration; or whether to allow two separate arbitrations to be consolidated into one; and who is responsible for making those decisions.

Even when there are no issues relating to the addition of other parties to the arbitration, construction arbitrations can involve dozens or even hundreds of discrete claims, such as a long list of disputed change orders, each involving questions of entitlement, damages, and (many times) resultant delays or disruption to the overall project. Maintaining an orderly and timely process is a foundational priority and a continuing task for all parties involved in an arbitration, if costs and the time to resolution are to be kept within reasonable bounds. In both administered[1] and in nonadministered arbitrations, the applicable arbitration rules provide both rules that govern adding parties and consolidating proceedings and multiple tools to manage the arbitral process efficiently.

Consultation and collaboration among counsel for the parties, outside proceedings in the presence of the arbitrator,[2] are generally the most effective and efficient methods to shape the complex or multiparty arbitration to assure its efficient and orderly progress. While the arbitrator is directly responsible for determining how to optimize the efficient progress of the arbitration, the arbitrator will be guided in significant part by agreements of counsel in this regard. Experienced arbitration counsel generally recognize that agreement among counsel with respect to adding parties, consolidating arbitrations, and adopting case management procedures adapted to the specifics of each complex dispute is ultimately very much in the interests of all parties and the preferred and efficient way to proceed.

I. Organizing the Case at the Initial Scheduling Conference

The initial prehearing conference (also called the scheduling conference or case management conference, depending on the applicable arbitration rules) is the first and best opportunity to establish the organizational structure for the progress of the arbitration and to raise any issues with respect to joining additional parties to the arbitration or consolidating the proceeding with another one. Decisions on such issues are generally not reached at that initial conference, but a procedure for resolving them is, such as establishing deadlines for filing requests to join additional parties or to consolidate separate pending arbitration proceedings and submission of responses to such requests.

The AAA Construction Rules include a checklist of possible initial prehearing conference topics at Rule P-2, and the JAMS Construction Rules have

1. Administered arbitrations are those managed by an independent administering organization, such as the American Arbitration Association (AAA) or JAMS, and nonadministered arbitrations are those where some combination of the arbitrator and the parties handles the administrative tasks, without involvement of an arbitral institution.

2. For convenience, the term "arbitrator" as used in this chapter references both sole arbitrators and panels of multiple arbitrators.

a similar but shorter list at Rule 16 (which also includes "[s]uch other matters as may be suggested by the Parties or the Arbitrator"). The arbitrator will often use these lists to identify the issues needing discussion at the initial conference. Issues commonly addressed include the following:

1. *Detailed Statements of Claims and Defenses.* Arbitration rules usually require only initial pleadings that meet minimum requirements, such as "a statement setting forth the nature of the claim including the relief sought and the amount involved."[3] As a result, the initial demand for arbitration and response often do not provide the opposing party with sufficient detail as to the claims and damages to efficiently prepare its defense. Where this is the case, the arbitrator can expedite matters by establishing early deadlines for the filing of detailed statements of claims, counterclaims, defenses, and damages, with the objective of minimizing subsequent discovery requirements. Early disclosure of the details of claims, damages calculations, and defenses is a powerful tool to clarify the scope of the arbitration and allow the parties to focus their subsequent discovery efforts.

2. *Discovery Needed.* Exchanges of information, particularly relevant documents, is a standard feature of construction arbitrations, and the initial conference is an appropriate time for discussion of how extensive such exchanges need to be, as well as the timing of requests, responses, and actual document production. Similarly, while fact witness depositions in arbitration tend to be limited in number and extent, many construction cases reasonably require a small number of depositions of key witnesses relevant to the actual issues in dispute. The need for, number, and timing of such depositions are generally established at the initial conference, subject to potential change at a later point as the case develops for good cause shown.

3. *Expert Testimony, Reports, and Depositions.* Construction cases most often involve expert testimony, in many instances multiple experts covering different subjects. A preliminary discussion of whether expert testimony is anticipated and in what areas is usually productive at the initial conference, and deadlines for disclosure of experts and filing of expert reports can be established. The potential need for expert depositions is also a fertile subject for discussion, although in many cases detailed expert reports should obviate the need for expert depositions.

Other case-shaping issues that can productively be raised at the initial prehearing conference include potential bifurcation of the proceedings, phased

---

3. American Arbitration Association Construction Industry Arbitration Rules (July 1, 2015) [hereinafter AAA Construction Rules], Rule 4.

hearings, and separate presentations of discrete claims (such as subcontractor pass-through claims), all addressed in more detail later. As with joinder and consolidation issues, generally no decision on such major shaping questions will be made at the initial hearing, but raising the issue at that point for determination a bit later in the proceedings gives all parties and the arbitrator an early opportunity to consider the issue and the most practical alternatives.

II. Joinder and Consolidation: General

In construction arbitrations, the practical advantages of either adding additional parties to an existing arbitration (joinder) or combining two different arbitrations into one (consolidation) are readily apparent. In an owner–contractor dispute, the issues in dispute often involve the interests of one or more subcontractors, and those subcontractors frequently have claims of their own against the contractor that stem from actions or omissions of the owner. Similarly in a contractor–subcontractor dispute, the contractor may believe that the subcontractor's claims are properly the responsibility of the owner. A contractor claim against the owner may, in the owner's view, be the result of a deficiency in the design prepared by the owner's architect or engineer or one of its consultants. In each of these frequently encountered situations, there are often considerable efficiencies to be gained by having the claims of the three or more relevant parties resolved in a single arbitration proceeding. Such a multiparty proceeding also eliminates the potential for inconsistent results that can easily result when the parties' respective rights and obligations are determined in two or more separate proceedings.

In court litigation, the applicable procedural rules provide for the addition of other parties who are needed to achieve an efficient resolution of a multiparty dispute with relatively few barriers, other than jurisdictional requirements and a showing of common issues of fact or law that justify adding the additional parties. The procedural rules similarly provide for allowing a third party to intervene and participate in the litigation. The consensual nature of arbitration, however, which is based on contractual agreements to arbitrate, makes joinder and consolidation a more complex and chancier proposition than in court actions. Construction contracts, and the arbitration agreements they contain, are usually between two parties only; adding a party who has not agreed to arbitrate is generally not possible unless that party consents to be included in the arbitration. However, where there are agreements to arbitrate disputes in each of the relevant contracts among the parties (or consent is later given separately), then consolidation or joinder can, in some but not all instances, be accomplished, although the rules and laws governing this can be complex.

There are two basic issues to be considered in understanding consolidation and joinder in arbitration. The first is whether consolidation or joinder is permissible and obtainable in a particular situation, and the second is whether the determination to join or consolidate is appropriately made by the arbitrators, the arbitral institution, or a court having jurisdiction. The relevant legal principles to be considered are found in the Federal Arbitration Act, any applicable state statute or case law, the rules of the specific arbitral institution, and of course the terms of the parties' contracts.

Starting with the last of these, contractual arbitration agreements vary widely in whether and how they address potential joinder and consolidation. Not infrequently, the issue is not addressed at all. At the other extreme, it is sometimes addressed in considerable detail, specifying particular situations where consolidation or adding additional parties may occur. The most commonly encountered standard form contracts (AIA and ConsensusDocs) both state a general openness to consolidation and joinder in circumstances where there are sufficient common issues of fact or law to support such action. The ConsensusDocs provision is unambiguously supportive of consolidation and joinder wherever appropriate:

> MULTIPARTY PROCEEDING All parties necessary to resolve a matter agree to be parties to the same dispute resolution proceeding, if possible. Appropriate provisions shall be included in all other contracts relating to the Work to provide for the joinder or consolidation of such dispute resolution procedures.[4]

By contrast, the comparable AIA provision allows consolidation but specifies important limitations as to when this can be done:

> Subject to the rules of the American Arbitration Association or other applicable arbitration rules, either party may consolidate an arbitration conducted under this Agreement with any other arbitration to which it is a party provided that (1) the arbitration agreement governing the other arbitration permits consolidation, (2) the arbitrations to be consolidated substantially involve common questions of law or

4. ConsensusDocs 200, Agreement and General Conditions between Owner and Constructor (Lump Sum), art. 12.6 (2017).

fact, and (3) the arbitrations employ materially similar procedural rules and method(s) for selecting arbitrators.[5]

Per the AIA provision, (1) joinder is not addressed, (2) consolidation must be sought by the party that is common to both arbitrations sought to be consolidated, and (3) the other arbitration agreement must affirmatively permit consolidation. As will be seen later, the two limitations on consolidation are more restrictive than what state law in many states would permit.

Where consolidation of arbitrations or joinder of third parties is specifically prohibited, either as a general matter or in the particular circumstances, that agreement is generally respected, precluding joinder or consolidation in the absence of a subsequent agreement to the contrary between those contracting parties. Where the contract is silent on the subject, however, or permits joinder or consolidation in particular circumstances without expressly prohibiting it in others, the issue is likely to be determined on the basis of applicable state law or the rules of the arbitral institution.

The Federal Arbitration Act (FAA) applies to any arbitration agreement in a contract "evidencing a transaction involving [interstate] commerce," and this covers most contracts for significant construction projects.[6] That said, the FAA contains no provisions applicable to joinder or consolidation. Under the 2003 decision in *Green Tree Financial Corp. v. Bazzle*,[7] however, the U.S. Supreme Court clarified that in cases governed by the FAA, the arbitrator and not the court has the power to determine whether an arbitration agreement permits class-action arbitration. Similarly, decisions relating to joinder and consolidation are left to the arbitrator (or arbitral institution, as addressed later), unless the arbitration agreement provides otherwise.[8] This delegation to the arbitrator can, however, be overridden if the parties have specified arbitration rules that allocate this authority otherwise, as is the case (discussed later) in both the AAA and JAMS Rules with respect to consolidation. In cases where the FAA is not applicable, the situation is less clear, and the applicable state law—generally a version of either the Uniform Arbitration

---

5. AIA Document A201-2017, § 15.4.4.

6. 9 U.S.C. § 2. *See* Allied-Bruce Terminix Cos., Inc. v. Dobson, 513 U.S. 265, 269, 272 (1995) (discussing application of the FAA's interstate commerce requirement).

7. 539 U.S. 444, 452–53 (2003).

8. Certain Underwriters at Lloyd's London v. Westchester Fire Ins. Co., 489 F.3d 580 (3rd Cir. 2007); Shaw's Supermarkets, Inc. v. United Food & Com. Workers Union, Local 791, AFL-CIO, 321 F.3d 251 (1st Cir. 2003).

Act (UAA) or the Revised Uniform Arbitration Act (RUAA)—determines whether the court or arbitrator is to decide the issue.

A. Joinder

State statutes do not commonly address joinder of additional parties to an arbitration, and neither the UAA nor the RUAA has any specific provision relating to joinder. Accordingly, issues of joinder are principally determined in accordance with the applicable arbitral institution rules.

Rule R-7 of the AAA Construction Rules governs both consolidation of arbitrations and joinder of additional parties to an arbitration. The hallmark of the AAA process is the appointment of a separate arbitrator (the "Rule 7 arbitrator") to determine issues of joinder or consolidation, and this arbitrator is ineligible to serve as an arbitrator on the merits of the dispute. A request to join an additional party must be filed within 90 days after notice from AAA that the administrative filing requirements regarding the arbitration are satisfied (submitting a conforming demand for arbitration and a copy of the arbitration agreement and paying the initial filing fee) or before appointment of the merits arbitrator, whichever is later. After that point, a joinder request is not permitted "absent a determination by the Merits Arbitrator that good cause was shown for the late request." The comparable Rule 6 of the JAMS Construction Rules, by contrast, has no express time limitations on raising either joinder or consolidation.

Rule R-7 requires service of the request on the party sought to be joined, as well as existing parties, and allows 14 days for a response. If the party sought to be joined is already a party to another AAA arbitration, failing to respond to the joinder request within 14 days is a waiver of any objection to joinder. If the party to be joined is *not* a party to an ongoing AAA arbitration, then the party requesting joinder must initiate an arbitration against the party to be joined. Rule R-7(c) then concludes: "If no response to the joinder request is received *by a party that is not a party to an ongoing arbitration*, that party will be deemed to have denied the joinder request."[9]

So, in effect, joinder is really only available under the AAA Construction Rules as to entities that are already a party to an ongoing AAA arbitration or can be made one. Otherwise, the party sought to be joined can effectively defeat the joinder request simply by ignoring it. That party may also have reasonable grounds to object to being joined, as discussed later.

9. Emphasis added.

The JAMS Construction Rules address joinder in Rule 6(f), as follows: "Where a third party seeks to participate in an Arbitration already pending under these Rules or where a Party to an Arbitration under these Rules seeks to compel a third party to participate in a pending Arbitration, the Arbitrator shall determine such request, taking into account all circumstances he or she deems relevant and applicable." In other words, the merits arbitrator makes the determination, and there is no provision for appointment of a special arbitrator to determine joinder issues.

No matter what rules are applicable, late efforts to join additional parties generally have a disruptive effect on the progress of an ongoing arbitration and may well affect the likelihood of success of a contested request for joinder. The later in the proceedings the request is filed, the greater the challenge to the requesting party to demonstrate good cause for the joinder.

Legal and jurisdictional issues also may affect the determination as to whether to allow joinder. To assist in determining these issues, the arbitrator is likely to request briefing from the affected parties. A threshold issue is whether there exists a written arbitration agreement between a current party to the arbitration and the prospective party sought to be joined. Often, although there is a written arbitration agreement between a party and a prospective party, the terms of the arbitration agreements are in conflict. For example, the various arbitration agreements may specify different jurisdictions' laws to govern the arbitration, or different sites of the arbitration hearings, or different arbitration rules, or different administering arbitral institutions, or different numbers of arbitrators to resolve disputes arising under each contract. These misalignments may prevent a party from achieving joinder of other parties who may be responsible directly or by indemnification for the damages claimed in the arbitration. As a general rule, a disconnect of this type where the joining party would need to forego what is deemed an important substantive right will be sufficient grounds to deny joinder, in the absence of an agreement on how the disconnect will be resolved.[10]

Factual issues pertinent to a request for joinder include such considerations as the level of involvement of the prospective party and whether the party sought to be joined was involved in the issues already identified as being in dispute in the arbitration. If, for example, no electrical defects or delays

---

10. *E.g.*, Hyundai Am., Inc. v. Meissner & Wurst GmbH & Co., 26 F. Supp. 2d 1271 (N.D. Cal. 1998) (consolidation denied because of differing applicable state law and specified arbitration venues in different states).

associated with the installation of electrical components are alleged in the pending arbitration, joinder of the electrical subcontractor to resolve separate disputes with that subcontractor will be difficult to justify.

Also significant is the extent to which the joinder of the prospective party would detract from the efficiency of the arbitral proceedings. While adding additional parties may serve important goals such as eliminating the need for duplicative separate proceedings and enhancing the ability of the arbitrator to order complete relief, increasing the number of parties involved in a single arbitration almost always extends and complicates the proceedings, although partial consolidation measures (as discussed later) can mitigate this effect. This is due to the likely increased volume of discovery, increased difficulty in finding agreeable dates for the hearing and other pre- and posthearing actions, an extended hearing due to each witness being subject to cross-examination by multiple parties, and the potential for multiplying prehearing motions. These are not trivial considerations, and the benefits of adding the party need to clearly outweigh the increased complexity of the proceeding. The same is true, of course, when consolidating two separate arbitrations.

An arbitral institution does not have the power to compel a party to join an arbitration unless it is party to another arbitration at the same institution (or can be made one, in which case the two arbitrations become subject to possible consolidation), and arbitrators alone cannot force parties not before them to participate in the arbitration. The College of Commercial Arbitrators' "Best Practices Guide" also cautions: "When arbitrators who have parties before them contend that other parties who did not sign the arbitration agreement should be added to the arbitration (e.g., on a theory of alter ego, corporate affiliation or otherwise), such relief is ordinarily available only from a court."[11] This advice follows from the reality that the arbitrator has no power over a nonparty unless the nonparty consents to participate, unlike a court with legal authority over parties properly served and within its jurisdiction, whether or not they actually appear.

Clearly joinder (as well as consolidation) is much facilitated if the key contracts for execution of a construction project contain dispute resolution provisions that are consistent in specifying arbitration, under the same set of arbitration rules and same governing law. This congruence should include the contracts between owner and contractor, contractor and subcontractor, owner

11. The College of Commercial Arbitrators Guide to Best Practices in Commercial Arbitration 139–40 (4th ed. 2017).

and design professional, and design professional and subconsultants. Perfect congruence is not necessarily required, and some disconnects can be overcome, depending on the specific situation. The inability to require the joinder of a downstream party or a party who may have contributed to the damages asserted by the claimant means potential exposure to conflicting outcomes in different proceedings, plus the added costs of having to participate in two or more separate dispute resolution proceedings instead of one multiparty proceeding. While joinder or consolidation in appropriate circumstances is to be hoped for, it is an objective often not capable of being realized due to such disconnects, at least absent agreement by the parties involved.

B. Consolidation

The situation with consolidation of two separate arbitrations involves many of the same issues as joinder but is often significantly more complex than the issue of joinder. To begin with, almost half of the states have provisions in their arbitration statutes that address consolidation of separate arbitrations, either in stand-alone statutory provisions (as in California) or via the RUAA. These provisions often add another layer of complexity to consolidation issues. The RUAA, unlike its predecessor the UAA, does specifically allow for consolidation in section 10, which provides:

> (a) Except as otherwise provided in subsection (c), upon motion of a party to an agreement to arbitrate or to an arbitration proceeding, the court may order consolidation of separate arbitration proceedings as to all or some of the claims if:
>
> > (1) there are separate agreements to arbitrate or separate arbitration proceedings between the same persons or one of them is a party to a separate agreement to arbitrate or a separate arbitration proceeding with a third person;
> >
> > (2) the claims subject to the agreements to arbitrate arise in substantial part from the same transaction or series of related transactions;
> >
> > (3) the existence of a common issue of law or fact creates the possibility of conflicting decisions in the separate arbitration proceedings; and
> >
> > (4) prejudice resulting from a failure to consolidate is not outweighed by the risk of undue delay or prejudice to the rights of or hardship to parties opposing consolidation.

(b) The court may order consolidation of separate arbitration proceedings as to some claims and allow other claims to be resolved in separate arbitration proceedings.

(c) The court may not order consolidation of the claims of a party to an agreement to arbitrate if the agreement prohibits consolidation.

The RUAA has been adopted, as of this writing, in 21 states and the District of Columbia.[12] Two important aspects of RUAA section 10 are worth noting. First, it provides that the *court* may order consolidation and does not address whether arbitrators *also* have the power to order consolidation. However, there is precedent for the proposition that the court's authority is not exclusive and the arbitrator (or arbitral institution) also has concurrent power to consolidate.[13] Moreover, as the RUAA's assignment of consolidation authority to the court conflicts with the Supreme Court decision in *Green Tree Financial* that under the FAA this authority is delegated to the arbitrator, this aspect of RUAA section 10 may also be preempted by the FAA when the FAA applies. Second, section 10 does not require that either of the two pertinent agreements to arbitrate expressly permit consolidation, but it does expressly prohibit consolidation where the arbitration agreement prohibits this.

With respect to the very similar consolidation statute in California,[14] it has been held that since the FAA is silent on consolidation and consolidation does not contravene the underlying principles of the FAA, the FAA does *not* preempt the state statute expressly allowing for consolidation.[15]

In sum, in light of section 10 of the RUAA, *Green Tree Financial* does not fully remove the courts from making consolidation decisions, most clearly in situations where the FAA does not apply.

---

12. Alaska, Arizona, Arkansas, Colorado, Connecticut, District of Columbia, Florida, Hawaii, Kansas, Michigan, Minnesota, Nevada, New Jersey, New Mexico, North Carolina, North Dakota, Oklahoma, Oregon, Pennsylvania, Utah, Washington, and West Virginia. *Arbitration Act (2000)*, UNIF. L. COMM'N, https://www.uniformlaws.org/viewdocument/final-act-2 (last visited Apr. 12, 2023).

13. Yuen v. Super. Ct., 121 Cal. App. 4th 1133, 1135 (2004).

14. CAL. CODE OF CIV. PROC. § 1281.3. Similar stand-alone consolidation statutes can be found at GA. CODE § 9-9-6(e) and MASS. GEN. LAWS ch. 251, § 2A.

15. Garden Grove Cmty. Church v. Pittsburgh-Des Moines Steel Co., 140 Cal. App. 3d 251, 262–63 (1983). In *New England Energy, Inc. v. Keystone Shipping Co.*, 855 F.2d 1 (1st Cir. 1988), it was similarly held that a state law consolidation provision is not preempted by the FAA.

Both the AAA Construction Rules and the JAMS Construction Rules deal expressly with consolidation, and in both cases the authority to decide whether consolidation is appropriate is removed by rule from the merits arbitrator. Under Rule R-7 of the AAA Construction Rules, the procedure for consolidation in AAA cases, as noted previously, is to appoint a separate Rule 7 arbitrator to consider solely the question of consolidation. The JAMS Construction Rules address the question of consolidation specifically in Rule 6(e) and provide that JAMS, and not the arbitrator, will decide whether consolidation is appropriate.

Each approach has its benefits and drawbacks. The AAA approach of appointing a separate Rule 7 arbitrator inevitably causes potentially significant delay to the proceedings, as the special arbitrator must be selected and then typically the parties are allowed time to brief the issues before a decision can be rendered. The JAMS approach puts the decision in the hands of JAMS administrators rather than an arbitrator selected from "a panel of construction attorneys who have experience with consolidation or joinder issues" per Rule R-7 but usually avoids much of the delay inherent in the AAA Rule 7 process.

The considerations involved in resolving requests to consolidate separate arbitrations are similar to those that arise in the question of joinder. The central issue is always whether there are sufficient common issues of fact or law to justify consolidation, either on the basis of efficiency (deciding the common issues once instead of twice in separate proceedings) or to avoid the risk of inconsistent outcomes.[16] JAMS Rule 6(e) also identifies "the links between the cases and the progress already made in the existing Arbitrations" as relevant considerations. Clearly, consolidating a newly filed arbitration with one that has substantially progressed toward the merits hearing is significantly more disruptive and likely to prolong the proceedings than combining two arbitrations that have both been recently filed. This factor is what motivates the AAA rule that consolidation or joinder must generally be raised before appointment of the arbitrators, absent good cause, and it strongly counsels seeking consolidation at the earliest available opportunity in all situations.

The concern identified in RUAA section 10(a)(4) regarding the "prejudice resulting from a failure to consolidate [not being] outweighed by the risk of undue delay or prejudice to the rights of or hardship to parties opposing consolidation" always comes into play as well. The decision-maker will weigh

16. Case law under Federal Rule of Civil Procedure 42 on consolidation of actions in federal court is frequently persuasive on the factual situations where consolidation would be appropriate.

the advantages of consolidation against the disadvantages, whether expressly stated in the applicable rule or not. The disadvantages of consolidation include not only the more cumbersome proceeding that typically results from consolidation (and the delay in resolution this often entails) but also the potential prejudice to the usual rights of each party to participate in the appointment of arbitrators and to have the hearing held at the site agreed in its arbitration agreement.

If the arbitrators have already been appointed in one proceeding and a second is consolidated with it, the added party in the consolidated proceeding may well lose any right to appoint an arbitrator or address the site of the hearing. JAMS Rule 6(e) deals with this expressly via a deemed waiver:

> Unless applicable law provides otherwise, where JAMS decides to consolidate a proceeding into a pending Arbitration, the Parties to the consolidated case or cases will be deemed to have waived their right to designate an Arbitrator as well as any contractual provision with respect to the site of the Arbitration.

The preamble to JAMS Rule 6(e), "Unless applicable law provides otherwise," is also significant, as there is case law in some states to the effect that a need to compromise important substantive rights like the right to constitute the arbitration panel in the agreed manner is sufficient by itself to defeat consolidation.[17] AAA Rule R-7, by contrast, deals with the issue of appointing arbitrators in a different manner. It provides that the Rule 7 arbitrator, if consolidation is directed, "may also establish a process for selecting merits arbitrators for any ongoing or newly constituted case and, unless agreed otherwise by the parties, the allocation of responsibility for arbitrator compensation among the parties."

Both the AAA Construction Rules and JAMS Rules contain serious limits on the situations where cases will be considered for consolidation that stem from the limits of what is under the arbitral institution's control. JAMS Rule 6(e) illustrates the problem:

---

17. Hyundai Am., Inc. v. Meissner & Wurst GmbH & Co., 26 F. Supp. 2d 1217 (N.D. Cal. 1998); *Garden Grove Cmty. Church*, 140 Cal. App. 3d at 263 (consolidation permitted "[w]here no substantive or substantial procedural contractual rights or obligations are affected"); Parker v. McCaw, 125 Cal. App. 4th 1494, 1506 (2005) (consolidation was appropriate, but trial court erred by resolving conflicting arbitration provisions in favor of a single arbitrator, because the right to a three-arbitrator panel is a substantial contractual right that needed to be honored).

(e) Unless the Parties' Agreement or applicable law provides otherwise, JAMS, if it determines that the Arbitrations so filed have common issues of fact or law, may consolidate Arbitrations in the following instances:

(i) *If a Party files more than one Arbitration with JAMS*, JAMS may consolidate two or more of the Arbitrations into a single Arbitration.

(ii) Where a Demand or Demands for Arbitration is or are submitted naming Parties already involved in another Arbitration or Arbitrations *pending under these Rules*, JAMS may decide that the new case or cases shall be consolidated into one or more of the pending proceedings and referred to one of the Arbitrators or panels of Arbitrators already appointed.

(iii) Where a Demand or Demands for Arbitration is or are submitted naming parties that are not identical to the Parties in the existing Arbitration or Arbitrations, JAMS may decide that the new case or cases shall be consolidated into one or more of the pending proceedings and referred to one of the Arbitrators or panels of Arbitrators already appointed.[18]

Neither JAMS nor AAA has any authority or control over parties who are not involved in an arbitration subject to its rules. Accordingly, neither has the ability to consolidate a JAMS arbitration with an AAA arbitration (or one pending under another arbitral institution's rules) or vice versa. While there is little to no case law on point, it is questionable whether a court would order consolidation in such a situation either, given the reality that at least one party would arguably be prejudiced significantly by denying it the ability to arbitrate under the arbitration rules to which it agreed.

Another key issue is whether two arbitrations can be consolidated where consolidation is not precluded by the arbitration agreements but not expressly authorized either. This situation arises both where the arbitration agreement authorizes consolidation in some specific instances, without prohibiting it in other situations, and where the arbitration agreement is simply silent on the subject of consolidation. Put another way, does the failure to prohibit consolidation imply consent to consolidation where the key element of common issues of fact or law exists, or alternatively, does it imply the opposite?

---

18. Emphasis added.

There is case law supporting both positions. In older federal cases (predating *Green Tree Financial*, decided in 2003, which clarified that this is not a decision for the court), the majority rule appears to have been that silence on the issue of consolidation in the particular circumstances presented precludes consolidation.[19]

Bruner & O'Connor on Construction Law is notably critical of cases holding that silence on the issue precludes consolidation:

> The reasoning that if parties have not expressly consented to consolidation they must have rejected it is peculiar. In the construction industry, it is just as likely that parties intend to be able to resolve disputes between multiple parties involving common questions of law and fact in one proceeding. . . . The cases that rush to a conclusion that the lack of language expressly permitting consolidation is alone sufficient to conclude that consolidation should not be ordered are unwise. At a minimum, inquiry should be made into what the parties intended at the time they entered into their agreement.[20]

There are certainly cases holding that silence does not imply prohibition and consolidation in an otherwise proper case is permissible unless specifically prohibited, as well as cases to the contrary.[21]

---

19. *E.g.*, Baesler v. Cont'l Grain Co., 900 F.2d 1193 (8th Cir. 1990). *See also* cases cited in Philip L. Bruner & Patrick J. O'Connor, Bruner & O'Connor on Construction Law § 20:76 (Westlaw 2022) [hereinafter Bruner & O'Connor].

20. Bruner & O'Connor, *supra* note 19, § 20:76. *See also* Ian R. McNeil et al., Federal Arbitration Law: Agreement, Awards & Remedies under the Federal Arbitration Act § 33.3.1 (1999 Supplement).

21. *Approving consolidation*: Lyndoe v. D.R. Horton, Inc., 287 P.3d 357 (N.M. Ct. App. 2012) (RUAA factors for consolidation satisfied, although arbitration agreements silent on consolidation); *New Eng. Energy, Inc.*, 855 F.2d 1; Gavlik Constr. Co. v. H.F. Campbell Co., 526 F.2d 777 (3rd Cir. 1975), *abrogated on other grounds*, Zosky v. Boyer, 856 F.2d 554 (3rd Cir. 1988); Sullivan Cnty. v. Edward L. Nezelek, Inc., 42 N.Y.2d 123 (1977) ("parties signing an agreement to arbitrate must be held to do so in contemplation of the announced authority of the courts to direct consolidation"); *Garden Grove Cmty. Church*, 140 Cal. App. 3d at 263; United Elec., Radio & Mech. Workers of Am. v. Honeywell Inc., 522 F.2d 1221, 1226 (7th Cir. 1975). *Contra* Bay Cnty. Bldg. Auth. v. Spencer Bros., 140 Mich. App. 182, 362 N.W.2d 739 (1984); Pueblo of Laguna v. Cillessen & Son, Inc., 101 N.M. 341, 682 P.2d 197 (1984) (no authority to consolidate in the absence of consent, a state statute authorizing consolidation, or an applicable arbitration rule authorizing consolidation).

C. Variations on Complete Consolidation

Consolidation of two previously separate arbitrations does not mean that the case going forward will necessarily be administered as a single proceeding with an added party. Where separate arbitrations are not suitable for complete consolidation, various forms of partial consolidation are possible. Arbitrations can be consolidated for prehearing purposes only, preserving separate merits hearings in each (but typically before the same arbitrator). Even more limited, consolidation can encompass only exchanges of certain information or documents, so that the information or documents exchanged in one arbitration may be introduced in the other proceeding, but otherwise case administration and the merits hearings proceed separately. Or there can be a single, consolidated merits hearing that is effectively subdivided into two or more parts, so that all parties need not attend and participate in the entire hearing, only the portion that involves their interests. Other partial consolidation structures are also possible, utilizing arbitration's inherent flexibility to tailor an arbitration process that maximizes efficiency and leads to prompt resolution.

III. Bifurcated Proceedings

The flexibility available in arbitration extends to the order of proof and the protocols for presenting evidence. Bifurcation of the issues—separating the contested issues into separate, sequential hearings—can promote overall efficiency and likely reduce the cost of a complex arbitration proceeding. The most common form of bifurcation is into separate issues of entitlement, which are heard and determined initially, and issues of damages, determined in a subsequent hearing after the entitlement rulings are issued. This streamlines the effort and expense involved in the damages phase, by eliminating the need for damages evidence on issues where no entitlement is found. Often more importantly, the quantum of damages may be capable of resolution by settlement once the entitlement issues are determined, eliminating the need for a second hearing altogether.

In other situations, the bifurcation may involve separating the presentation of evidence on one or two central issues first, followed, if needed, by a second hearing encompassing all remaining issues. This is most effective when the parties can agree that once the central issues are resolved, a settlement of the remaining issues should be reasonably achievable. Similarly, an initial hearing regarding technical issues (such as questions of asserted defective or nonconforming work), followed by a separate hearing covering resultant schedule impact issues, can offer the prospect of significant efficiencies.

Where claims for indemnification are asserted in the same arbitration as claims of direct breach of contract, a bifurcated hearing that addresses the direct claims first, deferring the indemnity claims to a second hearing, can similarly offer efficiencies. Oftentimes, the determination of liability and damages on the direct claims will establish the parameters for claims of indemnification based on damages incurred by third parties that are related to the same conduct or event. Exchanges of information can then be sequenced so that records relating to the indemnification claims need not be provided until after the initial determination of the related direct claims, with significant potential cost savings in the event that the related direct claims are denied.

By no means are all complex cases suitable for bifurcation in any of these ways. As a general rule, if there is no settlement after the initial hearing, then the overall time to final resolution of a bifurcated case will almost certainly be extended as compared to a single merits hearing encompassing all issues. The added time to resolution and added transaction costs associated with two hearings may well outweigh any savings from reducing the scope of the second hearing or discovery deferred until after the initial hearing. The specifics of each case must be carefully evaluated before bifurcation. The arbitrator will generally request the parties to confer as to their respective views on the bifurcation options and to present their joint or divergent recommendations before making any determination about whether bifurcation would enhance the efficiency of the arbitration.

IV. Phased Arbitration Hearings

Closely related to bifurcation is dividing a single merits hearing into distinct phases. The evidentiary hearings in complex construction arbitrations may often be streamlined by implementing a nontraditional structure regarding the order of the presentation of evidence on the various topics to be addressed. Where the arbitrator is required to determine a long list of discrete issues (such as a list of disputed change orders or disputed punchlist and warranty items), phasing or sequencing the presentation of evidence to address a single item or group of related items at a time, before moving on to the next item or group, both enhances the efficiency of the proceedings and avoids the ready possibility of confusion on the part of counsel and arbitrator alike in understanding the whole of the evidence relating to a particular issue.

Phasing can also be utilized where the resolution of some disputed issues is dependent on the determination of others, at least if the parties and arbitrator agree that a decision on the predicate issue is capable of being rendered on a "real time" basis, shortly after the evidence on that item is presented, without need for posthearing briefing or a significant pause in the hearing before proceeding further.

V. Presentation of Related Subcontractor/ Supplier Claims or Defined Scopes of Work

In cases where there are numerous subcontractors or suppliers that will participate in the hearing, each presenting its individual claims that are alleged as "pass-through" claims for which the owner is responsible (whether the subcontractors are actual parties to the proceeding or just appearing by permission or agreement to present their specific issues), a version of phasing the merits hearing is often appropriate to address the subcontractor/supplier claims in an efficient manner. Evidence regarding a specific scope of work (concrete, HVAC, electrical, or interior finishes, for example) can be presented together and addressed in a focused manner during the arbitration hearing. The advantage of such a presentation structure is that counsel and witnesses for the individual subcontractors or suppliers with only limited participation in the project need not be involved in the entire hearing and can be excused from attending other portions of the hearing before and after their specific issues have been presented. In an extended hearing, this can significantly reduce the costs of the arbitration for those with limited involvement in the overall dispute, who would otherwise need to be present continuously to deal with questions relating to their limited work scope that surface only in bits and pieces as the testimony proceeds.

Other useful techniques for streamlining the arbitration hearing, such as joint testimony of expert witnesses and the use of witness panels, are covered in detail in Chapter 7.

VI. Managing the Sequence and Scheduling of Components of the Arbitration

Any of the aforementioned options for efficiently shaping the arbitration proceedings should be determined well in advance of the evidentiary hearings, not left to the last minute. Counsel reasonably require a sufficient opportunity to plan the presentation of evidence effectively within the arbitration procedure that is determined, and leaving such decisions to the start of the merits hearing, for example, does little to promote efficiency and is unlikely to yield any significant savings in costs or schedule. Issues relating to shaping the arbitration accordingly should be raised as early as possible, preferably at the initial preliminary hearing, so that they can be considered carefully and determined in accordance with a reasonable process in the months before the merits hearing, with input from all parties. The process as so determined should then be memorialized in a written prehearing order so that counsel are all on the same page in their hearing preparations and preparation of witnesses.

CHAPTER 4

Document Exchange and Discovery

DEBORAH S. BALLATI

Although arbitration was historically designed and lauded as a dispute resolution option that largely dispensed with, or completely avoided, the extensive, costly, and sometimes burdensome discovery pursued in traditional litigation, that has not been the case for construction arbitrations for many decades. Especially in more complex construction disputes, but also in many simpler ones, some level of traditional fact discovery is generally contemplated and desired by the parties. The form of fact discovery that is most often seen is the primary subject of this chapter—document discovery. An exchange of relevant documents, including, where applicable, e-discovery of electronically stored documents like emails, is an almost universal element of construction arbitrations.

Recognizing this fact, many of the arbitral institutions that administer construction arbitrations have promulgated rules and protocols that permit such discovery; however, the institutions have also included in their rules requirements that are intended to limit the discovery process to preserve the efficiency and cost-effectiveness of arbitration. Despite the effort directed toward this goal in the rules, arbitrators are often asked to address requests for expanded discovery from one or more parties. Those requests can include everything from minor modifications of the limitations imposed by the applicable rules to allowing the parties to use most or all of the discovery options available in the relevant state court or under the Federal Rules of Civil Procedure. When the parties cannot agree on the scope of discovery, arbitrators are increasingly called upon to hear and decide discovery motions to resolve such disagreements. After establishing the arbitration schedule at the initial preliminary conference, discovery motions are often one of the first significant issues presented to the arbitrator for resolution.

This chapter first discusses the document discovery–related rules promulgated by the various arbitral institutions that administer arbitrations, the other discovery tools most commonly applied in construction arbitrations, and how the rules of some major institutions differ from or are similar to one another. The chapter then turns to some practice tips for arbitration discovery and suggestions for arguing discovery issues to the arbitrator.[1] We focus on the arbitral rules most frequently used by construction practitioners in domestic cases—specifically, those promulgated by JAMS, the American Arbitration Association (AAA), FedArb, and (particularly in California) ADR Services. In contrast, Chapter 5 addresses depositions and other discovery techniques, and Chapter 10 addresses discovery as it is practiced in international arbitrations.

I. Comparing and Contrasting the Arbitral Rules and Guidelines Pertaining to Document Discovery

Each of the different bodies that routinely administer construction arbitrations has rules pertaining to discovery. Those rules vary somewhat from organization to organization and sometimes within each organization depending on the nature or magnitude of the dispute being arbitrated.

The JAMS Engineering and Construction Arbitration Rules and Procedures (JAMS Construction Rules), the JAMS Comprehensive Arbitration Rules and Procedures (JAMS Comprehensive Rules), and the JAMS Engineering and Construction Arbitration Rules and Procedures for Expedited Arbitration (JAMS Expedited Construction Rules) are all commonly used in construction arbitrations (collectively, the JAMS Rules).[2] Within the JAMS Comprehensive Rules, there are also expedited procedures that the parties can adopt either in their contract or at the time a dispute arises (the JAMS Expedited Procedures).[3] JAMS explains that the goals of its expedited arbitration

1. For clarity, "arbitrator" as used here refers to both sole arbitrators and panels of three arbitrators.

2. JAMS Engineering and Construction Arbitration Rules and Procedures (June 1, 2021) [hereinafter JAMS Construction Rules]; JAMS Comprehensive Arbitration Rules and Procedures (June 1, 2021) [hereinafter JAMS Comprehensive Rules]; JAMS Engineering and Construction Arbitration Rules & Procedures for Expedited Arbitration (June 1, 2021) [hereinafter JAMS Expedited Construction Rules].

3. JAMS Comprehensive Rules, *supra* note 2, Rules 16.1, 16.2.

procedures are "to save clients time and money" and to allow the clients to "craft[] a process that is commensurate with the dispute," creating "an efficient process" that "limits depositions, document requests and e-discovery" if the party chooses.[4]

In addition to what is specifically provided in the JAMS Rules, JAMS has published Recommended Arbitration Discovery Protocols for Domestic, Commercial Cases (JAMS Discovery Protocols) since 2010. The purpose of these protocols is to "provide JAMS arbitrators with an effective tool that will help them exercise their sound judgment in furtherance of achieving an efficient, cost-effective process that affords the parties a fair opportunity to be heard." The Discovery Protocols note that "the experience, talent and preferences brought to arbitration will vary with the arbitrator. It follows that the framework of arbitration discovery will always be based on the judgment of the arbitrator, brought to bear in the context of variables such as the applicable rules, the custom and practice for arbitrations in the industry in question, and the expectations and preferences of the parties and their counsel."

The JAMS Discovery Protocols provide useful guidance for tailoring discovery to get the parties what they need to prepare their case, while also staying focused and narrow enough to achieve the efficiency that arbitration is intended to provide.[5] The guidance provided in the JAMS Discovery Protocols covers document requests and exchanges and e-discovery, as well as other discovery matters. Exhibit A to the JAMS Discovery Protocols also provides a fairly detailed roadmap to those considerations JAMS arbitrators may focus on in resolving discovery issues, such as the nature of the dispute, the parties' agreement, relevance, privilege, and confidentiality, and the characteristics and needs of the parties.

Like JAMS, the AAA has promulgated a set of Discovery Best Practices for Construction Arbitration (AAA Discovery Best Practices) that provide helpful guidance for arbitrators and counsel. The 2021 version highlights the AAA's guiding principles that "construction arbitration should provide a less

---

4. *Arbitrators & Arbitration Services*, JAMS, https://www.jamsadr.com/arbitration (last visited Apr. 12, 2023). JAMS also has a set of streamlined rules for use in cases where the parties agree to use them or, in the absence of an agreement, where no disputed claim or counterclaim exceeds $250,000, not including interest or attorneys' fees. JAMS Streamlined Arbitration Rules and Procedures (June 1, 2021) [hereinafter JAMS Streamlined Rules]. Although these rules are not often specifically designated by parties in construction disputes, they may be useful for smaller cases.

5. *Arbitration Discovery Protocols*, JAMS (Jan. 6, 2010), https://www.jamsadr.com/arbitration-discovery-protocols/ [hereinafter JAMS Discovery Protocols].

expensive, more expeditious and final form of dispute resolution than that offered in state or federal litigation" and that "discovery decisions should be proportional to the size and complexity of the matter being heard."[6] As to document exchanges, the AAA Discovery Best Practices note that, "due to the number of documents, discovery in a construction dispute is different than in a typical commercial dispute." Thus, "except for privileged or possibly proprietary documents, each side should be afforded the opportunity to examine the other party's project files that are relevant and material to the resolution of the issues in dispute." However, this exchange of information "is not intended to be a Federal Court-style document exchange, as the language of the Rules makes clear (Construction R24, R25 and F8/Commercial R22, R23 and E5). Rather, the scope of document requests and the exchange of documents should be narrowly tailored and proportionate to the disputes at hand."

The AAA Discovery Best Practices provide useful, specific tips regarding limitations on discovery tailored to the nature and complexity of the dispute; they also remind arbitrators of their discretion and management authority as it can be exercised in dealing with discovery issues. For example, the AAA Discovery Best Practices note that the arbitrator "should consider ordering that the parties immediately initiate a litigation hold, if they have not done so already, to avoid later fighting about document-retention issues."

The AAA, like JAMS, has different sets of rules for different types of arbitrations, which "cover the spectrum of industries and fields."[7] The AAA rules most commonly used in construction cases are the AAA Construction Industry Arbitration Rules (AAA Construction Rules) and the AAA Commercial Arbitration Rules (AAA Commercial Rules).[8]

Two additional arbitration institutions, ADR Services, Inc. (ADR Services) and Federal Arbitration, Inc. (FedArb), also include rules specific to discovery. ADR Services has only one set of arbitration rules.[9] FedArb has a

---

6. *American Arbitration Association Discovery Best Practices for Construction Arbitration: Recommendations for AAA Construction Advocates and Arbitrators* (2022) [hereinafter AAA Discovery Best Practices], https://go.adr.org/rs/294-SFS-516/images/AAA341_AAA_Discovery_Best_Practices_Construction_Arbitration.pdf.

7. *What We Do*, Am. Arb. Ass'n, https://www.adr.org/Arbitration (last visited Apr. 12, 2023).

8. American Arbitration Association Construction Industry Arbitration Rules (July 1, 2015) [hereinafter AAA Construction Rules]; American Arbitration Association Commercial Arbitration Rules (Sept. 1, 2022) [hereinafter AAA Commercial Rules].

9. ADR Services, Inc. Arbitration Rules (Jan. 29, 2021) [hereinafter ADR Services Rules].

set of basic arbitration rules[10] and a set of procedures for expedited disposition.[11] Neither of these organizations has different sets of rules based on the type of case or subject matter.

Although the rules of these various organizations are similar on many topics, they have differences that may end up being significant depending on the nature of the construction dispute, the level of rancor in the proceeding, and the oftentimes competing goals of the parties once a dispute arises. The most significant areas for comparison of the various rules include the extent to which the rules are self-executing, the role of the arbitrator in discovery at the beginning and throughout the proceeding, the limitations and deadlines included in the discovery rules, issues related to e-discovery, third-party discovery, and the consequences of discovery violations. Each of these areas is discussed next.

A. Self-Execution of the Rules

One of the most pronounced differences between the rules of the various organizations is the extent to which they are self-executing. The JAMS Rules expressly place the initial burden on the parties to move forward with the discovery process, advising the parties to "cooperate in good faith in the voluntary and informal exchange of all non-privileged documents and other information (including electronically stored information (ESI)) relevant to the dispute or claim *immediately after commencement of the Arbitration*."[12] They provide that the parties "shall complete an initial exchange of all relevant, non-privileged documents . . . and names of individuals whom they may call as witnesses at the Arbitration Hearing."[13] Moreover, the JAMS Rules provide that as the parties become aware of new documents or information, they "continue to be obligated to provide relevant, non-privileged documents to supplement their identification of witnesses and experts and to honor any informal agreements or understandings between the Parties regarding documents or information to be exchanged."[14]

---

10. FedArb Arbitration Rules (Aug. 9, 2021).

11. *Id.* Rule 16 (Expedited Disposition), app. C (Expedited Arbitration Agreement).

12. JAMS Construction Rules, *supra* note 2, Rule 17; JAMS Comprehensive Rules, *supra* note 2, Rule 17; JAMS Expedited Construction Rules, *supra* note 2, Rule 17 (emphasis added).

13. *Id.*

14. *Id.*

Under the AAA Rules, by contrast, the arbitrator manages discovery from the onset of the process. Specifically, the AAA Rules state that "the arbitrator shall manage any necessary exchange of information among the parties with a view to achieving an efficient and economical resolution of the dispute, while at the same time promoting equality of treatment and safeguarding each party's opportunity to fairly present its claims and defenses."[15] The practical effect of this difference is to postpone the start of document exchange until after the arbitrator is appointed and the initial preliminary conference is held.

The AAA Rules provide that the "arbitrator may, on application of a party or on the arbitrator's own initiative," require the parties to (1) exchange documents in their possession or custody on which they intend to rely, (2) update their exchanges of the documents as such documents become known to them, (3) make documents available to the other party in response to reasonable document requests, and (4) make documents available in electronic form if they are maintained in that fashion.[16] It is also noteworthy that the AAA Rules are less mandatory and more permissive than the JAMS Rules; they state that the arbitrator "may" require the exchange of documents, but there is no assurance of this, whereas the JAMS Rules require the initial exchange of relevant documents and information. Additionally, under the AAA Rules, the arbitrator has the power to enforce discovery rights by issuing an order to preserve confidentiality, impose reasonable search parameters for electronic documents, allocate the costs of producing documentation, and impose sanctions.[17]

Under the JAMS Rules, arbitrators also have ultimate control over the discovery process, especially when a dispute arises. For example, Rule 17(d) of both the JAMS Comprehensive Rules and the JAMS Construction Rules instructs the parties that once a dispute arises regarding discovery issues, the parties must inform JAMS so that a conference can be arranged with the arbitrator, "and the Arbitrator shall decide the dispute." Further, pursuant to the Expedited Procedures of the JAMS Comprehensive Rules, the "Arbitrator shall require compliance with Rule 17(a) prior to conducting the first Preliminary Conference"; it is up to each party under the Expedited Procedures to "confirm in writing to the Arbitrator that it has so complied or shall indicate any limitations on full compliance and the reasons therefor."[18] Finally,

15. AAA Commercial Rules, *supra* note 8, Rule R-24; AAA Construction Rules, *supra* note 8, Rule R-24.

16. AAA Construction Rules, *supra* note 8, Rule 24.

17. AAA Construction Rules, *supra* note 8, Rule 25; AAA Commercial Rules, *supra* note 8, Rule 23.

18. JAMS Comprehensive Rules, *supra* note 2, Rule 16.2(a).

Rule 13 of the JAMS Streamlined Rules states that the arbitrator shall determine "[t]he necessity of additional information exchange . . . based upon the reasonable need for the requested information, the availability of other discovery options and the burdensomeness of the request on the opposing Parties and the witness."

ADR Services' approach to control of discovery is more similar to the JAMS approach than to the AAA approach. ADR Services Arbitration Rule 21 states: "The parties shall cooperate in good faith to voluntarily, promptly and informally exchange all nonprivileged documents and other information relevant to the dispute or claim."[19] As with the JAMS Rules, however, the ADR Services arbitrator has the ability to assert control over the discovery process; specifically, he or she has the power to order discovery "by way of deposition, interrogatory, document production, or otherwise, as the arbitrator considers necessary to a full and fair exploration of the issues in dispute, consistent with the expedited nature of arbitration."[20]

FedArb's rules take a much more streamlined approach. FedArb Rule 10.07 only states that the "Tribunal shall closely supervise discovery."[21] It also states that the Tribunal shall "appoint a Discovery Master [to supervise discovery]" if necessary.[22]

B. Authorization for Specific Discovery

Another key area of comparison among the various organizations' rules is the level of detail and specificity provided with respect to the types of discovery that may be undertaken, including depositions, written discovery (such as interrogatories), expert discovery, discovery involving third parties, and e-discovery. Each of these is addressed next.

1. Depositions

JAMS explains its organizational philosophy with respect to depositions in the JAMS Discovery Protocols:

> JAMS recognizes that the size and complexity of commercial arbitrations have now grown to a point where more than a single deposition can serve a useful purpose in certain instances. Depositions in a complex arbitration, for example, can significantly shorten the

---

19. ADR Services Rules, *supra* note 9, Rule 21.
20. *Id.*
21. FedArb Arbitration Rules, *supra* note 10, Rule 10.07.
22. *Id.*

cross-examination of key witnesses and shorten the hearing on the merits. If not carefully regulated, however, deposition discovery in arbitration can become extremely expensive, wasteful and time-consuming. In determining what scope of depositions may be appropriate in a given case, a JAMS arbitrator balances these considerations.[23]

Consistent with this philosophy, the JAMS Comprehensive Rules provide that "[e]ach Party may take one deposition of an opposing Party or of one individual under the control of the opposing Party," adding, however, that the "necessity of additional depositions shall be determined by the Arbitrator," based on various factors.[24] The JAMS Construction Rules allow for two such depositions,[25] while the JAMS Expedited Construction Rules prohibit depositions "except upon showing of exceptional need for [them] and with the approval of the Arbitrator."[26]

The AAA Rules, on the other hand, do not set any presumptively authorized number of depositions. Similarly, the FedArb Rules are silent on depositions and other specific forms of discovery. Nevertheless, when the FedArb rules and procedures for an Expedited Disposition apply, those procedures specifically prohibit the taking of depositions except by agreement of the parties or upon a showing that the interests of justice require the prehearing testimony of a particular witness.[27] The issues related to depositions in arbitration are addressed more fully in Chapter 5.[28]

2. *Document Requests and Other Written Discovery*

The AAA Discovery Best Practices discourage the use of formal document demands. As the Best Practices explain: "[I]n lieu of the parties serving formal document demands and to save the time and expense associated with preparing and responding to such demands, consider requiring that parties disclose (1) the identity of persons likely to be witnesses or who have discoverable

---

23. JAMS Discovery Protocols, *supra* note 5, Depositions at 6.

24. JAMS Comprehensive Rules, *supra* note 2, Rule 17(b).

25. JAMS Construction Rules, *supra* note 2, Rule 17(b).

26. JAMS Expedited Construction Rules, *supra* note 2, Rule 17(a).

27. FedArb Arbitration Rules, *supra* note 10, Rule 16 (Expedited Disposition), app. C (Expedited Arbitration Agreement).

28. ADR Services Rules, *supra* note 9, Rule 21 ("The arbitrator shall have the authority to order such discovery, by way of deposition, interrogatory, document production, or otherwise, as the arbitrator considers necessary . . . .").

information, (2) a copy or full description of all documents the party is likely to present at hearing, and (3) a computation of damages claimed with supporting documentation."[29] The AAA Rules also grant the arbitrator authority to order the production of documents "in response to reasonable document requests."[30] The AAA Rules do not provide for interrogatories, requests for admission, or other types of written discovery typically available in court actions.

The JAMS Rules and Discovery Protocols do not address the subject of document requests as such, given that the JAMS Rules proactively require the parties to "exchange . . . all non-privileged documents . . . immediately after commencement of the Arbitration."[31] The JAMS Expedited Construction Rules do not require the proactive production of documents but specifically allow parties to request documents to be produced at a time set in the initial telephone conference.[32] The JAMS Discovery Protocols contemplate document requests, but with the following limitations: (1) the requests shall be limited to documents that are directly relevant to the matters in dispute or to its outcome; (2) the requests shall be reasonably restricted in terms of time frame, subject matter, and persons or entities to which the requests pertain; and (3) the requests shall not include broad phraseology such as "all documents directly or indirectly related to." Further, under the JAMS Expedited Procedures, document requests "shall not be encumbered with extensive 'definitions' or 'instructions,'" and the arbitrator may edit or limit the number of requests.[33] Finally, like the AAA Rules, the JAMS Rules do not provide for interrogatories, requests for admission, or other types of written discovery.

The FedArb Rules are silent on specific forms of discovery, but when the FedArb Expedited Rules apply, those Rules specifically prohibit requests for admissions.[34] And as noted earlier, the ADR Services Rules give the arbitrator authority to expand the scope of discovery to document requests, among other forms of discovery.[35]

---

29. AAA Discovery Best Practices, *supra* note 6, at 2.

30. AAA Construction Rules, *supra* note 8, Rule 24(b)(iii); AAA Commercial Rules, *supra* note 8, Rule 23(b)(iii).

31. JAMS Construction Rules, *supra* note 2, Rule 17(a); JAMS Comprehensive Rules, *supra* note 2, Rule 17(a).

32. JAMS Expedited Construction Rules, *supra* note 2, Rule 17(a).

33. JAMS Comprehensive Rules, *supra* note 2, Rule 16.2(b).

34. FedArb Arbitration Rules, *supra* note 10, app. C (Expedited Arbitration Agreement).

35. ADR Services Rules, *supra* note 9, Rule 21.

3. *Experts*

The AAA Rules include no provisions directed at expert discovery, nor do the FedArb Rules. The same is true for the JAMS Rules, except that under the JAMS Expedited Rules expert depositions are limited: "Where written expert reports are produced to the other side in advance of the Hearing, expert depositions may be conducted only by agreement of the Parties or by order of the Arbitrator for good cause shown."[36]

4. *Third-Party Discovery*

JAMS, AAA, ADR Services, and FedArb rules all include provisions dealing with securing discovery or information from third parties, and each provides for the issuance of subpoenas. For example, Rule 21 of the JAMS Rules provides: "The Arbitrator may issue subpoenas for attendance of witnesses or the production of documents either prior to or at the Hearing." It also adds that "[t]he subpoena or subpoena duces tecum shall be issued in accordance with the applicable law." Third parties have not agreed to any rules of arbitration, so the maximum scope of discovery available from them is generally defined by statute, not the parties' agreement.

The AAA Discovery Best Practices recognize that

> [a] non-party to a construction arbitration may have documents or knowledge that is material and relevant to the arbitration . . . . When such third parties are reluctant to cooperate voluntarily, a party may ask the arbitrator to execute a subpoena directed to the third party. Generally, the AAA rules do not contemplate third-party document discovery. This discovery guideline recommends that third-party document discovery should only be considered . . . if the party requesting the information demonstrates that the information sought is material and relevant to the resolution of the issues in dispute and cannot be obtained from other sources (such as from the other party).[37]

Once materiality and relevance are shown, the Best Practices state that "it is appropriate to sign a subpoena requiring testimony and/or documents at the hearing." But the Best Practices acknowledge that it is "more controversial" whether to issue a subpoena for a third party to produce documents or to appear for a deposition outside the arbitrators' presence. The AAA therefore

---

36. JAMS Comprehensive Rules, *supra* note 2, Rule 16.2(e).

37. AAA Discovery Best Practices, *supra* note 6, at 6.

suggests that "[i]t is appropriate to require the parties [to] brief the issues relating to enforceability of subpoenas in the relevant jurisdiction."[38]

Rule 10.09 of the FedArb Rules similarly recognizes this tension regarding third-party discovery in arbitration proceedings, noting: "Nothing in these Rules shall be construed to give the Tribunal the authority to compel the production of documents by third parties not subject to the arbitration, unless the Tribunal is so authorized by applicable law." Finally, Rule 32 of the ADR Services Rules states that the "Arbitrator may issue subpoenas for the attendance of witnesses or the production of documents pursuant to Code of Civil Procedure Section 1282.6."

5. E-Discovery

The AAA Rules do not establish detailed rules for e-discovery. Instead, Rule R-24(b)(iv) of the AAA Construction Rules and Rule R-22(b)(iv) of the AAA Commercial Rules state that the arbitrator may, on application of a party or on the arbitrator's own initiative, "require the parties, when documents to be exchanged or produced are maintained in electronic form, to make such documents available in the form most convenient and economical for the party in possession of such documents, unless the arbitrator determines that there is good cause for requiring the documents to be produced in a different form."

Additionally, however, unlike the other organizations' rules, the AAA Rules provide some input on search terms used in e-discovery, a topic that often requires involvement by the arbitrator if the parties cannot agree. Specifically, Rule 24 of the AAA Construction Rules and Rule 22 of the AAA Commercial Rules state that the "parties should attempt to agree in advance upon, and the arbitrator may determine, reasonable search parameters to balance the need for production of electronically stored documents relevant and material to the outcome of disputed issues against the cost of locating and producing them."[39] That said, some arbitrators lack experience in the complexities of e-discovery. One way to address this issue in the appropriate cases is for the arbitrator to request authority, at the parties' expense, to retain an expert on e-discovery to advise the arbitrator in resolving such disputes.

The AAA Discovery Best Practices also provide some practice tips for e-discovery; these include suggestions for prehearing planning by the parties

---

38. *Id.*

39. AAA Construction Rules, *supra* note 8, Rule R-24(b)(iv).

as well as the arbitrator.[40] In addition, the Best Practices suggest that if the cost of producing electronic documents appears excessive, the arbitrator may consider requiring the party demanding them to pay for the associated cost, subject to a possible reallocation of the costs in the final award.[41] And they suggest directing the parties to keep their electronically stored information requests narrowly focused and structured to make searching for such information as economical as possible.[42]

The JAMS Expedited Procedures also provide significant guidance on conducting e-discovery.[43] For example, production of electronic documents should only occur "from sources used in the ordinary course of business," and absent a showing of compelling need, no such documents should be required to be produced "from backup servers, tapes or other media."[44] The JAMS Expedited Procedures also provide that, "absent a showing of compelling need," the production of electronic documents should normally be made on the basis of generally available technology in a searchable format and metadata need not be produced.[45] Finally, the description of custodians from whom electronic documents may be collected should be narrowly tailored to include only those individuals whose electronic documents may reasonably be expected to contain evidence material to the dispute.[46]

C. Deadlines for Specific Discovery

Another notable difference among the rules of the various organizations relates to the specification of deadlines for certain activities. The ADR Services Rules state that "[e]ither party shall within fifteen (15) calendar days of receipt of notice of the arbitration hearing date, but no later than seventy (70) calendar days before the arbitration, have the right to demand in writing that the other party provide a list of witnesses, including designation of expert witnesses, it intends to call and a list of documents it intends to introduce at the hearing provided that the demanding party provides such lists at the time of its demand."[47] The responding party then has 15 days from receipt of the demand

40. AAA Discovery Best Practices, *supra* note 6, at 3.
41. *Id.* at 4.
42. *Id.*
43. JAMS Comprehensive Rules, *supra* note 2, Rule 16.2(c).
44. *Id.*, Rule 16.2(c)(ii).
45. *Id.*
46. *Id.*, Rule 16.2(c)(iii).
47. ADR Services Rules, *supra* note 9, Rule 21.

to produce the lists. These obligations can be modified by the arbitrator at the preliminary conference.

FedArb's Rules state that all parties shall "provide full discovery of all documents discoverable under federal discovery standards within 45 days of the final pleading."[48] They also require that the parties submit an Agreed Statement of Facts and expert testimony in writing at least 30 days before the hearing.[49]

The JAMS Rules require the parties to complete their initial exchange of information, including documents on which they rely in support of their positions and names of individuals whom they may call as witnesses, within 21 days[50] after all pleadings or notice of claims has been received.[51] These obligations can be modified by the arbitrator at the preliminary conference or thereafter.

The JAMS Expedited Procedures require the parties to comply with the disclosure requirements of Rule 17(a) prior to the first preliminary conference and require the arbitrator to set a discovery cutoff not to exceed 75 calendar days after the preliminary conference for fact witness discovery and not to exceed 105 calendar days for expert discovery.[52] Moreover, the JAMS Construction Rules require the exchange of final expert reports of testifying experts as scheduled in the preliminary conference or within 14 calendar days after the close of discovery.[53] The AAA Rules, by contrast, do not generally impose time deadlines.

D. Consequences of Discovery/Disclosure Violations

The JAMS, AAA, ADR Services, and FedArb rules all have one key discovery rule in common: provisions addressing the consequences of a party's failure to exchange documents and/or identify witnesses. For example, Rule 17(c) in the JAMS Rules states that documents not previously exchanged, or witnesses and experts not previously identified, may not be considered by the arbitrator at the arbitration hearing unless agreed by the parties or upon a showing of

48. FedArb Arbitration Rules, *supra* note 10, Documentary Discovery.

49. *Id.*, Agreed Statement of Facts.

50. The JAMS Expedited Construction Rules reduce this time to 14 days. JAMS Expedited Construction Rules, *supra* note 2, Rule 13.

51. JAMS Comprehensive Rules, *supra* note 2, Rule 17; JAMS Construction Rules, *supra* note 2, Rule 17.

52. JAMS Expedited Procedures, *supra* note 2, Rule 16.2(g).

53. JAMS Construction Rules, *supra* note 2, Rule 17(a).

good cause. ADR Services Rule 21 contains nearly identical language, as do the FedArb Expedited Rules.[54]

Rule 29 of both the JAMS Comprehensive and Construction Rules allows the arbitrator to impose sanctions for a party's failure to comply with its obligations under the Rules or with an order of the arbitrator. Sanctions can include (1) assessment of arbitration fees and arbitrator expenses, (2) assessment of any other costs occasioned by the actionable conduct, (3) exclusion of certain evidence, (4) drawing adverse inferences, or (5) determining an issue or issues submitted to arbitration adversely to the party that has failed to comply.

The AAA Construction Rules, Rule 25, and the AAA Commercial Arbitration Rules, Rule 23, both state that arbitrators may draw adverse inferences, exclude evidence and other submissions, and/or make special allocations of costs or an interim award of costs in the case of willful noncompliance with any of the arbitrator's orders. They do not permit determining an issue adversely as a sanction, however. Nevertheless, under all the rules, the arbitrator has broad latitude to impose penalties for violations of discovery rules.

II. Practice Tips Regarding Frequently Sought Discovery

Most arbitrators feel an obligation when addressing discovery disputes to consider the overall goals, focus, and guidance provided in the applicable rules governing the arbitration. Although arbitrators generally have discretion under both applicable rules and law to go beyond those rules in an appropriate case, the parties have the right to expect that the arbitrator will be guided by the rules, law, and requirements they have adopted.

While the sets of rules described in the first part of this chapter outline the permitted document discovery, the parties frequently choose to modify those requirements by agreement either at the time of contracting or once in arbitration. Additionally, once disputes arise, one party may seek to get around the limitations in the applicable rules by citing the arbitrator's broad discretion to control the proceeding. The arbitrator must strike a balance between making sure that the key information that is necessary for the parties to pursue their claims and defenses (and for the arbitrator to decide them) is made available

54. FedArb Expedited Rules provide, under the headline "Documentary Discovery," that "only documents produced in discovery shall be permitted to be introduced into evidence absent a showing that the document was unavailable for earlier production."

and at the same time making sure the goals of efficiency and cost effectiveness are achieved. The following section includes some tips for balancing these considerations.

A. Document Discovery

It is almost universally accepted in modern construction arbitration proceedings, and the rules discussed previously recognize, that an exchange of at least the key construction documents and project communications is appropriate and should occur as early as reasonably possible in the dispute resolution process. Complex construction cases, or even those that are not so complex, generally benefit from some level of document discovery that gets the key, clearly relevant information exchanged by the parties.

A limitation of required disclosure to only those documents that a party intends to use to prove its case is not likely to be as useful to the resolution process as a somewhat broader requirement for document production, because the documents a party will use to prove its case are by nature favorable to that party and only occasionally also reveal the basis of a defense to that party's claims. If this limited exchange is all that is required, the opposing party has no means of finding any damaging documents that are also to be found in the other party's project files. This particularly can prejudice a party who, because of its role on the construction project, naturally has significantly less of the detailed project documentation in its own files. When seeking more than the rules provide for, however, parties should be specific, focused, and limited in what they seek. Moreover, reminding the arbitrator that the materials sought are likely to be easy to gather and provide can be persuasive.

In general, the following guidelines for document requests will apply in most arbitrations and be productive, while minimizing costs and disputes:

- A formal pleading containing the requests for production of documents, along with detailed definitions and instructions, is only rarely called for in arbitration. Document requests can usually be set out simply in letter form or as an email attachment.
- Broadly phrased requests, seeking "any and all documents relating or pertaining to" a general subject, should be avoided whenever possible. The more specific the request is, and the more focused on a clearly relevant topic, the more likely the documents will be obtained without having to resort to motion practice.
- Be careful what you ask for. Sometimes a broadly worded request will not be objected to but instead used as an excuse for a massive "data dump," where the relatively few key documents are buried in

thousands of irrelevant or marginally relevant documents that must then be reviewed.

- Keep the total number of requests as low as practicable. Many arbitrators will see a list of 60 or 70 document requests and reflexively suspect that this is far more than reasonably necessary.
- Especially where a request by its nature must be worded somewhat broadly, indicate your intent to narrow the request as much as possible by providing reasonable date ranges and a reasonable list of the persons involved in the request.
- Addition of an explanatory phrase or sentence in respect to a request where the relevance may not be readily apparent can head off objections and potential motion practice. Making the relevance connection on the face of the request makes it that much easier for the arbitrator to see the need for the requested documents.

Stressing issues of fairness, on the part of the party seeking production, and contractual limitations or provisions of applicable rules agreed to by the parties, on the part of the party resisting production, is a common battleground when seeking broader document discovery than the applicable rules specify. Arbitrators may feel compelled to be less restrictive in what they allow if convinced that to do so is the right thing under the circumstances. In making this determination, the arbitrator may be inclined to balance the features parties give up in the arbitration process—including a jury trial and the right to appeal—against the restrictions to which they have agreed.

B. E-Discovery

The most complex discovery issues that arise in modern construction arbitrations are those involving e-discovery. Therefore, it is important for the arbitrator and counsel to focus on those issues early and with a clear understanding of both the issues and the relevant technology. As with many things, when it comes to e-discovery, one size will not fit all; there are many issues that must be either agreed by the parties or directed by the arbitrator where not agreed. Because the resolution of these issues may take time and can delay the proceedings if they are not resolved quickly, they should be addressed at the preliminary hearing conference, either by counsel or by the arbitrator.

One of the biggest issues that can bog things down is the protocols surrounding e-discovery. Unfortunately, many arbitrators are not as familiar with the many vagaries of e-discovery and electronic searches as counsel are. When that is the case, the arbitrator may ask, or counsel may suggest, that the arbitrator engage an e-discovery consultant to help the arbitrator understand and resolve the issues.

The costs of unchecked e-discovery can be staggering. To minimize complaints from the opposing party regarding costs, focus is again the key. Limiting the number of custodians whose electronic files must be retrieved and searched is one important way to keep costs under control. In small to medium-size construction organizations (including most owners), almost all significant emails are directed to or copied to a relatively small group. The chances of an underling having a key email in his or her inbox that the supervisor never received are often small enough to avoid adding the underling to the custodian list. Even in larger organizations, the protocol most often is that communications flow through, or at least are copied to, the department head or functional lead. Search their electronic files and you will get a very high percentage of what the others in that department either received or generated.

Similarly, focusing and narrowing search terms, and avoiding common terms that will doubtless return many irrelevant hits, help keep e-discovery costs under control. Reasonable date ranges for documents to be searched, and agreeing not to search backup tapes, servers, and the like, are other ways to minimize costs.

As the AAA Discovery Best Practices suggest, where a party is insisting on overly expensive e-discovery, the arbitrator may require the party demanding the e-discovery to pay for the cost to produce it, subject to a possible reallocation of the costs in the final award. The JAMS Expedited Procedures similarly provide for this.[55]

Arbitrators often have to decide whether the complexities of e-discovery are being used by one party to delay the resolution process. Offering ways to streamline the process and keeping control of it are tools the arbitrator can use to avoid this. Parties seeking to avoid delay should be creative in suggesting ideas for shortening and/or streamlining the e-discovery process, especially in matters presided over by an arbitrator who is not particularly conversant in e-discovery practices.

C. Discovery from Third Parties

Seeking discovery from third parties is generally contemplated by the applicable rules but often raises numerous complex issues. Third parties are not parties to the arbitration and so not subject to the arbitrator's control; accordingly,

---

55. JAMS Comprehensive Rules, *supra* note 2, Rule 16.2(c)(iv).

counsel need to understand and utilize the legal tools available to them for third-party discovery in the relevant jurisdiction. These will most importantly include any applicable state statutes, as well as case law.

Assuming the rules permit discovery to be taken from third parties, counsel should be even more careful to focus their requests on documents and other evidence that are essential, not available easily or at all from other sources, and relevant to the claims and defenses at issue in the dispute. Arbitrators are increasingly wary of requested subpoenas that seem likely to impose significant costs on nonparties to the arbitrated dispute. The party seeking such third-party discovery should be prepared to respond to objections that it is either on a fishing expedition or seeking the discovery to disrupt a business relationship between the third party and the opposing party.

III. Arguing Document Discovery Issues

Because arbitrators are given broad discretion in determining the scope of permitted discovery, the arbitrator is the last avenue of recourse for a party who wishes to get around discovery restrictions to which it previously agreed but that are not well suited to the actual dispute that has arisen. In light of this, it is useful for parties to learn as much as they can about whether proposed arbitrators are more or less inclined to expand on, or enforce the limitations in, the parties' agreement regarding discovery. Such information is generally not found on their resumés and requires a deeper level of diligence. This can include talking to those who have prior experience with the arbitrator and counsel asking for a brief interview with proposed arbitrator candidates in the selection process.

It is a fair area for inquiry to ask about an arbitrator candidate's general views with respect to allowing, limiting, or blocking altogether the use of standard litigation discovery tools, like interrogatories, requests for admission, and formal requests for production of documents. Often arbitrators feel strongly that part of their role is to attempt to limit or avoid the most significant disputes that often arise when using traditional discovery methods in litigation. One question to consider when doing your due diligence on an arbitrator is whether he or she is likely to permit such discovery as standard form interrogatories, or requests for admissions followed by focused interrogatories on denials, which are generally not provided for in either arbitration agreements or the applicable arbitration rules.

Before presenting any discovery matter to the arbitrator, counsel would be well advised to

- know what the parties' prior agreement or the applicable arbitration rules permit or require;
- consider carefully how each discovery ruling the party seeks fits within that agreement or the governing rules, if it does, or why it is essential to the case that the arbitrator extend allowable discovery beyond what the agreement or rules permit; and, if possible,
- consider any information available as to the arbitrator's views on the subject or how the arbitrator approached similar issues in earlier cases.

While the first two pieces of information are readily available to both sides, arbitrators are regularly surprised by the failure of counsel to understand them before bringing a discovery dispute to the arbitrator. And while the third piece of information may be more difficult to acquire, it may be the most important component in determining what the overall outcome of the discovery dispute will be. The easiest route to the information in many instances is a call to counsel you know who have had similar prior cases with your arbitrator; another route is articles or other writings authored by the arbitrator. And if the arbitrator is a former judge, prior published decisions while he or she was on the bench may be useful.

In seeking broader document discovery from arbitrators, be prepared to explain in detail why the particular documents sought are not just potentially relevant or likely to lead to the discovery of admissible evidence but instead are essential, not readily available to the party seeking them from other sources, and important to a full and fair resolution of the case. Once this case is made, most arbitrators are reluctant to preclude their production.

Both the JAMS Discovery Protocols and the AAA Discovery Best Practices recognize that in construction cases, allowing more discovery than traditionally contemplated in arbitrations can in fact further the goals of efficiency, cost effectiveness, and final resolution.

The AAA Discovery Best Practices put it this way:

> The American Arbitration Association ("AAA") is committed to the principle that construction arbitration should provide a less expensive, more expeditious and final form of dispute resolution than that offered in state or federal litigation. While costly and time consuming, pre-trial discovery devices such as depositions, interrogatories and requests for admission are readily available in litigation, their use in arbitration should be limited consistent with the goals of arbitration as a speedy, cost effective and final means of resolving disputes.

> Absent specific agreement by the parties regarding the scope of prehearing discovery, the arbitral process the parties have chosen does not allow them to engage in unlimited discovery. Therefore, arbitrator should, consistent with their authority, manage arbitration proceedings to achieve the goal of providing a simpler, less expensive and more expeditious process, and discovery decisions should be proportional to the size and complexity of the matter being heard. The arbitrator should stress how, due to the number of documents, discovery in a construction dispute is different than in a typical commercial dispute.

Both the AAA and JAMS stress the overarching goals of efficiency and cost effectiveness. Parties should focus on those goals in making their case for—or arguing against—more expanded discovery than provided for in the parties' agreement or applicable rules.

Another important focus in presenting discovery motions is to address the cost and time implications for the arbitration of either permitting or rejecting the discovery sought. Parties seeking expanded discovery should be prepared to explain why allowing the discovery sought is, in fact, the speediest way to get issues framed, positions clarified, and resolution fairly achieved and, most importantly of all, why allowing the discovery will not result in a postponement of the arbitration hearing.

While arbitrators vary in their views on this issue, many arbitrators who spent their careers as lawyers for parties in construction disputes have a strong predisposition with respect to the usefulness and value of interrogatories and requests for admission in particular. Many litigators feel that interrogatories are the least useful, and have the least value for the cost expended, of all discovery tools and that the truly valuable information gained is limited and not worth the cost and effort expended to secure it. On the other hand, parties are increasingly seeking to use a limited number of focused requests for admissions, with follow-up interrogatories on those requests that are denied, to narrow the issues in dispute and get vital information on the disputed matters. As is true in litigation, focused requests for admissions can be a very efficient way to get useful information important to resolution of the case.

An additional important consideration in arguing discovery issues is determining the format for presenting those issues. For example, the JAMS Discovery Protocols and Comprehensive Rules provide that "lengthy briefs on discovery matters should be avoided. In most cases, a prompt discussion or submission of brief letters will sufficiently inform the arbitrator with regard to the issues to be decided."[56] This is sound advice in most construction arbitration situations.

Because the parties ostensibly have chosen arbitration, at least in part, because of its presumed efficiency and cost effectiveness, most arbitrators take seriously their responsibility to move the process along and to provide the parties with what they bargained for when they chose arbitration. Confronting a significant discovery issue as early in the process as possible is important; when the problem arises midway through the arbitration process, the schedule can get disrupted in ways that are not to the benefit of the process, the arbitrator, or one or more of the parties.

Discovery in construction disputes is often important to ensuring full preparation of claims and defenses. In arbitration, however, the process often limits how much and what types of discovery can be obtained. Navigating those limitations successfully is aided by keeping discovery requests focused, specific, and as streamlined as possible to achieve the legitimate goals of the party seeking discovery.

---

56. JAMS Discovery Protocols, *supra* note 5; JAMS Comprehensive Rules, *supra* note 2, Rule 16.2(f)(ii).

CHAPTER 5

Depositions and Other Discovery Methods

JAMES DUFFY O'CONNOR

The availability of discovery in arbitration proceedings depends on the parties' arbitration agreement and the arbitration rules that are specified. The word "discovery" does not even appear in the Federal Arbitration Act[1] and rarely in state arbitration acts.[2] The parties can insert specific discovery rights in their arbitration agreement, and some do, such as by expressly incorporating the Federal Rules of Civil Procedure into the dispute resolution procedure. This is rare, however, since the general view is that arbitration ought not to be as expensive and drawn out as litigation in the courts often is. More commonly, the arbitration agreement will identify an administering organization to administer the arbitration and expressly incorporate that organization's procedural rules—for example, the American Arbitration Association (AAA), JAMS, or CPR arbitration rules. Each of these organizations has published a

1. 9 U.S.C. §§ 1–14 (1990).

2. California, for example, preserves a statutory right to discovery in contractual arbitrations in certain limited circumstances, such as bodily injury and wrongful death cases. *E.g.*, CAL. CODE CIV. PROC. §§ 1283.05, 1283.1. *See also* Cole v. Burns Int'l Sec. Servs., 105 F.3d 1465 (D.C. Cir. 1997); Armendariz v. Found. Health Psychcare Servs., Inc., 24 Cal. 4th 83 (2000). Both cases mine a right to certain forms of discovery essential to protecting the statutory rights of the litigant. *Cf. Employment Due Process Protocol*, AM. ARB. ASS'N (May 9, 1995); AAA National Rules for Resolution of Employment Disputes, Rule 7.

set of procedural rules that address when and how discovery is permissible. They are addressed further later.

The recurring complaint among litigators that "there is no discovery in arbitration" is a myth. Each of the administering organizations identified (and others) expressly permits discovery that is essential to a fair, yet efficient, arbitral process. Additionally, the parties to the dispute can generally expand the scope of discovery by agreement to accommodate their perceived needs, so long as they do not compromise the fundamental goals of arbitration, which are to minimize the cost of the dispute, accelerate the timing of its resolution, and preserve the fairness and integrity of the process and the parties' legal rights. The trick is to satisfy each of these goals.

Without question, prehearing discovery mechanisms such as depositions, interrogatories, and requests for admissions can be costly and time consuming—especially when discovery disputes arise in connection with their use. Absent specific agreement by the parties regarding prehearing discovery, the use of these discovery devices may be restricted or prohibited by the arbitrator, especially when the intended use of such devices is not proportional to the size and complexity of the dispute. There is no formulaic solution to when they may or should be allowed. Certainly, cooperation between counsel can go a long way to finding a solution that advances and preserves each of the stated goals of arbitration.

The AAA's Discovery Best Practices for Construction Arbitration is a set of general guidelines for conducting prehearing discovery in a construction arbitration.[3] The AAA Best Practices discourage unfettered discovery, recommending it be limited to where a party can demonstrate that it can promote the speed and efficiency of the arbitral process. If the parties jointly request the use of particular discovery devices, then the arbitrator[4] is much more likely to allow the parties to engage in their preferred discovery process but may still push back if the requested scope of discovery seems excessive for the particular case. The AAA Best Practices also note that the arbitrator is vested with the authority to order appropriate sanctions, including sanctions for discovery abuses, albeit a default award is never considered an appropriate sanction under the AAA rules.

---

3. *American Arbitration Association Discovery Best Practices for Construction Arbitration: Recommendations for AAA Construction Advocates and Arbitrators* (2022) [hereinafter AAA Discovery Best Practices]. The AAA Discovery Best Practices address document exchange and e-discovery, which are addressed in Chapter 4.

4. References to "the arbitrator" for purposes of this chapter include both sole arbitrators and panels of three arbitrators.

The College of Commercial Arbitrators (CCA) has also published a Best Practices Guide, including best practices relating to prehearing discovery in commercial arbitrations.[5] The CCA Best Practices emphasize the importance of ensuring a fundamentally fair hearing in which the parties are treated equally, while at the same time endeavoring to limit the scope of discovery to that which is proportional to the nature of the case and the needs of the parties. It acknowledges that "controlling discovery has long been seen as one of the great advantages of arbitration."[6] Both the CCA and the AAA Best Practices showcase the importance of the preliminary procedural conference, where the parties can discuss and the arbitrator can order whatever scope of discovery is best suited to the specific dispute. This can both obviate the need for some of the traditional discovery devices like interrogatories and also provide the parties with access to the information essential to developing their claims and defenses. These can include more particularized statements of claims and defenses, precise damages calculations/claims, expert reports, and witness statements.

I. The Rules

A. The AAA Construction Industry Arbitration Rules (AAA Construction Rules)

The AAA Construction Rules are organized into four tracks: the Regular Track; the Large, Complex Construction Dispute Track; the Fast Track; and the Document Submission Track. The Fast Track is just what it sounds like, a very quick process for claims under $100,000, with the hearing scheduled

---

5. James M. Gaitis, A. Holt Gwyn, Laura A. Kaster & John J. McCauley, The College of Commercial Arbitrators Guide to Best Practices in Commercial Arbitration (JurisNet, LLC, 4th ed. 2017) [hereinafter CCA Guide to Best Practices]. While other "best practices" resources are provided free online, the CCA Guide to Best Practices is offered for sale from JurisNet, LLC. Amazon offers it for sale new for $75, and as of the time of this writing, a used version can be purchased for under $10. While now somewhat dated, it is still a very useful and comprehensive text on commercial arbitration and well worth the cost.

6. *Id.* at 179. The authors caution that "parties sometimes have become disaffected with arbitration when the scope of discovery has been needlessly broad, occasionally to the point of being indistinguishable from litigation." *Id. See also* Richard J. Tyler, *Discovery*, *in* Construction ADR 159–60 & nn.1–5 (Adrian Bastianelli & Charles Sink eds., ABA 2014) (Chapter 5 of *Construction ADR*, authored by Rich Tyler, is a very thorough analysis of discovery in arbitration).

within 45 days of the filing of the arbitration demand. There is virtually no discovery allowed, and the hearing time is typically a day, with an award to follow within two weeks of the close of the hearing. The Document Submission Track is typically used for claims under $25,000 and likewise contemplates no discovery.

The Regular Track Rules pertaining to discovery are found in R-23, R-24, R-25, and R-37, as well as P-1 and P-2 (the Preliminary Hearing Procedures and Checklist). Rule R-23 provides that "as soon as practicable" the arbitrator, the parties, and their counsel should come together to "discuss and establish a procedure for the conduct of the arbitration," including any discovery. This is the Preliminary Conference, and Rule R-23 directs the arbitrator and the parties to specifically address the issues listed in Rules P-1 and P-2 at this conference. This is the first and best opportunity for the parties to actively tailor their discovery needs to fit the scope and complexity of their dispute. The portions of AAA Rule P-2, the Preliminary Hearing Checklist, that relate to discovery are as follows:

> P-2. Checklist
>
> (a) The following checklist suggests subjects that the parties and arbitrator should address at the preliminary hearing, in addition to any others the parties or the arbitrator believe to be appropriate to the particular case. . . .
>
> > (i) whether a party will seek a more detailed statement of claims, counterclaims, or defenses;
> >
> > (ii) whether the parties will exchange documents, including electronically stored documents, on which they intend to rely in the arbitration, and/or make written requests for production of documents within defined parameters;
> >
> > (iii) whether to establish any additional procedures to obtain information that is relevant and material to the outcome of the disputed issues;
> >
> > (iv) how costs of any searches for requested information or documents that would result in substantial costs should be borne;
> >
> > (v) whether any measures are required to protect confidential information;

(vi) whether the parties intend to present evidence from expert witnesses, and if so, whether to establish a schedule for the parties to identify their experts and exchange expert reports;

(vii) whether, according to a schedule set by the arbitrator, the parties will:

(a) identify all witnesses, the subject matter of their anticipated testimonies, exchange written witness statements, and determine whether written witness statements will replace direct testimony at the hearing;

(b) exchange and pre-mark documents that each party intends to submit; and

(c) exchange pre-hearing submissions, including exhibits;

(viii) whether any procedure needs to be established for the issuance of subpoenas;

(ix) any other matter the arbitrator considers appropriate or a party wishes to raise; and

(x) whether any site visit will be required and timing of said visits.[7]

AAA Construction Rule R-24 deals specifically with prehearing exchange and production of information, an issue addressed in depth in Chapter 4. Suffice it to say here that Rule R-24 addresses the type of discovery that is presumed sufficient for most construction disputes—the exchange of documents and other information, including electronically stored information. Rule R-25 empowers the arbitrator to impose restrictions on discovery otherwise available and to impose sanctions on parties who abuse the discovery process.

The AAA Large, Complex Construction Disputes (LCC) Rules complement and expand upon the discovery allowed under the Regular Track Rules. The LLC Rules apply when the parties' claims exceed $1,000,000 or otherwise when the parties agree to use the LCC Rules. The LLC Rules expressly provide a limited opportunity for depositions. Rule L-4(f) states that "[i]n exceptional

7. American Arbitration Association Construction Industry Arbitration Rules (July 1, 2015) [hereinafter AAA Construction Rules], Rules P-1, P-2.

cases, at the discretion of the arbitrator, upon good cause shown and consistent with the expedited nature of arbitration, the arbitrator may order depositions to obtain testimony of a person who may possess information determined by the arbitrator to be relevant and material to the outcome of the case." This is the only place that the AAA Construction Rules mention depositions, and the language emphasizes that their role should be limited.

B. JAMS Construction Arbitration Rules and Procedures (JAMS Construction Rules)

The JAMS Construction Rules address discovery procedures in Rule 17, entitled Exchange of Information. It emphasizes that successful discovery is dependent upon good-faith cooperation of the parties in the voluntary and informal exchange of "documents and other information." Rule 17 directs the parties to produce copies of documents in their possession or control on which they intend to rely in the arbitration, as well as the identities of all witnesses they may call during the hearing, within 21 days of the filing and receipt of the request for arbitration and without awaiting the preliminary conference.[8] Each party is entitled by rule to take two depositions of an opposing party or individual under its control. Additional depositions are permitted on a case-by-case basis: "The necessity of additional depositions shall be determined by the arbitrator based upon the reasonable need for the requested information, the availability of other discovery options and the burdensomeness of the request on the opposing Parties and the witness." Third-party discovery is not expressly allowed, except in consumer and employment disputes, and then only with the approval of the arbitrator.

JAMS has also published a discovery guide to assist in applying the scope and intent of Rule 17.[9] The JAMS Discovery Protocols highlight the importance of early and active arbitrator participation in determining the discovery process to be utilized, while acknowledging that it remains subject to the joint agreement of the parties: "where all participants truly desire unlimited discovery, JAMS arbitrators will respect that decision."[10] When the parties are not of equal minds on the needed scope of discovery, the arbitrator is charged with setting meaningful limitations on discovery.

8. JAMS Engineering and Construction Arbitration Rules and Procedures (June 1, 2021) [hereinafter JAMS Construction Rules], Rule 17(a).

9. JAMS Recommended Arbitration Discovery Protocols for Domestic, Commercial Cases (2010) [hereinafter JAMS Discovery Protocols].

10. *Id.* at 2.

The JAMS Discovery Protocols caution that "deposition discovery in arbitration can become extremely expensive, wasteful and time consuming."[11] However, it also notes that the size and complexity of the case may call for multiple depositions and that their use in the hearing can often reduce the hearing time necessary to resolve the dispute. JAMS highlights the importance of restricting discovery and discovery disputes if the arbitrator determines that they might jeopardize the scheduled hearing dates. In this way the JAMS Rules and Discovery Protocols mirror the AAA Construction Rules. Similarly, the JAMS Discovery Protocols make clear that Rule 17 is intended to be flexible enough to allow the use of discovery devices that are not expressly referenced in the Rule when the parties make a good case for their use or when the arbitrator independently determines that such is the case.

C. CPR Rules

The International Institute for Conflict Prevention & Resolution (CPR) publishes arbitration rules for both administered and nonadministered domestic U.S. arbitrations. Rule 11 regarding discovery is identical in both sets of Rules. CPR Rule 11 addresses the scope of discovery in a single sentence: "The Tribunal may require and facilitate such discovery as it shall determine is appropriate in the circumstances, taking into account the needs of the parties and the desirability of making discovery expeditious and cost-effective."

CPR has also published its own discovery guidelines, the CPR Protocol on Disclosure of Documents and Presentation of Witnesses in Commercial Arbitration (CPR Protocol). While the CPR Protocol is similar to the JAMS Discovery Protocols in establishing general principles for document production and other discovery and contemplates some discretion of the parties in developing a discovery strategy, it generally adopts a conservative approach to permitting extensive discovery in all but the most unusual cases. With respect to depositions, it provides:

> Depositions should be permitted only where the testimony is expected to be relevant and material to the outcome of the dispute and usually where one or more of the following circumstances apply: Witness statements are not being used, the parties agree to the taking of the deposition and/or the witness may not be available to testify, in person or by telephone- or videoconference, before the tribunal. The tribunal should impose strict limits on the number and length of any

---

11. *Id.* at 3.

depositions allowed, taking into account any agreement between the parties. If appropriate, the tribunal may issue subpoenas for depositions of third parties in accordance with applicable law.

II. Managing the Use of Discovery Devices

Managing the use and scope of discovery devices in domestic arbitration involves evaluating multiple complex and sometimes conflicting considerations. These include the arbitrator's authority pursuant to the parties' arbitration agreement; the relevance and materiality of the information sought; the time, cost, and difficulty inherent in obtaining the information; and the need to ensure a fair and equal opportunity for each party to present its claims and defenses. While each arbitrator approaches the effort from a unique personal perspective, virtually every arbitrator will endeavor to ensure that the discovery allowed is proportional to the nature and value of the dispute.

Arbitrators in the United States have been taught to find creative ways to balance all these considerations in determining whether to allow or restrict discovery in an arbitration. Many arbitrators will discourage the parties from employing traditional discovery methods when one or the other raises them as a discovery option during the preliminary hearing. Instead, the arbitrator may suggest the parties explore the use of alternative methods to obtain what they may consider essential to presenting their claims and defenses.

For example, the arbitrator may insist that the parties provide the panel and the parties with early Detailed Statements of Claims and Defenses, a timely ordered Comprehensive Damage Summary (complete with exhibits), and early comprehensive Witness Disclosure submissions (identifying all known fact witnesses). When it comes from the arbitrator, such a request may result in a more candid and useful presentation of discovery information and obviate the need for formal discovery between the parties.

If the arbitrator feels that a response is less than sufficient for the purposes of the dispute, he or she can require submissions to be supplemented without need for a formal motion. This can short-circuit disputes and focus the parties on developing their cases, not distracting discovery disputes. Likewise, the use of Witness Statements and Stipulations can obviate the need for depositions to satisfy factual elements of proof that are uncontested.

If the arbitrator still cannot talk counsel out of their perceived need for the use of some traditional prehearing discovery, the arbitrator is likely to press them to balance the use of litigation-style discovery against the goals of arbitration that their clients formalized in their construction agreement. Part of the balancing process is to require the party requesting the discovery to "make a case" for it—to demonstrate why it is necessary and how it is material and possibly outcome determinative to a claim or defense.

The remainder of this chapter will address how counsel may best advocate for the use of discovery devices in an arbitrated dispute, including interrogatories, requests for admission, depositions, and site inspections. While document exchange is an essential discovery process—particularly in arbitration—that process is covered in depth in Chapter 4 and will not be addressed here.

A. Interrogatories and Requests for Admissions

Interrogatories and requests for admissions are disfavored discovery devices in arbitration. Their reputation for burdensome and inefficient "make-work" has preceded them in the modern world of ADR. It is true that a *fairly* drafted interrogatory can elicit relevant and material information if *fairly* answered. The problem is the "fairly" part. Nobody wants to fairly answer an unfair question. Contention interrogatories will almost always elicit evasive or obstructive answers, especially when the contention is skewed toward demonstrating the other party's failures or default. Interrogatories crafted in that manner will almost never be allowed. Likewise, if the interrogatory is preceded by pages of "instructions," the arbitrator will automatically recognize it as "make-work" and likely dismiss the request out of hand.[12]

The lesson to be gleaned from this is to *unlearn* litigation discovery strategies. Focus instead on identifying for the panel the shared need for the fair and reasonable exchange of information. When the request for information is not shaded by a perceived strategic advantage, the arbitrator is more likely to recognize the request as legitimate and one that will advance the goal of minimizing the costs of the arbitration for everyone. Another lesson is to rename the request. Do not present the arbitrator with a list of requested interrogatories. Instead, write a simple letter (to the parties and the arbitrator) listing precisely the information that each party should acknowledge as essential from

12. The CCA Guide to Best Practices notes that some arbitrators may allow a broader use of interrogatories in arbitration on the theory that they will "require the responding party to conduct a reasonable investigation to provide information not immediately known to the responding party." CCA Guide to Best Practices, *supra* note 5, at 188. This still begs the question whether after the investigation the responding party will produce useful and responsive answers. Generally speaking, if the arbitrator foresees that the effort will likely just result in motion practice, he or she will nip the discovery effort in the bud.

the other. The list should be short—don't overreach—and call it a proposed joint "exchange of information"—after all, that is the title of the rule authorizing this kind of discovery in the AAA and JAMS Construction Rules and Discovery Protocols. Don't tell the arbitrator you need it because you don't have it. Instead, demonstrate persuasively that you need it to counterbalance an unfair imbalance in access to project data, that you are unable to develop the information through an exchange of documents only. And don't insist that your form of interrogatory must be used. It is the information that's important, not how it is delivered to you. That is the ball to keep your eye on.

Requests for admissions are generally even more disfavored than interrogatories in arbitration because they are almost always drafted to elicit outcome-determinative admissions against interest or admissions of liability. Such discovery devices are nonstarters. A request to utilize them will almost certainly be denied and sooner or later (or sooner *and* later) generate a discovery motion or a motion for sanctions, something the arbitrator very much seeks to avoid. A legitimate request for admission must be directed to a matter of fact and not a matter of conclusion. For example, the authenticity of a document is a matter of fact. That the document arguably demonstrates the other party's bad faith/breach of contract/default is a matter of legal conclusion and will almost never be admitted. In a construction arbitration, there often are many facts that both parties can reasonably agree are undisputed. The lesson to be learned here is to rename the discovery device. Give it a name that isn't sullied by years of litigation abuse. Give it a name the arbitrator is likely to welcome.

B. Stipulations of Fact; Early Detailed Statements of Claims and Defenses; Witness Statements

While not exactly a discovery device, stipulations of fact can have the intended effect of a request for admission. Both parties in the arbitration are subject to the same limits on available hearing time. Both parties benefit from not having to dedicate hearing time to proving what is not disputed. The arbitrator will welcome a time-saving mechanism. Here is where counsel may jointly develop and submit to the arbitrator a set of agreed facts that may advance their claims and defenses. Construction arbitrators are typically very good at observing the obvious. Arguing against the obvious is not only a waste of time, but it is also a distraction from your case in chief. It can also become an obstacle to satisfying your burden of persuasion relating to a claim or defense. The lesson here is to spend more time working on producing a fair and equitable stipulation of facts and avoid spending time on a set of argumentative requests for admissions.

It is incredibly easy to commence an arbitration. All you need to do is fill out a single-page demand for arbitration, identify the parties (and counsel if known), describe generally the nature of the dispute, and state an amount in controversy. It is so easy that the arbitrator will read it once and forget it immediately, hoping that additional filings will be more informative. The trade-off for the ease of commencement is the lack of persuasive effect. Counsel should take the time to compose a descriptive and persuasive Statement of Claim/Answering Statement. It is the first and last "softball" pleading you get to file, when you can say what you want, how you want, and why you want it to the arbitrator. Don't resist the opportunity, thinking it is better to keep your facts and theories close to the vest until you are forced to present them to your adversary.

The next logical step to a fully fleshed-out statement of claims and defenses is a "supplement" to it that is generally called a "detailed" statement of claims/defenses. When this filing is called for, you should be prepared to supplement the previous narrative with names and dates and documents and photos, meaning all the nuts and bolts of your claims and defenses. Prepared counsel will have much to say in the detailed statement, and the arbitrator will read and reread it to understand the parties' claims and defenses, because it may be the last time he or she gets the chance to learn the specifics of the case until the submissions just prior to the hearing. What is more, a well-prepared detailed statement of claims and defenses will obviate the need for the very kind of discovery mechanisms most arbitrators dislike—such as requests for admissions, interrogatories, and the like.

Witness statements are a very efficient mechanism for the submission of evidence, but they can also be a great mechanism for prehearing disclosure of information, including production of physical and documentary evidence. The fact that the witness statement is prepared largely by counsel will not surprise the arbitrator, but if it turns out that the witness statement is essentially the counsel's testimony, and not the witness's, then the arbitrator will likely give it *exactly* the weight it deserves—none. A well-prepared witness statement is clear and concise, consists of information and insights that are not evident from the written exhibits, identifies the source of the witness's testimony, and of course is the sworn, truthful testimony of the witness. From a discovery perspective, it dots the *i*'s and crosses the *t*'s of essential information required by opposing counsel. The key, of course, is to agree to timely schedule the submission of witness statements, which necessitates that counsel know their case and present it early. Early submission of the witness statements will not inhibit later supplementation and will go a long way to eliminate the need for extensive prehearing discovery.

C. Depositions

Depositions are not normally considered an essential part of prehearing discovery in arbitration. The predominant view in arbitration is that depositions ought to be allowed only sparingly because they are too time consuming and costly.[13] The AAA Regular Track Rules do not mention them, and the LCC Rules allow depositions to be ordered by the arbitrator only in exceptional cases. JAMS Rules authorize only two depositions per side, and then only a party witness or a person under the control of the party.

Arbitrators will frequently authorize depositions only when the requesting party can demonstrate a clear and compelling need and that the deposition will promote a speedy and efficient arbitration. Too often the "good" reasons offered to justify depositions are anything but. Counsel ought to think through the actual need, real number, and true scope of depositions necessary to obtain information not available from other sources, then present a written explanation to the arbitrator that "makes the case" for the arbitrator. A well-thought-out justification for depositions will address the following issues:

- Particularize the need with a specific number.
- Identify the deponents by name and title.
- Describe what information is likely known by the deponent and why it is important to an essential element of your claim/defense.
- Explain why the deponent's presumed knowledge is not otherwise obtained from the exchange of project documents—for example, the witnesses' particularized knowledge is needed to contextualize statements made in project documents; testimony is necessary to explain precisely when/why/where durations were impacted by predecessor/follow-on trades—something not explained by the project schedule itself; etc.
- Concentrate on the need to explore *facts*, not legal issues.
- Explain how and why different witnesses' knowledge do not overlap/repeat.

---

13. Between deposition preparation time, travel time, and the time in the deposition itself, it is not uncommon for a single deposition to take a day or more of lawyer time. Multiply that by the number of depositions both parties may wish to take, and one can easily see that the time and effort of conducting deposition discovery can exceed the scheduled time for the hearing on the merits.

- Explain how the need for testimony dovetails with the factual complexity of the information sought.
- Particularize the issue of cost in relation to the size and scope of the dispute.
- Address how the number of proposed depositions can be mitigated by a limited duration of examination and scheduling of witnesses to reduce the hourly effort relating to the entirety of discovery sought—knocking off four witnesses in a day takes the sting out of the number four.
- Propose staging the process to emphasize that the need for certain information is contingent upon the testimony of others, thus postponing the decision to order more expansive deposition discovery.

Not-so-well-thought-out justifications include the following:

- Depositions are necessary to ascertain the intent of the parties when they entered into the construction agreement.
- The number requested is "the normal" number in cases like this.
- The applicable Rules allow it.
- The parties (actually, in almost all cases, their lawyers) have agreed on the number of depositions "they want."
- This is a seven-figure case.
- Depositions are necessary to explore possible dispositive motion practice.
- We don't know enough to know what we don't know, and depositions are the quickest way to learn the case.

When depositions are permitted, it is common that the arbitrator will impose restrictions on the number of depositions permitted and the time allowed to complete them.[14] At most, only a few key witnesses are deposed in arbitration. You will not have the luxury of a deposition transcript to aid in preparing cross-examination of every witness, but then neither will opposing counsel.

Arbitrators are also often reluctant to allow depositions of expert witnesses, especially when the expert's written report and exhibits should suffice to prepare for cross-examination. However, many large construction

---

14. The AAA's Discovery Best Practices also propose "limiting the depositions to the main fact-witness each party intends to call and imposing costs of deposition on parties insisting to go beyond main fact-witnesses." AAA Discovery Best Practices, *supra* note 3, at 4.

arbitrations involve multiple and complex forms of expert testimony. Counsel may make a case for deposing experts in such a situation on the basis that the time and effort will likely result in a significant reduction in the hours of hearing time required for cross-examination.

The arbitrator will also be interested in whether the deponent is a party witness or a nonparty witness.[15] Arbitrators are typically concerned about imposing upon nonparties the requirement to appear at the hearing to give testimony and are sensitive to the fact that they may not have the legal authority to compel a nonparty witness to sit for a discovery deposition. Arbitrators accordingly are often reluctant to issue subpoenas for discovery purposes if they are uncertain about the ability of the requesting party to compel the nonparty to comply with its terms.[16] The arbitrator will often require the party asking for the subpoena to demonstrate that it has the legal authority to enforce the subpoena in a court with jurisdiction over the nonparty. Generally, an arbitrator has authority only to subpoena a witness to appear at the hearing and even then must rely on local courts to enforce that subpoena if the nonparty is not compliant.

The arbitrator has authority over nonparties to the arbitration agreement only to the extent such authority is granted under the FAA or the applicable state arbitration act. Section 7 of the FAA expressly empowers the arbitrator to compel a witness to appear and testify at an arbitration hearing at a locale and bring with him or her documentary evidence that will be admitted as evidence in the hearing.[17] Section 7 is silent as to whether the arbitrator has the authority to compel the witness to appear with documents and give testimony at a discovery deposition, where the arbitrator is not literally sitting. There is currently a split in the federal circuits regarding whether an arbitrator has the

---

15. Rule 17(b) of the JAMS Construction Rules states that the depositions allowed must be of a party witness. Rule L-4 of the AAA Construction Rules does not limit deposition discovery to party witnesses only, but it does restrict depositions to "exceptional cases, at the discretion of the arbitrator, upon good cause shown." Moreover, the AAA Best Practices recommend a complementary limitation on depositions of nonparties. AAA Discovery Best Practices, *supra* note 3, at 4–5. *See also* Tyler, *supra* note 6, at 180–83 & nn.102–12.

16. The arbitrator will likely direct the party seeking the subpoena to draft it in such a fashion as to promote its enforceability and conform to applicable state laws. The arbitrator will entertain objections from any party regarding the issuance of the subpoena and may require the requesting party to demonstrate that what it is asking for is legally permissible and enforceable.

17. 9 U.S.C. § 7. *Cf.* CCA Guide to Best Practices, *supra* note 5, at 192.

legal authority to compel a witness to appear at a deposition. The Third Circuit has ruled that the arbitrator has no such authority.[18] The Eighth Circuit has ruled that the arbitrator is empowered "implicitly" under the FAA to compel a witness to appear for a discovery deposition.[19]

There are possible workarounds, which can extend to the arbitrator agreeing to convene a limited merits hearing at a site near the third-party witness, solely for purposes of taking his or her testimony (including cross-examination). The widespread availability of video depositions where the witness can testify from any convenient location, and the arbitrator can also be "present" by video, also offers possibilities for honoring the boundaries of FAA section 7 in substance if not in letter, although the courts have not yet ruled on this.

Suffice it to say that counsel desiring to depose a nonparty witness ahead of the hearing needs to carefully weigh the need for the testimony against the complications and expense involved in obtaining it. It is not simply a matter of requesting a subpoena to compel a nonparty to appear for a discovery deposition, as such a subpoena may have no practical legal effect. Part of the answer depends on whether the arbitrator is "sitting" in a federal circuit that permits the arbitrator to issue a subpoena for a discovery deposition.[20] Additionally, counsel should determine whether applicable state law imposes restrictions or limitations on the arbitrator's authority to summon nonparty witnesses.[21]

III. Site Inspections

Construction disputes often involve questions regarding the status or condition of the project or the project site. Site visits are a useful tool in many instances, giving the arbitrator a firsthand look at the specific physical layout and conditions regarding the issues in dispute. The notion of an arbitrator visit to the project site is often overlooked by parties in the midst of a dispute.

Site visits can be beneficial for several reasons. First, hands-on familiarity with the project site can enlighten the arbitrator's understanding of the

18. Hay Grp., Inc. v. E.B.S. Acquisition Corp., 360 F.3d 404, 411 (3d Cir. 2004).

19. *In re* Sec. Life Ins. Co. of Am., 228 F.3d 865, 871 (8th Cir. 2000).

20. *See generally* Comment, *Balancing Burdens: Clarifying the Discovery Standard in Arbitration Proceedings*, 117 Yale L.J. 159 (2008).

21. State arbitration acts may differ materially from the FAA and each other. For an excellent and thorough analysis of the most frequent state law issues affecting arbitrator authority to summon nonparty witnesses, see CCA Guide to Best Practices, *supra* note 5, at 199–217. *See also* Tyler, *supra* note 6, at 161, 175–83 & nn.75–112.

issues in dispute—the size of the project, the general environmental conditions, access, etc. Second, a site visit can eliminate perceptional biases about otherwise purely legal arguments. Observing the reality of the site can either confirm or refute preliminary views formed from oral and written testimony. Third, a site visit may better inform the parties' experts, rendering their testimony more helpful to the arbitrator. Sometimes seeing is believing—or not believing.

Before requesting a site visit, counsel should consider the current condition of the site, logistical obstacles to observing the relevant conditions at the site, and whether the cost of getting there is justified. The timing of a useful site inspection can be before, during, or after the merits hearing, depending on access, safety, and other issues. Counsel may consider a site inspection to be strategic, but the arbitrator is likely to make every effort to remove strategic presentations from the effort and condition the site visit upon an appropriate and particularized site visit and inspection protocol.

When a site visit is requested, counsel should anticipate a discussion with opposing counsel and the arbitrator about whether and how it may be conducted in a fair and orderly manner. Typically the issues to be addressed include:

1. Who is going?
2. Who will do the talking and who will answer the arbitrator's questions?
3. Who is paying the costs?
4. Is the attendance of experts necessary or appropriate?
5. How, if at all, may the parties highlight particular conditions and locations during the inspection?
6. Is any testing intended to be part of the inspection?
7. What safety measures will be in effect during the inspection?
8. How will the arbitrator and parties be delivered to the site and returned after the inspection?
9. Will any testimony be presented during the site inspection, and how will that be recorded?
10. Will all or part of the inspection be recorded?

A site inspection can provide the arbitrator with opportunities for first-hand observation that photos and project records cannot provide—a direct impression of the physical work or conditions that are at the heart of the parties' dispute. Consider, for example, a disruption claim that emphasizes in significant part the congestion of the work areas involved and the limited available space for maneuvering and installing the work. A visit can convey the site working conditions far better than a video or an animation, much less what photos or testimony could ever hope to provide. It is important to ensure that the site inspection is relevant and helpful to the arbitrator in resolving the dispute, while also protecting the fairness of the process and the parties' rights to adequately present their positions. Accordingly, the arbitrator will welcome a jointly developed inspection protocol, the most common elements of which are described next.

A. The Party Representatives

Each party should designate a representative who will act as that party's "guide" during the site visit. In multiparty disputes (especially those involving ten or more parties), one designee often serves to represent multiple parties. The representative should know the site and the precise issues in the case that will be highlighted by the site observations and be respectful of the need for private observations and discussions among the panel when there is more than one arbitrator. The party representative is a guide and not an advocate. In some cases, the party representative may be a technical expert who can help ensure that the arbitrator sees the precise conditions that are most relevant and important.

B. The Scope and Route of the Visit

The parties will sometimes disagree about just what the arbitrator ought to see. In that case, the typical compromise is to include all parts of the project structure and systems that each party wants the arbitrator to view. The arbitrator is likely to reject the requested inspection if it appears it is being used to gain an advantage for one party over the other. The sole purpose of a site inspection is to help the arbitrator better understand the issues that separate the parties, not to advance one party's position. Likewise, neither party should "lead" the inspection or be the sole decider as to what the arbitrator sees. Both parties should jointly agree on the scope and route of the site inspection. To that end, it is important to schedule a previsit to the project site by the party representative and counsel to ensure that conditions at the project site will enable the arbitrator to see the features that all of the parties collectively want to be included on the visit.

While helping the arbitrator better understand the issues is the objective, an inspection can do this in varying ways: it can include education about the issues, provide technical understanding necessary to evaluate the oral and written testimony, allow the arbitrator to gather facts relating to the project site to assist in formulating the arbitration award, or a combination of these elements. This should be discussed and agreed upon by the parties in advance. The arbitrator should be provided with an agreed itinerary addressing transportation to and from the site, security access requirements, personal protective equipment, and the identity of the site guides who will conduct the site tour. Additionally, the itinerary should include an orientation map of the overall project and a route map, ideally accompanied by photos of what will be seen along the way. Photos are useful because they permit the arbitrator to independently compare his or her site observations with photographic evidence in the case. Where appropriate, the parties can also supply the arbitrator in advance with relevant contract drawings and specifications for key elements of the project that are in dispute.

C. Interactions with the Arbitrator

Communication among counsel, potential witnesses, and the arbitrator during the site visit should also be addressed and agreed in advance. Ex parte communications are universally forbidden in arbitration, as in court. Yet, while at what can often be a somewhat chaotic project site, the casualness of the moment can lead to spontaneous exchanges at points where both counsel may not be in hearing range. A careful site visit protocol will emphasize the importance of avoiding such instances to protect the integrity and independence of the arbitrator. The arbitrator also should be careful to abide by the protocol and not engage in such casual conversations but may sometimes need to be gently reminded of this. A site visit is an extension of the hearing room, where casual conversations with the arbitrator outside the presence of all counsel are not permitted.

Accordingly, rules for questions and discussion should be established. What is the proper timing and format for this interaction? Generally speaking, it is usually most effective to allow a moment for questions and discussion before leaving each specific area of the tour, limited to that section of the work, at a location where the arbitrator, counsel, and the designated guides can all hear and participate in responding to questions. This is generally not the time to allow counsel to ask questions of representatives of the other party, other than straightforward factual questions about what has just been viewed (e.g., "where is that pipe coming from?").

The risk is that the inspection can sometimes be turned into its own mini-hearing, and this is very much to be avoided. A site visit is not the time for cross-examination, arguments, motions, or countermotions. Discussion and questions should be limited to assuring that everyone has seen what counsel wanted them to see and, just as importantly, understood what it is that they are looking at.

D. On-Site Discussions and Evidentiary Submissions

Counsel should consider whether and how to preserve evidence collected at the site inspection. This is by no means always necessary, but in some cases it is important. A court reporter will not be of much use during a site inspection. Taking video and photographs is most often used when there is a need to have a record in some form of what occurred. Still, sound and reproduction quality of video shot at the site may be poor, to the point of being unreliable or misleading. The angle of the video capture, the order of presentation, the witness's characterization of the subject matter: these are all potential subjects for disagreements between counsel.

In an unusual case, such as where the site visit will include testing of components or systems in real time, counsel should consider designating an independent videographer. But even then, the end product may be unclear, inadequate, or otherwise objectionable. Alternatively, each party can arrange its own inspection process, capture its own images, and develop its own presentation.

E. Safety

Construction sites present myriad opportunities for injuries to persons and property. The site visit protocol should address safety and security measures necessary to protect all the participants. Compliance with project site safety criteria, OSHA requirements, safety site training, warm-up/conditioning, clothing and footwear requirements, etc., should all be clarified well in advance of the site inspection, as well as who is going to provide any needed personal protective equipment such as hard hats, safety goggles, gloves, and safety vests. All participants must agree to abide by all such applicable restrictions and safety requirements. The site superintendent should be included in developing this part of the protocol, as it may be necessary to cordon off certain hazardous areas or install special signage, including instructions on emergency procedures.

CHAPTER 6

Motions in Arbitration

WENDY KENNEDY VENOIT

As a starting point, motions (of all types) are typically less common—and often less accepted by arbitrators—in the arbitration setting as compared to state and federal court practice. This is not because the applicable arbitration rules or agreed-upon procedures necessarily forbid them. Rather, much like discovery and other litigation-oriented procedures, robust motion practice is often frowned upon in arbitration because, when overused or misused, it is the antithesis of the efficient and cost-effective process that arbitration is intended to provide.

In discussing motions in this chapter, we are referring to all types of motions that may arise in the arbitration setting, including (1) jurisdictional motions; (2) pleading-related motions (such as motions for greater particularity in the pleadings and motions to amend the pleadings); (3) joinder and consolidation motions; (4) venue-related motions; (5) discovery-related motions, including motions to compel, to subpoena third parties, or requesting additional discovery beyond what is afforded by the applicable rules or procedural order;[1] (6) motions for dispositive relief; (7) motions in limine or to strike evidence; (8) motions for sanctions; (9) motions to amend or to correct an award; and (10) motions for continuance or modifications to procedural orders. This list is by no means exhaustive of the motions that a party may seek to bring in arbitration, but these are the most commonly encountered. As we address each of these types of motions, we will endeavor to identify their suggested uses, the applicable rules relevant to each, and likely outcomes.

---

1. Discovery-related motions are addressed in greater depth in Chapter 4, Document Exchange and Discovery, and Chapter 5, Depositions and Other Discovery Methods.

I. Motion Practice Generally

Motions are generally permitted by most institutional arbitral rules to varying degrees and for varying purposes, at the discretion of the arbitrator.[2] For example, the American Arbitration Association Construction Industry Arbitration Rules (AAA Construction Rules) expressly authorize the arbitrator to allow dispositive motions to be brought, upon prior written application to and approval of the arbitrator, that may dispose of all or part of a claim or narrow the issues in a case.[3] Notably, the AAA Construction Rules are otherwise silent regarding motion practice, leaving the issue to the discretion of, and within the broad authority of, the arbitrator in his or her management of the arbitration.

II. Types of Motions Utilized in Arbitration

A. Jurisdictional Motions

It is quite common in arbitration for one of the parties to object to the jurisdiction of the arbitrator to hear and decide some or all of the issues in dispute. Because the right and obligation to arbitrate are creatures of contract and/or party agreement, jurisdiction is a fundamental aspect of the arbitration process, as it provides the basis for the arbitrator's authority to hear and decide the dispute.[4] Absent jurisdiction, the arbitrator is without authority to rule.

A party considering whether to file a jurisdictional motion should evaluate the following questions: (1) Is there a basis to contest jurisdiction? (2) If so, *should* you contest jurisdiction? (3) If so, when is the appropriate time and what is the appropriate procedure for making such a motion?

1. Is There a Basis for a Jurisdictional Objection?

The starting point for any analysis of jurisdiction is determining whether there is a valid agreement to arbitrate and, if so, what the scope of that arbitration agreement is. Although courts strongly favor arbitration, they will not compel the arbitration of claims that are outside the scope of a valid and enforceable arbitration agreement. In the construction context, the arbitration agreement is typically contained in the contract between the parties, and it is that agreement

---

2. The singular "arbitrator" as used in this chapter refers to both sole arbitrators and panels of three arbitrators.

3. American Arbitration Association Construction Industry Arbitration Rules (July 1, 2015) [hereinafter AAA Construction Rules], Rule R-34.

4. Steelworkers v. Warrior & Gulf Nav. Co., 363 U.S. 574, 582 (1960).

that defines the jurisdictional basis for submission of a dispute to arbitration. Less commonly, the parties may agree to submit a dispute to arbitration after the dispute arises and without a preexisting contractual agreement to arbitrate.

Jurisdictional challenges are most commonly raised where (1) there is no agreement to arbitrate at all or the respondent is not a party to the agreement to arbitrate; (2) the arbitration agreement is narrowly defined or otherwise limited in scope; (3) the party demanding arbitration has not satisfied a jurisdictional prerequisite to arbitration (e.g., mediation); (4) a party is asserting extracontractual claims (e.g., claims sounding in tort) that arguably fall outside the arbitration agreement; or (5) the party demanding arbitration has waived its right to arbitrate by pursuing its claims in litigation.

The most clear-cut scenario is where there is no arbitration agreement at all—and, therefore, no basis to invoke the jurisdiction of the arbitrator. Rarely, if ever, do we see arbitrations brought under this circumstance, however. The more likely scenario is where it is not clear that the respondent is a party to the arbitration agreement or has not otherwise agreed to be bound by the arbitration agreement. An example is a dispute initiated by the beneficiary of a surety bond seeking payment from the surety for a default by the principal on the bond, when the underlying construction contract contains an arbitration clause. In this circumstance, there is little question that the principal on the bond would be subject to arbitration, but the surety may argue that it is not a signatory to that arbitration agreement and that it never agreed to arbitrate its obligations under the surety bond. Most courts that have considered this issue have held that because the underlying contract is incorporated into the terms of the bond, the surety has agreed to the arbitration agreement in the underlying contract.[5] The key consideration in determining whether the respondent is subject to arbitration is whether, through words, conduct, or incorporation by reference, the respondent actually or impliedly agreed to arbitrate.

Another scenario where jurisdictional challenges can be raised is where the arbitration agreement is narrowly defined to include resolution of only certain types of claims or claims between certain parties. In this situation, the respondent (or the claimant with respect to a counterclaim) argues that the claims asserted in the arbitration fall outside the scope of the arbitration agreement and, therefore, are not arbitrable. The resolution of this issue typically

5. G. Winkler Cranley & T.M. Kocke, *Arbitration: Participation of the Surety as a Named Party*, ABA Tort Trial & Ins. Prac. Section, 2018 Fid. & Sur. L. Midwinter Conf. 2 (Jan. 26, 2018) ("A majority of jurisdictions require a surety to arbitrate when the bond incorporates a contract containing a mandatory arbitration clause.").

turns on the language of the arbitration agreement itself.[6] "Under a narrow arbitration clause, a dispute is subject to arbitration only if it relates to an issue that is on its face within the purview of the clause, and collateral matters will generally be beyond its purview."[7] In contrast, where an arbitration clause is broad, "there arises a presumption of arbitrability and arbitration of even a collateral matter . . . if the claim alleged implicates issues of contract construction or the parties' rights and obligations under it."[8] While there are no magic words needed to make an arbitration clause "broad," the most common formulation that reliably achieves this result is language providing that "any controversy or claim arising out of or relating to this contract, or the breach thereof, shall be settled by arbitration."

---

6. *E.g.*, Hearn v. Comcast Cable Commc'ns, LLC, 416 F. Supp. 3d 1155 (N.D. Ga. 2019) (plaintiff's claims for relief under the Fair Credit Reporting Act did not relate to the service agreement between the plaintiff and defendant and therefore did not fall within the scope of their arbitration agreement); Anderson v. Deere & Co., 393 Mont. 157 (2018) (where arbitration agreement covered only disputes "between Dealer and Company" and the claims at issue were for torts against the plaintiff personally, not as part of "Dealer," there was no obligation to arbitrate); Perez v. DirecTV, 740 F. App'x 560 (9th Cir. 2018) (claims filed by a consumer for violations of the Communications Act were not subject to the arbitration clause in DirecTV's customer agreement, which specifically exempted disputes "involving a violation of the Communications Act").

7. Chelsea Fam. Pharmacy, PLLC v. Medco Health Sols., Inc., 567 F.3d 1191, 1262 (10th Cir. 2009).

8. *Id.* Examples of cases involving broad arbitration clauses: C & L Enters., Inc. v. Citizen Band Potawatomi Indian Tribe of Okla., 532 U.S. 411, 415 (2001); Oracle Am., Inc. v. Myriad Grp. A.G., 724 F.3d 1069, 1071 (9th Cir. 2013); Petrofac, Inc. v. DynMcDermott Petroleum Operations Co., 687 F.3d 671, 674 (5th Cir. 2012); Fallo v. High-Tech Inst., 559 F.3d 874, 876 (8th Cir. 2009); Qualcomm Inc. v. Nokia Corp., 466 F.3d 1366, 1369 (Fed. Cir. 2006); Terminix Int'l Co. v. Palmer Ranch Ltd. P'ship, 432 F.3d 1327, 1329 (11th Cir. 2005); Getzelman v. Trustwave Holdings, Inc., No. 13-cv-02987-CMA, 2014 WL 3809736, at *3 (D. Colo. Aug. 1, 2013); Julian v. Julian, No. 4137-VGP, 2009 WL 2937121, at *5 (Del. Apr. 23, 2009) ("related to" language "explicitly extends the scope of the arbitration provision 'beyond the four corners of'" the agreement); Brown v. Coleman Co., Inc., 220 F.3d 1180, 1184 (10th Cir. 2000) (arbitration clause encompassing "all disputes or controversies arising under or in connection with this Agreement" constituted "a broad arbitration clause as it covers not only those issues arising under the employment contract, but even those issues with any connection to the contract"); Qwest Corp. v. New Access Commc'ns, LLC, No. 03-N-1278, 2004 U.S. Dist. LEXIS 28523, at *3 (D. Colo. Mar. 31, 2004) (arbitration clause covering "any claim, controversy or dispute between the parties" with no restriction found to be broad).

A final example of a jurisdictional challenge is where the contract requires mediation (or other preceding procedural step) as a prerequisite to arbitration, and the claimant files arbitration without first exhausting the mediation process. Resolution of this issue will typically turn on the language of the arbitration agreement (i.e., is mediation truly a jurisdictional prerequisite?). But even where mediation or another procedural step, such as a meeting of the parties' senior executives, is a clear precursor and jurisdictional prerequisite to arbitration, the challenge generally will only postpone the arbitration (which is stayed until the condition precedent is satisfied) but generally will not cause it to be dismissed.

2. *If There Is a Basis, Should You Assert a Jurisdictional Objection?*

Of course, even if a party does have a valid basis to object to the jurisdiction of the arbitrator, that party should weigh not only the merits of the motion but also the pros and cons of proceeding with the arbitration notwithstanding the basis for an objection. Some parties believe that if they object to the arbitration, the dispute may simply go away. That is rarely the case. So, the party considering raising a jurisdictional objection should first ask itself: "What is my alternative to proceeding with the arbitration?" It may be that arbitration is actually a more appealing alternative than litigation or that prevailing on the jurisdiction issue will likely result in arbitrating the arbitrable portion and having to litigate the nonarbitrable portion, thereby significantly increasing the overall cost. This is the "be careful what you ask for, you might just get it" question.

Because there is a general presumption of arbitrability that can be difficult to overcome, extended motion practice on this threshold issue carries a distinct risk that it will only delay resolution of the dispute and add to the costs for both parties. As such, a party considering a jurisdictional challenge should carefully weigh all factors before proceeding with the objection.

3. *When and How to Assert a Jurisdictional Motion*

Jurisdictional objections should be raised at or near the commencement of the arbitration. If the respondent does not object at the commencement of the arbitration and instead avails itself of the arbitral process without objection to the arbitrator's jurisdiction, it will likely be deemed to have waived any right to object later.[9] This concept is not dissimilar to what occurs in state and federal

9. Steven H. Reisberg, *Objections to the Jurisdiction of the Arbitration Tribunal under the U.S. Federal Arbitration Act: How to Preserve the Right to Judicial Review*, 13 INT'L A.L.R. 148, 150 (Issue 4, 2010) ("It is well settled that a party who

courts when a party fails to raise a jurisdictional objection at the outset of the litigation through either submission of a motion to dismiss or assertion of an affirmative defense. In the arbitration context, however, jurisdictional objections are typically first made directly to the arbitral institution administering the proceeding or at the very latest to the arbitrator once selected.

A party seeking to object to jurisdiction is well advised to raise the objection as early in the process as possible. Because of the relative informality of arbitration, the objection is often raised initially by letter to the case administrator at the arbitral institution. This gets the objection on the table, but except in the most clear-cut circumstances, the case administrator will not decide the issue but rather defer the issue for decision by the arbitrator once selected. In other words, the jurisdictional objection will typically not avoid or stall the arbitral process. Appointment of the arbitrator will likely proceed notwithstanding the ongoing jurisdictional objection.

In order to preserve its jurisdictional objection, the objecting party must at the latest assert its objection in its answering statement or other initial pleading. The jurisdictional objection should also be raised at the initial procedural conference, so a briefing schedule can be set for addressing the jurisdictional issues and any other threshold issues or objections. The arbitrator will generally resolve any jurisdictional issues early in the process, but the process will continue in the interim.

Another potential option open to the party challenging jurisdiction is to file an action in a state or federal court seeking to enjoin the arbitration on the basis that the arbitrator is without jurisdiction to hear the dispute. Except in the most clear-cut circumstances (such as where there is no arbitration agreement at all), such collateral attacks on arbitration are rarely successful, because courts recognize a strong presumption in favor of arbitration.[10] In addition, while the general rule is that questions of arbitrability are ordinarily decided

---

participates in an arbitration without asserting an objection to the jurisdiction of the arbitrator will be held to have waived any such objection."). *See also* Jones Dairy Farm v. Local No. P-1236, United Food & Com. Workers Int'l Union, AFL-CIO, 760 F.2d 173, 175–76 (7th Cir. 1985); Gvozdenovic v. United Air Lines Inc., 933 F.2d 1100, 1105 (2d Cir. 1991).

10. Moses H. Cone Mem'l Hosp. v. Mercury Constr. Corp., 460 U.S. 1, 24–25 (1983); Mastrobuono v. Shearson Lehman Hutton, Inc., 514 U.S. 52, 62 (1995); Diamond Materials, LLC v. Tutor Perini Corp., No. N20C-05-162, MAA, 2021 WL 1716969, at *2 (Del. Super. Ct. Apr. 30, 2021) ("A strong presumption exists in favor of arbitration and, accordingly, contractual arbitration clauses are generally interpreted broadly by the courts.").

by a court,[11] this can be overcome where the parties have decided that arbitrability questions will be decided by the arbitrator. The arbitral institution rules that are most often specified in the arbitration clause (including the AAA Construction Rules) authorize the arbitrators to decide their own jurisdiction. Specifically, most arbitral rules provide that the arbitrator will have the power to rule on his or her own jurisdiction, including any objections with respect to the existence, scope, or validity of the arbitration agreement or the arbitrability of any claim or counterclaim.[12] Most courts have held that by specifically incorporating these institutional rules into the arbitration agreement, the parties have "clearly and unmistakably" agreed to arbitrate questions of arbitrability.[13] Even if the arbitration agreement does not specifically incorporate a particular

11. Howsam v. Dean Witter Reynolds, Inc., 537 U.S. 79, 83–84 (2002).

12. *E.g.*, American Arbitration Association Commercial Arbitration Rules (Sept. 1, 2022) [hereinafter AAA Commercial Rules], Rule 7(a); AAA Construction Rules, *supra* note 3, Rule R-9; International Chamber of Commerce Rules of Arbitration, art. 6(5) (Jan. 1, 2021); UNCITRAL Arbitration Rules, art. 23 (rev. 2010); CPR Administered Arbitration Rules, Rule 8.1 (eff. Mar. 1, 2019); JAMS Engineering and Construction Arbitration Rules and Procedures (June 1, 2021) [hereinafter JAMS Construction Rules], Rule 11(b).

13. Awuah v. Coverall N. Am., Inc., 554 F.3d 7, 10–12 (1st Cir. 2009); Schneider v. Kingdom of Thai., 688 F.3d 68, 72–74 (2d Cir. 2012) ("Where parties explicitly incorporate rules that empower an arbitrator to decide issues of arbitrability, the incorporation serves as clear and unmistakable evidence of the parties' intent to delegate such issues to an arbitrator."); Richardson v. Coverall N. Am., Inc., Case Nos. 18-3393, 18-3399, 2020 U.S. App. LEXIS 13568 (3d Cir. Apr. 28, 2020) (agreeing to arbitrate under the AAA rules affording the arbitrators the right to rule on their own jurisdiction clearly and unmistakably delegates arbitrability questions to the arbitrators to resolve); Simply Wireless, Inc. v. T-Mobile U.S., Inc., 877 F.3d 522 (4th Cir. 2017) (by incorporating the JAMS arbitration rules into their arbitration clause, the parties "clearly and unmistakably" provided that the arbitrators would decide what issues were subject to arbitration); *Petrofac, Inc.*, 687 F.3d at 675 (parties' express incorporation of AAA rules constituted clear and unmistakable evidence that parties agreed to arbitrate question of arbitrability); Blanton v. Domino's Pizza Franchising LLC, Case No. 19-2388, 2020 U.S. App. LEXIS 18975 (6th Cir. June 17, 2020) (agreeing to arbitrate under the AAA rules affording the arbitrators the right to rule on their own jurisdiction clearly and unmistakably delegates arbitrability questions to the arbitrators to resolve); *Fallo*, 559 F.3d at 878; *Oracle Am., Inc.*, 724 F.3d at 1072–77 (in arbitration agreement between sophisticated parties to commercial contract, parties' incorporation of arbitration rules of United Nations Commission on International Trade Law delegates questions of arbitrability to arbitrator). *But see* Chesapeake Appalachia, LLC v. Scout

set of arbitration rules, but the agreement designates that the arbitration will be administered by a particular provider (such as the AAA), that provider's rules may state that by choosing the provider to administer the arbitration, the parties are deemed to have incorporated that provider's rules into their agreement[14] and have therefore agreed to submit issues of arbitrability to the arbitrator.

B. Pleading-Related Motions

Pleading-related motions are less frequently seen in arbitration because most arbitral institution rules and the arbitration acts governing arbitration proceedings do not have specific pleading requirements or do not require a great deal of particularity in the pleadings. In fact, the required detail is often less than what is required for "notice pleading" in federal court. For example, an AAA arbitration can be commenced by simply filling out the one- to two-page Demand for Arbitration form on the AAA website, which requires little detail about the dispute beyond the names of the parties, the amount in controversy and relief sought (because the filing fee is tied to that amount), the anticipated number of hearing days, the venue, the type of dispute (e.g., construction), and a copy of the arbitration agreement. The required AAA Answering Statement form to be filed in response is equally slim. Given the paucity of information and detail needed to commence a domestic arbitration, there is little opportunity to attack a party's initial pleading as insufficient on the basis of lack of detail or particularity.

While motions directed at filling out bare-bones pleadings are rare, the problem of lack of sufficient information regarding the claims and defenses being raised is often addressed in a different manner. Arbitrators will frequently direct the parties to serve detailed statements of claim, counterclaim, and defenses early in the process in order to ensure that the disputes and issues

---

Petroleum, LLC, 809 F.3d 746, 751 (3d Cir. 2016) (an incorporation of the AAA rules is not a clear and unmistakable delegation to the arbitrators).

14. *E.g.*, International Centre for Dispute Resolution, International Dispute Resolution Procedures (Mar. 2021), art. 1.1 ("Where parties have agreed to arbitrate disputes under these International Arbitration Rules ('Rules'), or have provided for arbitration of an international dispute by the International Centre for Dispute Resolution (ICDR) or the American Arbitration Association (AAA) without designating particular rules, the arbitration shall take place in accordance with these Rules as in effect at the date of commencement of the arbitration, subject to modifications that the parties may adopt in writing. The ICDR is the Administrator of these Rules.").

to be decided are adequately framed and to avoid procedural ambush. If this is not raised by the arbitrator, it is entirely appropriate for counsel to raise the subject at the initial procedural conference. Although there are no rules as to what these detailed statements must include, procedural orders may specify requirements for these submissions. For example:

> A concise written summary of their claims or counterclaims (including claims of offset) and defenses, stating with reasonable particularity each claim or defense; an explanation of the claim or defense; a concise summary of the legal and factual arguments underlying each claim, counterclaim, offset, or defense that each Party intends to raise at the arbitration hearing; and a breakdown of all damages or other relief sought in this Arbitration. All of the foregoing is subject to refinement by expert reports and testimony, as well as discovery.

The intent is to give the opposing party adequate notice of the claims being asserted so that it can defend itself properly, as well as to further define the scope of discovery that will be needed. In rare circumstances, one of the parties will complain about the level of particularity in the other party's statement of claim or defenses and may request the arbitrator to direct additional specifics to be provided. The success of such a motion will generally turn on whether the arbitrator agrees that greater particularity is reasonably necessary given the stage of the case and/or as a matter of fairness to the other party.

While motions attacking the sufficiency of pleadings are relatively uncommon and rarely successful, motions to amend the pleadings are more common and typically granted, much like their litigation counterparts. Most institutional rules allow for amendments as of right prior to appointment of the arbitrator but require arbitrator approval for any amendments made thereafter. For example, Rule 10 of the JAMS Construction Rules provides:

> After the filing of a claim and before the Arbitrator is appointed, any Party may make a new or different claim against a Party or any third party that is subject to Arbitration in the proceeding. Such claim shall be made in writing, filed with JAMS and served on the other Parties. Any response to the new claim shall be made within fourteen (14) calendar days after service of such claim. After the Arbitrator is appointed, no new or different claim may be submitted except with the Arbitrator's approval. A Party may request a Hearing on this issue. Each Party has the right to respond to any new or amended claim in accordance with Rule 9(c) or (d).

Similarly, Rule R-6 of the AAA Construction Rules provides:

R-6. Changes of Claim or Counterclaim

(a) A party may at any time prior to the close of the hearing or by the date established by the arbitrator increase or decrease the amount of its claim or counterclaim. Written notice of the change of claim amount must be provided to the AAA and all parties.

(b) Any new or different claim or counterclaim, as opposed to an increase or decrease in the amount of a pending claim or counterclaim, shall be made in writing and filed with the AAA, and a copy shall be provided to the other party, who shall have a period of 14 calendar days from the date of such transmittal within which to file an answer to the proposed change of claim or counterclaim with the AAA. After the arbitrator is appointed no new or different claim or counterclaim may be submitted without the arbitrator's consent.

The AAA Construction Rules for Preliminary Hearing provisions suggest that the parties and the arbitrator address "whether there are any anticipated amendments to the parties' claims, counterclaims, or defenses" at the initial procedural hearing in order to avoid undue surprise, and procedural orders may include a deadline for any such amendments.

In practice, motions to amend are liberally granted, particularly when made relatively early in the proceedings when there is more than adequate time for the respondent to respond to and defend against any new causes of action or allegations. Even late-filed motions will most often be granted unless the respondent can articulate some clear prejudice from the amendment that cannot be addressed otherwise.

C. Joinder and Consolidation Motions

The issues surrounding joinder and consolidation were addressed in greater detail in Chapter 3. Accordingly, these issues will be addressed only briefly here.

Joinder and consolidation motions have become increasingly frequent in arbitration—and particularly in construction arbitrations—given the number of interconnected parties on most construction projects. As a result, it has become increasingly common to see arbitration clauses that allow for the joinder and consolidation of other parties into a single proceeding (e.g., owner, contractor, subcontractors, architect, and other design professionals) in order to afford full and complete relief in a single proceeding.

Likewise, many institutional arbitral rules specifically address joinder and consolidation. For example, Rule R-7 of the AAA Construction Rules provides for the appointment of a separate arbitrator to determine solely the issues of joinder or consolidation, when the request is filed within the timeframes established in Rule R-7; subsequent to that time, joinder may be allowed by the merits arbitrator only for good cause shown. Moreover, failure to object to a joinder request will be deemed a waiver of the right to object.

Rule 6(f) of the JAMS Construction Rules, by contrast, leaves joinder to the sound discretion of the merits arbitrator "taking into account all circumstances he or she deems relevant and applicable." Rule 6(e) of the JAMS Construction Rules also identifies the circumstances when consolidation is appropriate, but the consolidation decision is made by JAMS and not by the merits arbitrator:

> (e) Unless the Parties' Agreement or applicable law provides otherwise, JAMS, if it determines that the Arbitrations so filed have common issues of fact or law, may consolidate Arbitrations in the following instances:
>
> > (i) If a Party files more than one Arbitration with JAMS, JAMS may consolidate two or more of the Arbitrations into a single Arbitration.
> >
> > (ii) Where a Demand or Demands for Arbitration is or are submitted naming Parties already involved in another Arbitration or Arbitrations pending under these Rules, JAMS may decide that the new case or cases shall be consolidated into one or more of the pending proceedings and referred to one of the Arbitrators or panels of Arbitrators already appointed.
> >
> > (iii) Where a Demand or Demands for Arbitration is or are submitted naming parties that are not identical to the Parties in the existing Arbitration or Arbitrations, JAMS may decide that the new case or cases shall be consolidated into one or more of the pending proceedings and referred to one of the Arbitrators or panels of Arbitrators already appointed.
>
> When rendering its decision, JAMS will take into account all circumstances, including the links between the cases and the progress already made in the existing Arbitrations. Unless applicable law provides otherwise, where JAMS decides to consolidate a proceeding

into a pending Arbitration, the Parties to the consolidated case or cases will be deemed to have waived their right to designate an Arbitrator as well as any contractual provision with respect to the site of the Arbitration.

While intended to achieve greater efficiency, the joinder of all potentially interested parties can easily make the proceedings less efficient and administratively challenging. Just scheduling the hearings to accommodate the calendars of not only the arbitrators and primary parties but also all of the ancillary parties can become a nightmare. Also, if every party insists on having its day in court—in terms of presenting evidence, making arguments, and so on—it can lead to prolonged hearings. Nonetheless, there are often valid reasons why joinder and consolidation will be appropriate and should be pursued.

D. Venue-Related Motions

In most cases, the parties will designate the venue of the arbitration, meaning the location (typically city and state) where the arbitration hearing will take place, in their arbitration agreement. In international arbitrations, the concept of venue has increased significance. This is because the designation of venue (or the "seat") of the arbitration usually determines the applicable procedural law, which can have important practical and legal implications, including the role of local courts in relation to the arbitration.[15]

Most arbitrators and courts will enforce the parties' designated choice of venue, even if the venue turns out to be inconvenient to one or both parties. The parties are, of course, free to agree to a shift in venue, and the arbitrator will typically accommodate such agreements. If the arbitration agreement is silent on the issue of venue, the arbitrator is expressly empowered under most arbitral institution rules to determine venue if the parties cannot agree.

There are circumstances, however, where a party will object to a given venue as being contrary to applicable law or on equitable grounds. For example, in some states, like Connecticut, a choice-of-venue provision designating a location outside of the state for hearing disputes arising out of a construction project in that state is void and unenforceable as a matter of statutory law.[16]

---

15. Claudia Salomon & Irina Sivachenko, *Choosing an Arbitral Seat in the United States*, LexisPSL Arb. (Mar. 2014), https://salomonarbitration.com/wp-content/uploads/2020/11/2014.03-choosing-an-arbitral-seat-in-the-us.pdf.

16. Conn. Gen. Stat. § 42-158m (part of the Fairness in Financing Act). This section provides: "Any provision in a construction contract for the performance of work on a construction site located in this state that purports to require that any dispute arising

This applies to both litigation and arbitration proceedings. By law, if a party wants to arbitrate a dispute arising out of a Connecticut construction project, that arbitration must take place in Connecticut. The parties are always free to agree otherwise, but a party cannot be forced to arbitrate elsewhere. Texas has a similar statute applicable to "a contract that is principally for the construction or repair of an improvement to real property located in [Texas]," which states: "If a contract contains a provision making the contract or any conflict arising under the contract subject to another state's law, litigation in the courts of another state, or arbitration in another state, that provision is voidable by the party obligated by the contract to perform the construction or repair."[17] Notably, while these statutes will likely control in a venue dispute in an arbitration proceeding, parties have been less successful in utilizing them to dismiss litigation that has been brought in another state.[18]

Parties may also argue that an inconvenient venue is unfair, unreasonable, or contrary to public policy. However, absent fraud or overreaching, venue selection provisions are generally enforced.[19] Courts as well as arbitrators are highly deferential to a contractual venue selection when determining whether a venue is proper.[20] The party opposing the enforcement of a venue selection clause has the burden to establish that the clause is unfair or unreasonable or that it is invalid for reasons such as fraud or overreaching.

---

under the construction contract be mediated, arbitrated or otherwise adjudicated in or under the laws of a state other than Connecticut shall be void and of no effect, regardless of whether the construction contract was executed in this state."

17. Tex. Bus. & Com. Code Ann. § 272 (2017).

18. *E.g.*, Inovateus Solar, LLC v. Polamar Precision, Inc., Cause No. 3:16-cv-00312-JD-MGG, 2017 WL 2971950 (N.D. Ind. July 10, 2017) (upholding forum-selection clause as valid despite Connecticut statute prohibiting such clauses that force litigation outside the borders of Connecticut); Whiting-Turner Contracting Co. v. Westchester Fire Ins. Co., No. JFM-13-348, 2013 WL 3177881, at *3 (D. Md. June 20, 2013) (upholding forum-selection clause notwithstanding Pennsylvania statute forbidding out-of-state forum-selection clauses in construction contracts); 62 Pa. Stat. and Cons. Stat. Ann. § 3937 (2022); Secured Sys. Tech., Inc. v. Frank Lill & Son, Inc., Docket No. 08-CV-6256, 2010 WL 11549354 (W.D.N.Y. June 17, 2010) (finding New York choice-of-law provision to be valid and enforceable notwithstanding the Connecticut statute that would render such provision invalid).

19. Michael J. Boxerman et al., *The Fight Over Where to Fight: Removal, Transfer of Venue and Compelling Arbitration*, ABA 34th Annual Forum on Franchising (Oct. 19–21, 2011).

20. *Id.* at 2–3.

Like jurisdictional motions, questions of arbitral venue (or seat of the arbitration) are presumptively for the arbitrator to decide, even in international arbitrations, and so long as the arbitrator "arguably interpreted the arbitral-venue provision," courts will defer to the arbitrator's interpretation.[21]

With the advent of the COVID-19 pandemic, a new question regarding venue arose—whether the arbitrator has the authority to shift an in-person hearing to a virtual hearing in the absence of both parties' agreement. While not technically a venue question, this issue does implicate the location of the proceeding. Many of the institutional rules already authorized the arbitrator to order virtual hearings either expressly or by implication, which provided a basis for arbitrators to order virtual hearings, even over the objection of one of the parties. Additionally, many arbitral institutions have amended their rules since 2020 to make this authority express. Section 10(a)(3) of the Federal Arbitration Act (FAA) affords broad latitude to arbitrators in the conduct of arbitral proceedings and even allows an arbitrator to forego oral hearings so long as each party is afforded an opportunity to present its evidence and arguments.[22] As such, the FAA has been interpreted by courts to mean that an arbitration award may not be vacated on this basis unless there is a violation of fundamental fairness.[23]

Typically, if one party or the arbitrator favors a virtual hearing over an in-person hearing, the arbitrator will invite argument as to why a virtual hearing should or should not be allowed. The parties are well advised to frame their arguments with specificity rather than vague generalities about fairness and due process, as most experienced arbitrators at this point consider, based on personal experience, that a virtual hearing can provide both fairness and due process to both parties. The parties should instead explain why a virtual hearing would assist or prejudice a party, rather than making vague statements regarding efficiency or the need to assess the demeanor of witnesses

---

21. Gustavo J. Membiela & Juan Olano, *Client Alert: Can I Dispute an Arbitrator's Arbitral Venue or Seat Decision?*, HUNTON & WILLIAMS (July 2017), https://www.huntonak.com/images/content/3/1/v2/31935/can-i-dispute-an-arbitrators-arbitral-venue-or-seat-decision.pdf. *See* Bamberger Rosenheim, Ltd. v. OA Dev., Inc., 862 F.3d 1284 (11th Cir. 2017), *cert. denied*, 138 S. Ct. 654 (2018).

22. 9 U.S.C. § 10(a)(3); Yonir Techs, Inc. v. Duration Sys. (1992) Ltd., 244 F. Supp. 2d 195, 209–10 (S.D.N.Y. 2002) ("[T]he lack of a formal, oral hearing does not violate [the FAA] and is not fundamentally unfair. . . . It does not violate due process principles to issue a decision based on written submissions alone.").

23. *Yonir Techs, Inc.*, 244 F. Supp. 2d at 209–10

generally.[24] The party requesting a virtual hearing should also demonstrate that the appropriate technical requirements will be met.[25] In the event a virtual hearing is ordered, it should be confirmed in writing that notwithstanding the decision to conduct the hearing virtually, the arbitration will be deemed to have taken place in the location specified in the arbitration agreement. This is because the venue of the arbitration may determine the procedural law that will govern the proceeding, absent agreement of the parties otherwise.[26]

E. Discovery-Related Motions

Probably the most commonly seen type of motion in arbitration is one relating to a discovery issue. Counsel should nevertheless be prudent with the issues they take to the arbitrator for decision and should first attempt to resolve any disputes amongst themselves before filing a discovery motion.

The general procedure is to first raise any discovery-related issues, disputes, or objections with opposing counsel and to make a good-faith effort at resolution without having to engage the arbitrator. Many procedural orders will make this a formal requirement, but it is advisable in any event. Counsel should keep in mind the time and efficiency goals of arbitration when considering discovery disputes and should refrain from overly aggressive discovery or motion practice unless warranted.

Counsel wishing to bring a discovery issue to the arbitrator's attention can accomplish that objective in any number of ways. First, counsel can send an email to the arbitrator requesting a telephone conference to discuss the discovery issue and potential resolution. This is often the preferable process for simple or discrete discovery issues that can be addressed expeditiously and without extensive briefing.

Second, counsel can file a formal motion to compel compliance with a discovery request or to object to the scope of the other party's discovery. A motion need not be overly formal and can generally be submitted in the form of a letter. Typically, the arbitrator will then allow the opposing party

---

24. J. Brian Casey & Grant Hanessian, *Ordering Virtual Hearings over the Objections of a Party*, ADR Inst. of Can., https://adric.ca/ordering-virtual-hearings-over-the-objections-of-a-party/ (last visited Apr. 18, 2023).

25. *Id.*

26. P. Jean Baker, *Utilizing Virtual Arbitration during the Pandemic*, Am. Bar Ass'n (May 26, 2020), https://www.americanbar.org/groups/litigation/committees/alternative-dispute-resolution/articles/2020/spring2020-utilizing-virtual-arbitration-during-the-pandemic/.

to respond to such submission within a defined time period. This may be followed by a right of reply and/or oral argument, although oral argument is typically reserved for significant disputes only.

Finally, some U.S. arbitrators are importing a practice from international arbitration and requiring parties to submit discovery disputes in the form of a "Redfern schedule." A Redfern schedule is defined as follows by Law Dictionary:[27]

> The Redfern schedule (originally devised by Alan Redfern) is a collaborative document, to which the claimant, respondent and tribunal all contribute. Different columns of the schedule are completed by the parties at various times.
>
> The purpose of the schedule is to create a user-friendly record of requests for disclosure, the parties' arguments on those requests, and the tribunal's decision.
>
> The schedule consists of four columns. Separate entries are made in each column in respect of every requested document or class of documents. . . .
>
> Column 1: Column 1 sets out the request for disclosure. Use a separate entry for each document or class of documents. Consider whether broad classes of documents can be divided into sub-classes or single documents.
>
> Column 2: Column 2 contains the requesting party's submissions, both in support of the request and in rebuttal of the opposing party's submissions. The submissions in support of the request should do two things: First, it should identify the paragraph of the written pleading or claim submission to which the requested document relates. If the claim submissions are formulated in a detailed and focused manner, this will be relatively easy. Secondly, it should explain why the documents sought are relevant. This will usually involve explaining exactly what the documents are, what information they are thought to contain, and how that information is likely to impact on the issues which the tribunal has to decide.
>
> Column 2 also contains the requesting party's submissions in rebuttal of the opposing party's objections. This section will be completed at [a] later date.

27. *See Redfern Schedule*, ACAD. DICTIONARIES & ENCYCS., https://law.en-academic.com/6270/Redfern_Schedule (last visited Apr. 18, 2023).

Column 3: Column 3 contains the objecting party's submissions. Of course, if the objecting party is happy to produce a specified document or class of documents, then this should be stated. Otherwise, the reasons for resisting production should be set out concisely. Typical grounds for resisting production include irrelevance, the request being too broad in its scope, immunity or privilege, or that the cost of producing the documents is disproportionate.

The requesting party will then respond by entering rebuttal submissions in column 2.

[After this point, the Redfern is sent to the tribunal for consideration of the remaining items in dispute between the parties.]

Column 4: Column 4 summarizes the tribunal's decision on each request, and sets out, in brief, the reasons for that decision. [The arbitrator will insert decisions only on disputed requests and will ignore any rows in the schedule that have been resolved or otherwise agreed to by the parties.]

A Redfern schedule can be an efficient and effective way to address individual discovery requests.

If there are three arbitrators, the initial procedural order should designate whether discovery disputes will require a decision of the full panel or whether discovery disputes will be addressed by the chair alone. In significant disputes, the parties will often want the decision of the full panel, whereas in smaller matters, parties may agree to a decision by the chair alone in order to reduce arbitrator expense. The arbitrator's decision may be conveyed to the parties via email, letter, or formal order.

See also Chapter 4 for further discussion of discovery in arbitration.

F. Motions for Dispositive Relief

A dispositive motion or motion for summary disposition is usually defined as a motion that would finally determine or dispose of any issue in dispute, much like a motion to dismiss or motion for summary judgment in court proceedings.

The use of dispositive motions in arbitration is a highly discussed and debated issue. The Revised Uniform Arbitration Act[28] and nearly all of the institutional arbitral rules allow for dispositive motions, subject to certain

---

28. Revised Uniform Arbitration Act § 15(b) (2000) ("An arbitrator may decide a request for summary disposition of a claim or particular issue.").

procedural safeguards and limitations.[29] For example, the AAA Construction Rules require the party seeking to file a dispositive motion to submit a prior written application to the arbitrator and provide that the arbitrator may permit such a motion if it will "dispose of all or part of a claim, or narrow the issues in a case."[30] Even where not specifically required by the applicable rules, arbitrators will often require the moving party to seek permission before filing a dispositive motion in order to avoid unnecessary time and expense associated with frivolous filings or motions that are unlikely to succeed.

It is good practice to discuss potential dispositive motions at the initial procedural conference. If there is some possibility that either party may seek to file a dispositive motion at some point, the procedure and the timing for doing so should be addressed in the initial procedural order. Typically, there will be no limit on how *early* in the arbitral process a dispositive motion can be filed. More commonly, as is the case in most courts, there will be a time limit on how *late* in the proceeding the dispositive motion can be filed. Where there is a clear-cut legal issue that will dispose of some (or all) of the issues in dispute, it is prudent to address and resolve that issue as early in the process as possible in order to reduce discovery and the hearing duration. For example, a statute of limitations issue may be appropriate for a dispositive motion early in the case.

A party requesting leave to file a dispositive motion should clearly articulate the basis for the proposed motion, the reasons why it is likely to succeed on the merits, and the reasons why a ruling on that motion will narrow the claims and issues to be decided. In determining whether to permit the dispositive motion, the arbitrator will consider whether the proposed motion appears to have merit or is clearly frivolous, whether there are likely to be issues of fact that will prevent the arbitrator from granting dispositive relief, and (most importantly) whether a decision on the motion will reduce hearing time, reduce the number of testifying witnesses or experts, or dispose of a significant part of the case. Arbitrators often grant permission to submit a requested dispositive motion, but that should not be taken as an indication of

---

29. *E.g.*, AAA Construction Rules, *supra* note 3, Rule R-34 ("Upon prior written application, the arbitrator may permit motions that dispose of all or part of a claim or narrow the issues in a case."); AAA Commercial Rules, *supra* note 12, Rule 33 ("The arbitrator may allow the filing of and make rulings upon a dispositive motion only if the arbitrator determines that the moving party has shown that the motion is likely to succeed and dispose of or narrow the issues in the case."); JAMS Construction Rules, *supra* note 12, Rule 18; JAMS International Arbitration Rules and Procedures, Rule 26 (June 1, 2021); CPR Administered Arbitration Rules, *supra* note 12, Rule 12.6.

30. AAA Construction Rules, *supra* note 3, Rule R-34.

merit or likely outcome. In fact, most dispositive motions will fail for the same reasons that they fail in court.

If permission to file the dispositive motion is granted, a briefing schedule will be set (by the arbitrator or agreement of the parties) for the dispositive motion that is similar to court practice, albeit without the same formality required in court filings. For example, a brief will typically suffice without the need for a statement of undisputed facts as required in federal court. Whether supporting affidavits are necessary will depend on whether there is a need to establish facts relevant to the disposition of the motion. Of course, the more facts a party needs to introduce, the more likely that the arbitrator will conclude there are relevant contested facts, leading to the motion being denied in favor of deciding the issue in connection with the hearing on the merits.

The success or failure of a dispositive motion will generally turn on whether there are issues of fact that can be resolved on the papers alone, the merits of any purely legal issues raised, and whether granting the requested relief is likely to reduce the issues to be decided and overall hearing time. Even if the requested relief will dispose of an issue but will not actually shorten the hearing, the arbitrator may be less likely to grant dispositive relief but to instead defer the issue to the hearing.

A nonexhaustive list of examples of circumstances where dispositive motions have been granted follows:

- The claims are barred by the applicable statute of limitations or statute of repose.
- The claims are barred by a release. Only where the release clearly covers the claims at issue will dispositive relief be granted, however. For example, dispositive motions on the basis that the contractor's claims are barred by the language in a partial lien waiver and release executed in exchange for progress payments are frequently seen. In most cases, the contractor defending such a motion will argue that it did not intend to release its claims and that the partial lien waiver and release was just an acknowledgment of payments made. Most often the contractor is able to raise issues of fact as to whether the lien waiver and release was intended to release all claims arising prior to the date of the release—particularly if the lien waiver and release was executed while the parties were engaged in ongoing discussions and negotiations of pending claims, precluding summary disposition.
- The claims are barred by a limitation of liability or exclusive remedies provision in the underlying contract that is applicable to the dispute.

- The claims are barred by applicable law. For example, in some states, a pass-through claim on behalf of a subcontractor may be barred by applicable state law if the proffering party has not admitted liability to the subcontractor. In other states, an owner's liquidated damages claim may be barred where the owner terminated the contractor for convenience (no fault), rather than for cause.
- One party seeks to enforce a written contract, change order, or agreement executed by the other party, and the other party denies the existence or enforceability of that contract, change order, or agreement.
- A party seeks to assert a state law or tort claim that is barred by that state's law or by the choice-of-law clause in the underlying contract.[31]

One of the few bases on which an arbitral award may be vacated under the FAA is where the arbitrator refuses to hear pertinent and material evidence.[32] This is a major reason why summary disposition is granted in arbitration even less than summary judgment in litigation. If an arbitrator grants a dispositive motion—thereby rendering the evidentiary hearing unnecessary or narrowing the evidence to be presented at the hearing—he or she is effectively excluding evidence. This may thus open a window for the losing party to claim that the final award should be vacated. In the interest of protecting the award against challenge, arbitrators tend to be quite conservative and to deny granting dispositive motions in favor of deferring the ruling until after the parties have an opportunity to present all relevant evidence at the hearing.

Counsel sometimes justify filing dispositive motions that are unlikely to be granted as an opportunity to educate the arbitrator regarding key issues in the dispute. Rather than providing a strategic advantage, this is more often a waste of time and resources better devoted to preparation for the hearing. If the legal issue and arguments can be addressed just as well in the prehearing brief (typically submitted closer to the hearing than a dispositive motion), the better course is usually to address the issue at that time. The arbitrator will generally appreciate this as well. Unless there is a clear benefit to raising the issue earlier *and* the motion is objectively likely to succeed on the merits, filing a dispositive motion is not recommended. The reality of construction disputes is that the great majority of issues are fact dependent and not usually suitable to resolution via dispositive motion.

---

31. Herbert H. Gray, III, et al., *Motion Practice in Arbitration* at 13, https://www.hpylaw.com/content/uploads/2019/03/214_Motion-Practice-in-Arbitration.pdf (last visited Apr. 18, 2023).

32. 9 U.S.C. § 10(a)(3).

G. Motions in Limine and/or to Strike Evidence

A motion in limine is a creature of court practice that provides a mechanism to exclude the introduction of specific evidence at trial that is irrelevant, inadmissible, or unfairly prejudicial. Such motions are also used in court to exclude or limit expert testimony.

Arbitral institution rules generally afford the arbitrator broad authority and discretion to determine admissibility, relevance, and materiality of evidence and to exclude evidence deemed cumulative or irrelevant.[33] That said, motions in limine are rarely seen in arbitration. The reason for this is twofold: unless agreed to by the parties, the rules of evidence typically do not apply in arbitration; and an arbitrator typically sees his or her role as being the fact-finder, rather than a gatekeeper in admitting evidence. Arbitrators are accordingly very likely to accept the evidence presented and to "give it the weight that it is due" (that is, exercise judgment as to what weight, if any, to give it).[34] While in limited situations objections can be helpful to alert the arbitrator to a party's concern with proposed evidence, evidentiary objections are most often denied. An arbitrator is typically far better equipped than a jury to determine what weight, if any, to give to the evidence. Also, by admitting the evidence and giving it "the weight that it is due," the arbitrator avoids a potential avenue of attacking the final award, since an arbitral award may be vacated under the FAA where the arbitrator refuses to hear pertinent and material evidence.[35]

So when made, motions in limine are generally overruled, often without comment. This does not mean, however, that the arbitrator is effectively saying that the evidence sought to be excluded will be given equal weight to other evidence. In fact, it may be given no weight at all.

If counsel chooses to file a motion in limine, there are no formalities to doing so in arbitration. Accordingly, a motion to exclude evidence can be submitted by letter, brief, or oral motion at the hearing. In fact, it is often more efficient to raise such matters orally at hearing because arbitrators are typically sophisticated enough to make admissibility determinations as they arise and without extensive briefing or written submissions.

Similarly, and for the same reasons, motions to strike evidence are rarely (if ever) granted by arbitrators. That said, there are times that such motions may be appropriate. For example, if a witness testifies about a privileged

---

33. *E.g.*, AAA Commercial Rules, *supra* note 12, Rule R-34; AAA Construction Rules, *supra* note 3, Rule R-35; JAMS Construction Rules, *supra* note 12, Rule 22(d).

34. Gray, III, et al., *supra* note 31.

35. 9 U.S.C. § 10(a)(3).

conversation or settlement discussion, or engages in bald speculation, the arbitrator may grant a motion to strike. Motions to strike are sometimes made with respect to expert testimony, where the expert report is offered in a way that is procedurally improper (such as the last-minute submission of an unauthorized reply report) or improperly relies on evidence not previously produced in discovery.

But there are typically ways for the arbitrator to address these concerns without excluding evidence, and these are often preferred. Arbitrators will often allow the evidence but will provide an opportunity for remedial measures to avoid prejudice to the complaining party. For example, the arbitrator may require the evidence not produced to be immediately produced and then be liberal in allowing the complaining party additional time to prepare for examination of the expert or fact witness involved. Or the arbitrator may grant the right to submit further evidence and/or a further reply expert report to respond to an unauthorized submission.

H. Motions for Sanctions

The issuance of sanctions in arbitration, like dispositive motions, is also a highly debated issue. Until recent years, an arbitrator's authority to impose sanctions was somewhat unclear and, when recognized, was deemed to arise primarily from broad language in the arbitration clause.[36] The AAA clarified this situation by adding provisions to its Rules affording arbitrators the authority to award "appropriate sanctions" where a party fails to comply with its obligations under the Rules or with an order of the arbitrator. The AAA Construction Rules address this at Rule R-60:[37]

> (a) The arbitrator may, upon a party's request, order appropriate sanctions where a party fails to comply with its obligations under these rules or with an order of the arbitrator. In the event that the arbitrator enters a sanction that limits any party's participation in the arbitration or results in an adverse determination of an issue or issues, the arbitrator shall explain that order in writing and shall require the submission of evidence and legal argument prior to the making of an award. The arbitrator may not enter a default award as a sanction.

---

36. *See* Superadio Ltd. P'ship v. Winstar Radio Prods., LLC, 446 Mass. 330, 844 N.E.2d 246 (2006) (holding that the power to award sanctions arises from a broad "all disputes" arbitration clause).

37. *See also* AAA Commercial Rules, *supra* note 12, Rule R-58.

> (b) The arbitrator must provide a party that is subject to a sanction request with the opportunity to respond prior to making any determination regarding the sanction's application.

Rule 29 of the JAMS Construction Rules similarly authorizes the arbitrator to order appropriate sanctions for failure of a party to comply with its obligations under the rules or an order. Sanctions may include assessment of fees, exclusion of evidence, drawing adverse inferences, or (in extreme cases) determining an issue adversely to the noncomplying party.[38]

I. Motions to Amend or to Correct an Award

After the arbitrator issues an interim or final award, a party dissatisfied with some or all of the award has a limited opportunity to move to amend or correct the award. Many arbitral institution rules expressly provide for modification of an award after issuance to correct clerical, typographical, technical, or computational errors *but not to revisit the merits of the award.*

For example, Rule R-51 of the AAA Construction Rules provides:

> (a) Within 20 calendar days after the transmittal of an award, the arbitrator on his or her initiative, or any party, upon notice to the other parties, may request that the arbitrator correct any clerical, typographical, technical or computational errors in the award. The arbitrator is not empowered to redetermine the merits of any claim already decided.

The JAMS Construction Rules contain a similar provision allowing a party to request correction of the award within seven calendar days after service of the award for "any computational, typographical or other similar error in the Award."[39]

Computational errors in the award in complex construction cases are not infrequent, as such cases often involve a substantial number of discrete claims.

---

38. JAMS Construction Rules, *supra* note 12, Rule 29 ("The Arbitrator may order appropriate sanctions for failure of a Party to comply with its obligations under any of these Rules or with an order of the Arbitrator. These sanctions may include, but are not limited to, assessment of Arbitration fees and Arbitrator compensation and expenses; assessment of any other costs occasioned by the actionable conduct, including reasonable attorneys' fees; exclusion of certain evidence; drawing adverse inferences; or, in extreme cases, determining an issue or issues submitted to Arbitration adversely to the Party that has failed to comply."). *See also* Gray, III, et al., *supra* note 31, at 15.

39. JAMS Construction Rules, *supra* note 12, Rule 24(j).

Such errors include adding up the damages incorrectly, inadvertently transposing figures, or some other clerical or typographical error. These types of mistakes are often clear from the face of the award but were overlooked by the arbitrator prior to issuance.

Given the limited bases on which awards may be modified after issuance, a dissatisfied party should consider whether the unsatisfactory aspect of the award is just a clerical or typographical error or something more. If it is something more, and the dissatisfied party believes there is a basis to have the award vacated by a court, it is likely better served by filing an appropriate action in court to modify or vacate the award rather than seeking correction from the arbitrator who issued the award.

J. Motions for Continuance or Modifications to Procedural Orders

Another motion often seen in arbitration is the motion for continuance or modification to the procedural order. Hearing dates and interim prehearing deadlines are typically established at the time of the first procedural conference of the parties and arbitrator. Because much can happen between the time of that first procedural conference and the merits hearing, one or both parties may seek an extension of certain interim deadlines or a continuance of the hearing.

Arbitral rules provide the arbitrator with authority to control the proceedings and to modify the hearing dates if necessary. For example, Rule R-31 of the AAA Construction Rules permits the arbitrator to postpone a hearing "for good cause shown . . . upon agreement of the parties, upon request of a party, or upon the arbitrator's own initiative." The AAA Commercial Rules contain a similar provision.[40] The granting or denying of an adjournment or postponement generally falls within the broad discretion of the arbitrator.[41]

If the parties agree as to proposed modifications to the prehearing deadlines, the typical practice is to request the appropriate modifications to the procedural order by email. If the proposed modifications do not appear unreasonable or unjustified, the arbitrator will typically agree to the modifications. However, if the proposed modifications appear unreasonable or unjustified, the arbitrator has the authority to refuse the proposed modifications, even if

40. AAA Commercial Rules, *supra* note 12, Rule 30.

41. Ceco Concrete Constr. v. J.T. Schrimsher Constr. Co., 792 F. Supp. 109, 110 (N.D. Ga. 1992); Nyall Storey v. Searle Blatt Ltd., 685 F. Supp. 80, 82 (S.D.N.Y. 1988); Fairchild & Co. v. City of Richmond, 516 F. Supp. 1305, 1313 (D.D.C. 1981); Dan River Inc. v. Cal-togs, Inc., 451 F. Supp. 497, 503–04 (S.D.N.Y. 1978).

the parties are otherwise in agreement, especially if the modifications would lead to undue delay. This is atypical, however.

In cases where the parties do not agree to a modification of interim deadlines, or do not agree as to length of the adjustment needed, a motion is generally necessary. The party seeking the modification should articulate a compelling case as to why good cause exists for the modification and why that party is not at fault for the proposed delay and (with respect to interim deadlines) confirm that the hearing date will not be affected by the proposed modification. Conversely, the party resisting the modification should articulate the reasons why a modification is unnecessary, unjustified, or caused by the dilatory tactics of the requesting party or would be prejudicial to the resisting party. If there is reasonable justification for the requested modifications, the arbitrator will typically look for a fair, middle-ground approach that grants appropriate schedule relief but does not unduly prejudice the other party.

Continuances of hearing dates, once established in the initial procedural order, are a different matter. Arbitrators are less apt to continue the hearing date absent a compelling reason and good cause for delay. A primary reason for this is that delays in the hearing date translate directly to prolonged duration of the time to resolution and to additional costs for both parties. There is also the often-difficult problem of finding new hearing dates when the parties and arbitrator can be available. The request may be for only a short postponement, but conflicting schedules often preclude a short postponement and require instead a four- to six-month (or greater) delay before acceptable new dates can be found.

Typical grounds where hearing dates have been continued are when due to illness/death of counsel or a key witness; unanticipated unavailability of a key witness that is not within the control of the proffering party; and other compelling and exceptional reasons.[42] Arbitrators are less apt to grant continuances where the requesting party has been less than diligent in progressing the case, does not have a legitimate and justifiable excuse for the requested continuance, has made a number of prior requests for postponements, or requests an unreasonably long delay or where the other party would be unduly prejudiced by the continuance.

---

42. *See* Allendale Nursing Home, Inc. v. Loc. 1115 Joint Bd., 377 F. Supp. 1208 (S.D.N.Y. 1974); Tube & Steel Corp. v. Chi. Carbon Steel Prods., 319 F. Supp. 1302 (S.D.N.Y. 1970); Chestnut Energy Partners v. Tapia, 300 S.W.3d 386 (Tex. App. – Dallas 2009).

While most arbitrators make every effort to maintain the established hearing date whenever possible, arbitrators are also aware that failing to grant a continuance can be a basis for seeking to overturn the award when good cause existed for the requested postponement. Under the FAA, it is a ground for vacating an arbitration award "where the arbitrators are guilty of misconduct in refusing to postpone the hearing upon sufficient cause shown."[43] That said, there have been few successful challenges to awards based on refusal to postpone the hearing.[44]

43. 9 U.S.C. § 10(a)(3).

44. Schmidt v. Finberg, 942 F.2d 1571 (11th Cir. 1991); *Ceco Concrete Constr.*, 792 F. Supp. 109 (arbitrator's refusal to postpone arbitration was not unreasonable and was not the product of misconduct).

CHAPTER 7

Structuring the Arbitration Hearing

ALBERT BATES, JR.
R. ZACHARY TORRES-FOWLER

I. Introduction

The hearing on the merits (other than in the relatively rare instance of a documents-only arbitration) is the centerpiece of a construction arbitration, as well as the most expensive part of the process by a considerable margin. The views that the arbitrators develop during the hearing will almost assuredly determine the outcome of the case. As a result, counsel rightfully spend considerable time and energy assessing how the structure and format of the arbitration hearing will enable them to most effectively present their case. However, the decisions concerning the structure of the hearing start almost at the outset of the arbitration and additionally affect the posthearing submissions that close the record following the hearing.

Structuring the hearing thus includes the basic organization of exhibits and order of witnesses, how experts and witnesses will testify, and how posthearing submissions will be organized. An arbitration hearing is not a trial; there are no mandatory rules of evidence, no juries, and few of the formalities that accompany federal or state court litigation. As a result, parties and arbitrators have far greater leeway to utilize procedures that would not otherwise be available in a court trial to streamline the proceeding and make it more efficient and cost effective. This flexibility is particularly important for complex construction disputes where the scale and substance of the dispute are very difficult to manage using traditional courtroom procedures and rules. The sprawling and often highly technical nature of construction disputes means that construction arbitrations present unique challenges that are distinct even from other forms of commercial arbitration.

Accordingly, this chapter aims to provide counsel with practical insight into the mechanics of a construction arbitration hearing and the many options users have as they move into the hearing phase of the proceedings. While basic norms and default assumptions have developed over time, no "one-size-fits-all" structure and format exist. As a result, the procedures that have come to embody construction arbitration hearings vary significantly and are worth careful consideration and discussion.

This chapter will first outline the prehearing considerations and tasks that parties must keep in mind in preparing for the hearing. Second, we will consider ways that counsel and arbitrators can streamline the presentation of evidence during the hearing. Third, we will set out some of the posthearing possibilities that can be used to summarize the evidence presented at the hearing in the most effective manner to persuade the arbitrators.

II. Prehearing Considerations and Tasks

Long before reaching the merits hearing, there are a variety of prehearing considerations and tasks that should be addressed in a complex construction case. These issues have a substantial influence on how, and the ease with which, counsel present their case at the hearing.

A. Roles of Counsel and Arbitrators in Prehearing Logistics

1. Claimant's Role in Prehearing Logistics

The arbitrators expect that counsel will engage in good-faith efforts to coordinate prehearing logistics; however, as a practical matter one party is almost inevitably responsible for leading any joint efforts. Unstated assumptions over which party will take responsibility for such tasks as scheduling the hearing venue often lead to wholly avoidable disputes that just increase the costs of the process unnecessarily. Thus, the question of which party should take the lead to coordinate hearing logistics is a common area of confusion where clarity from the outset is advantageous to both parties.

The general norm is that, unless otherwise agreed, the claimant will lead the coordination of joint prehearing logistical matters. Where one party must take the first step to address or raise an administrative or logistical issue that requires agreement between the parties, that usually falls to the claimant as a default practice. The claimant is generally the party seeking the majority of relief sought (although counterclaims that exceed the claim value are by no means unknown) and thus the party with the most to gain by pushing the process forward expeditiously.

Importantly, respondents remain responsible for cooperating in good faith and should proactively assist the claimant with prehearing administrative matters. Indeed, many logistical and administrative tasks require agreement between the parties. As a result, respondents cannot, for example, refuse to timely respond to claimant's proposals or make unreasonable demands on prehearing logistics that force claimant to shoulder an unnecessary administrative burden.

If appropriate cooperation between counsel is not occurring for any reason, counsel may wish to engage the assistance of the arbitrators before the lack of cooperation becomes an impediment to the proceedings. Indeed, the arbitrators are highly likely to notice the dysfunctional relationship between counsel before long and respond. Responses can vary, from making inquiries as to the cause of stalemate on particular issues to pushing overtly for greater cooperation or requiring client representatives to attend prehearing conferences so they can observe and draw their own conclusions regarding the behavior of counsel. In egregious cases, obstructive behavior may be addressed in the award, such as through allocation of arbitration costs against the obstructive party, an award of prehearing interest if such conduct delays the proceedings, or an award of attorneys' fees in circumstances where this is permitted.

2. *Arbitrators' Role in Prehearing Logistics*

The arbitrators will generally defer much of the management and coordination of hearing procedures and logistics to the parties, at least in the first instance. This approach is rooted in the notion that the parties should be allowed to decide how they wish to present their case and that the arbitrators' role is to manage the process and resolve any disputed procedural issues.

That said, it is increasingly frequent in complex construction cases that arbitrators take a more proactive role in managing prehearing and hearing issues, seeking to aid the process in a number of ways. First, making the arbitrators' preferences known concerning the logistics and organization of a hearing often simplifies the discussion where both parties are willing to go along with the arbitrators' preferences on issues such as prehearing briefs and other submissions and organization of exhibits. Second, arbitrators who propose procedural devices, including novel procedural devices, may help to improve either the efficiency of the hearing (saving the parties time and money) or the arbitrators' ability to assess the evidence presented. At a minimum, an arbitrator's willingness to propose the use of different procedural devices can stimulate discussion among counsel as to whether these proposals fit well with the circumstances of the case.

Without input from the arbitrators, many times counsel either default to practices that imitate those used in court proceedings or otherwise default to "tried and true" procedures that they have routinely used in the past. While these procedures may be familiar, they may also make the arbitration hearing more costly and cumbersome and constitute a missed opportunity to adopt a proposal that may save the clients' time and money with no loss to the integrity or quality of the arbitration process. Thus, good practice suggests that counsel seek and receive feedback from the arbitrators to ensure that the proposed hearing procedures align with the arbitrators' own expectations and preferences.

B. Prehearing Planning

1. *Prehearing Conferences and Orders*

A first order of business in most arbitrations is to agree upon the terms of an initial prehearing order that sets out the basic timeline and deadlines for prehearing events as well as the merits hearing dates. It is also common in complex construction disputes to schedule a series of prehearing status conferences at intervals before the hearing. Initially such conferences tend to focus on the progress of document exchange and other discovery, including any issues that may have arisen, but as the hearing nears the discussion often shifts to issues related to the structure and logistics of the actual hearing. The intent of these conferences is in part to provide an opportunity for counsel to raise with the arbitrators for discussion any emerging areas of disagreement regarding the hearing structure and receive the arbitrators' input. This often results in further procedural orders that guide the proceedings going forward.

The initial prehearing conference is generally an opportunity for the parties to raise high-level procedural expectations for the arbitration hearing that will affect the terms of the first procedural order. Common hearing-specific issues discussed at the initial conference are (1) whether a hearing is necessary at all, (2) how much time will be required to complete the hearing, (3) whether a bifurcated hearing approach would aid the process, (4) the scope and extent of document exchange and any other information exchange or discovery, (5) whether written witness statements will be used in lieu of live direct examination, (6) whether the use of a "chess clock" allocation of hearing time is appropriate in the case, and (7) other high-level procedural aspects, especially those that potentially affect the number of days reserved for the hearing. Additionally, dispositive motions and the need for other prehearing submissions (such as more detailed statements of claims or damages) that do not specifically concern the hearing itself are also often raised at the initial conference and can affect the structure of the hearing. Resolving such issues as close as possible to the outset of the arbitration is important to enable the parties to establish the arbitration schedule going forward.

The more granular procedural features of the hearing are generally reserved for one or more final prehearing conferences within a few weeks of the hearing date. At that point counsel typically have a better understanding of their claims and defenses, and their witnesses both fact and expert, and so a clearer understanding of how they plan to present their case.

To make the initial conference most efficient and productive, counsel should consult with one another in advance to reach agreement on prehearing procedures and identify any areas of disagreement to raise at the conference. To facilitate this process, the arbitral forum or the arbitrators often provide counsel with an agenda of topics to be addressed in advance or a template for the initial procedural/scheduling order to guide advance discussions. In the absence of specific guidance from the arbitrators, it is still good practice for counsel to agree upon and prepare an initial draft scheduling order that resolves as many issues as possible in advance of the initial conference. A relatively advanced draft scheduling order aids both counsel and arbitrators in identifying the key areas of disagreement and helping to focus discussion during the initial conference.

A simpler alternative to actually attempting to draft the scheduling order in advance of the initial conference is for counsel to develop a table or schedule of proposed prehearing deadlines, which can also be expanded to include proposed procedural terms. A formal way of addressing procedural terms, which is usually effective even when the dispute is particularly contentious, is to create a table with up to five columns—(1) Procedure, (2) Claimant's Proposal, (3) Respondent's Comments, (4) Claimant's Reply, and (5) Respondent's Reply. The claimant describes in columns 1 and 2 the specific procedures the claimant proposes for the hearing. The respondent then indicates in column 3 whether it agrees to the proposed procedure or offers a counterproposal. Counsel can then engage the arbitrators where there is no agreement, while presenting their specific alternative approaches. This approach is useful because it requires counsel to state their preferred approaches in writing and avoids any miscommunication that can occur during meet and confer sessions between counsel.

2. *Is a Hearing Even Necessary? Documents-Only Arbitrations*

Not every case requires an evidentiary hearing. Documents-only arbitrations are an available alternative under most arbitration rules and may be particularly appropriate for low-value disputes where the cost of a hearing may be prohibitively expensive.

Various formats for expedited arbitration proceedings are also offered under many sets of arbitral rules. Expedited arbitration rules usually impose specific procedural limits on hearings and prehearing procedures, such as limiting the length of the hearing. Under the American Arbitration Association (AAA), International Centre for Dispute Resolution (ICDR), and International Chamber of Commerce (ICC) rules, expedited arbitration rules will apply as a default to disputes whose amount in controversy falls below a specific threshold amount.

In cases that are potential candidates for a documents-only or other expedited proceeding, counsel should use the prehearing planning stage to consider whether a hearing is actually necessary or, alternatively, whether the hearing can be confined to a small list of factual issues in dispute. It is also possible that later in the proceeding, counsel may determine that the core issues in the case do not relate to issues of fact and that a more streamlined process would be more appropriate.

While entirely doing away with a hearing may not be acceptable to either party, it may also be the case that particular issues can be addressed more efficiently solely on the documents or other summary procedures. This approach enables the parties to focus their attention on the core issues and avoid spending expensive hearing time on claims involving relatively small sums of money.

3. *Remote Hearings vs. In-Person Hearings*

The COVID-19 pandemic required the arbitration community to adapt rapidly to the use of remote hearing technology to conduct arbitration proceedings. As a result, Zoom, WebEx, and Microsoft Teams, among others, have become common platforms on which to conduct arbitration hearings, prepare witnesses, and take depositions.

While remote hearings are imperfect substitutes for in-person hearings, the use of remote hearings is likely to continue for a number of reasons. The cost savings generated by remote hearings are significant. Remote hearings enable parties to avoid spending money on transportation, lodging, and other administrative expenses involved in an in-person hearing. Moreover, remote hearings avoid logistical challenges posed by the need to transport experts, witnesses, and counsel from various locations to appear in a hearing room in another city where scheduling conflicts might otherwise prevent their appearance.

Counsel now need to consider from the outset of the arbitration process whether the cost savings and logistical ease of remote hearings outweigh the benefits of an in-person hearing and alternatively explore whether a hybrid remote and in-person approach is an efficient alternative to a fully in-person hearing.

C. Prehearing Deliverables

1. Hearing Binders/Bundles

Among the most time-consuming but important prehearing tasks is the selection and organization of hearing exhibits and other materials to be referenced during the hearing itself—often referred to as "hearing binders" (or "hearing bundles" in international practice). These days, these compilations are typically electronic folders and files, rather than physical ones. Hearing binders provide the arbitrators, counsel, witnesses, and experts with a package of documents that all concerned can easily reference during the hearing without disrupting the flow of the testimony. They are critically important to a smooth-running hearing and worthy of careful consideration and care when compiling them in advance of the arbitration hearing.

a. Content

Hearing binders are most often used for the specific exhibits the parties intend to rely on during the hearing. While practices vary, exhibit binders are most commonly organized into three separate sets of documents: (1) claimant's exhibits, (2) respondent's exhibits, and (3) joint exhibits.

For purposes of coordinating the hearing exhibit binders, counsel commonly exchange their proposed sets of exhibits a week or two in advance of the hearing. Upon receipt of the opposing party's exhibits, each party then has the opportunity to object, by a deadline in advance of the hearing, to any exhibits they believe should not be admitted into evidence during the hearing. To the extent the parties cannot resolve an objection, the issue may be presented to the arbitrators for resolution. The arbitrators may rule upon the objections in advance of the hearing but often defer ruling until a party offers the exhibit during the hearing. Otherwise, all exhibits not objected to are generally admitted into evidence at the outset of the hearing.

Exhibits are numbered, and the exhibit number should be on the first page of the document. Various computer programs enable placing the exhibit numbers in the corner of a document just as they would a Bates number. The claimant's exhibits are typically numbered with the prefix C-#, the respondent's exhibits with the prefix R-#, and joint exhibits with the prefix J-#.[1] In cases where prehearing depositions have been taken, the exhibit binders also typically include all of the deposition exhibits as joint exhibits.

In addition to the exhibit binders, counsel less commonly prepare binders containing other documents relevant for purposes of the hearing, such as compilations of any briefing in the case, procedural orders, transcripts, and so on that may need to be referenced during the hearing.

Arbitrators generally request the parties to identify any duplicative exhibits that are proposed by both parties and to transfer those exhibits to the joint exhibit binder. This both cuts down the volume of exhibits and avoids confusion caused by a single document having two exhibit numbers. However, as a practical matter, the process of identifying and removing duplicative exhibits is time consuming and often falls by the wayside in the final prehearing rush. Counsel should resist the urge to avoid removing duplicative exhibits and should, as much as possible, allocate time and resources to address this last-minute task. Arbitrators tend to strongly prefer eliminating duplicative exhibits that can make their task in the award-writing process more difficult. The arbitrators will appreciate counsel's taking the time to reduce duplication of exhibits as much as possible.

b. Format

Counsel must also determine whether they will need to produce hard-copy or electronic sets of the hearing binders (or both). In most cases, arbitrators and counsel prefer to utilize electronic versions of the hearing binders during the hearing. The volume of material, ease of use, and search capability of electronic documents generally tip the scale in favor of dominant reliance on electronic copies, particularly in cases where the volume of exhibits is large. However, it is not uncommon to provide testifying witnesses and experts access to hard copies of their witness statements or reports and any exhibits expected to be used during the course of their examination. Even when the arbitrators prefer electronic hearing binders, providing the arbitrators as well with a compact

1. Where written witness statements or expert reports are used, other prefixes are sometimes utilized to enable the parties and arbitrators to quickly identify whether a particular exhibit relates to a witness statement or expert report. Witness or expert report exhibits can be assigned a prefix such as C-NAME-#, so that a witness statement for John Smith would be numbered C-SMITH-#. However, this risks multiplying the number of duplicative exhibits with different numbers.

hard-copy binder of these materials for a given witness or expert for easy reference during the testimony of that witness can be very effective.

Some arbitrators may prefer to use hard copies of exhibits, rather than utilize the electronic copies. The complexities associated with the preparation of multiple, identical physical copies of the exhibit binders are quite often overlooked, and the logistics should not be underestimated. Every binder should have a clear label on the spine and cover showing the volume number and range of exhibit numbers it contains, and every document must be separately tabbed so the desired exhibit may be quickly located.

Where hard copies are to be utilized during the hearing, each party typically organizes and produces its own respective exhibit binders. Either party can take the lead to produce joint exhibit binders and any nonexhibit hearing binders, with the parties sharing production costs.

While less time intensive to assemble, electronic hearing binders should be organized according to an intuitive folder structure that allows all concerned to quickly access the relevant documents. A common folder structure may include the following subfolders: (1) Written Submissions, (2) Claimant's Exhibits, (3) Respondent's Exhibits, (4) Joint Exhibits, (5) Witness Statements (if necessary), (6) Expert Reports, and (7) Procedural Orders. While claimant often takes the lead, the effort can readily be divided, and full cooperation of the respondent is expected and essential.

2. *Prehearing Submissions or Briefs*

"Prehearing submissions," generally titled as "prehearing briefs," are utilized to outline each party's position in writing and often to provide supporting legal authority for each party's positions. The need for prehearing briefs is typically agreed during the initial prehearing conference, while the briefs themselves are usually submitted in the weeks leading up to the arbitration hearing, giving the arbitrators ample time to review them in advance of the hearing.

Prehearing briefs are particularly important in cases where few, if any, written submissions have been exchanged during the course of the arbitration. The prehearing briefs enable the parties to explain their claims and defenses in detail, with the benefit of what has been learned through discovery, to better frame the dispute for the arbitrators in advance of the hearing.

However, prehearing submissions that total hundreds of pages of highly detailed legal and factual recitation and analysis are rarely seen in U.S. practice, and the prevailing practice is more of an outline of the case that will be presented by each party, along with legal arguments and authorities supporting what are anticipated as the key legal issues to be faced during the hearing.

When the subject of prehearing briefs is raised in a prehearing conference, counsel should make sure to clarify the arbitrators' expectations concerning length, exhibit references, format, specific issues to address, and related issues. For example, it is increasingly common for arbitrators to ask counsel to add hyperlinks to exhibit references to enable the arbitrators to quickly call up the exhibit while reviewing the submission. While hyperlinks can be very useful, the process of adding hyperlinks is time consuming, so counsel must plan accordingly to allow sufficient time for this prior to the deadline for submission.

3. *Joint Issue Lists*

Some arbitrators also require counsel to prepare joint lists of the issues that the arbitrators must decide when drafting their award. These enable the arbitrators to focus their attention on the core issues in the case and are particularly useful in complex construction cases with dozens of individual claims.

The disadvantage of an issue list is that it is often time consuming to prepare and may give rise to additional disputes between the parties. In other cases, the issue list can be so imprecise that it is of limited utility to anyone. As a result, the issue of whether developing such a list is worth the effort involved is worth discussion among counsel and arbitrators and is very case-dependent.

4. *Joint Stipulations of Facts*

Arbitrators often insert into the scheduling order a date to reach agreement on and submit a joint stipulation of undisputed facts. Such stipulations can significantly streamline the presentation of evidence at the hearing. It is often possible to stipulate to a substantial number of facts, such as the governing contract documents, applicable law, and basic facts such as a chronology of key events, without characterizing in any way the significance (or lack thereof) of any particular event. Complex construction cases also frequently lend themselves to stipulations on accounting issues, such as payment amounts, retention, amount of approved change orders, and actually incurred cost figures, in order to streamline the proof at the hearings.

Counsel frequently do not take advantage of the benefit of joint stipulations of fact, however, for a number of reasons. For one, stipulations take significant time to prepare and are often given low priority in the final rush of hearing preparations. Additionally, depending on the personalities of counsel involved, agreeing on stipulations can quickly become an exercise in gamesmanship and wordsmithing that end up watering down the usefulness of a joint stipulation.

D. Court Reporters and Interpreters

1. Transcripts

Absent an expressed preference by the arbitrators, having the hearing transcribed by a court reporter is generally optional in arbitration. A transcript enables both counsel and arbitrators to refer back to the record to understand a witness's precise testimony or clarify which exhibit was being referenced by the witness on a particular point. To the extent the parties intend to make posthearing written submissions, a transcript is particularly helpful to point the arbitrators to exactly when the key testimony on a point was presented. Additionally, a transcript is almost essential if preserving the right to vacate or challenge the award is important.

However, a transcript is a significant cost item, commonly totaling tens of thousands of dollars in lengthy hearings. As a result, a transcript can be prohibitively expensive in low-value cases.

That said, a transcript generally remains the norm in construction arbitrations where the amount in controversy exceeds $1,000,000. As a result, there are a number of practices that counsel should consider when engaging a court reporter.

- First, consistent with the general practice that claimants take the lead on logistical prehearing matters, it is normal for the claimant to engage the court reporter, with the approval of the opposing party. In addition, counsel should discuss whether to have the reporter produce daily rough transcripts and whether to obtain "real-time" reporting capability.
- Second, once the court reporter is engaged, counsel should prepare a list of the arbitrators, attorneys, witnesses, experts, company names, and so on that the court reporter will encounter. Failing to provide such a list at the outset of the hearing tends to create disruptions during the hearing and risks an inaccurate transcript.
- Third, following the hearing, parties sometimes submit errata sheets to correct any perceived errors in the transcript. This is a subject worthy of discussion between counsel, however. Preparing an errata sheet requires a careful study of the transcripts and takes considerable time and effort. Further, requests to correct errors in the transcript sometimes risk attempts by one party to inappropriately alter testimony. Given this, counsel in recent years have frequently determined to mutually waive submitting errata sheets.

2. *Interpreters*

While only rarely encountered in U.S. construction arbitrations, interpreters can be required in proceedings where a witness is not proficient enough to offer his or her testimony in English. If an interpreter will be required, there are a unique set of challenges for counsel to consider prior to the hearing date.

The first question to consider is whether the interpreter needs to translate both the questions presented to and answers provided by the witness. Proceeding in this manner both is time consuming and tends to disrupt the examiner's ability to question the witness. The alternative, if the witness understands English but is concerned about his or her ability to provide clear and precise responses in English, is to allow the examiner to question the witness in English and the witness to respond in his or her preferred language for the interpreter to translate.

Second, any examination through an interpreter will predictably last longer than an examination without an interpreter. This logistical issue needs to be anticipated when allocating hearing time.

Third, the arbitrators must be careful not to allow either party to utilize an interpreter to create mischief. It is incumbent on the opposing party to raise any concerns about the use of an interpreter with the arbitrators as soon as practicable and for the arbitrators to keep abuses within control. Counsel can, for example, insist on use of an interpreter with a witness who communicated in English throughout the project in jobsite meetings and other contexts, just so the witness effectively gets to hear the questions twice and has more time to frame an answer.

Another issue is when the interpreter misstates either the question or the answer. The opposing party may in some cases have a second interpreter attend, to confirm the accuracy of the translations and raise issues when they occur. As the court reporter will be transcribing only the English portion of the proceeding, if an interpretation error is not immediately challenged, the erroneous version will be all that is reflected in the record.

E. Hearing Venue and Related Logistics

Finally, the prehearing planning stage also requires counsel to consider a series of often overlooked administrative items. While usually straightforward in nature, they must be considered to ensure that the hearing proceeds smoothly. The following is a brief checklist of these issues.

- **Hearing Venue**—Arbitration hearings are normally conducted either at a neutral venue such as a hotel conference room or dedicated arbitration hearing venue (such as a JAMS resolution center or AAA office) or in the law offices of one counsel or the other. Using a law office conference room often saves significant costs and avoids some of the logistical issues required to reserve space at a neutral venue. However, counsel must consider whether a law office has the appropriate space, support, and other amenities necessary to host the hearing. Moreover, some counsel believe that having the hearing at the opposing party's law office places them at a perceived disadvantage.

- **Hearing Rooms**—As a practical matter, multiple rooms are required to host a hearing. The first requirement is a large hearing room that can hold all attendees comfortably and that has space and electrical connections available for laptops, other equipment, and hearing binders (to the extent hard copies are utilized). Additionally, at a minimum each party and the arbitrators will require their own breakout room (a minimum of three breakout rooms for a two-party arbitration). Preferably, at least one additional conference room should be available to use as an overflow room for private meetings, phone calls, food setup, and so on.
- **Technology and Equipment**—It is a safe assumption that all attendees will require high-speed internet access during the hearing day and may also require access to a high-speed printer. Attendees will generally bring their own laptops, requiring a large number of convenient electrical outlets. If exhibits are to be shown on a screen or monitor, each arbitrator, witness, and counsel need to be able to see the displayed exhibit, which often requires multiple screens. Technical support should be readily available to all attendees to resolve the inevitable technical problems that arise. For remote hearings, or individual witnesses appearing remotely, it is important for each party to ensure in advance that its witnesses and experts have all of the equipment necessary to appear at the hearing, as discussed further later.
- **Dress Code**—Given the increasing prevalence of business casual attire, it is good practice for counsel to confer on the dress code for the hearing and communicate any preference to the arbitrators. While business attire has traditionally been the norm, business casual attire has become more acceptable and commonplace in recent years.
- **Food**—Counsel need to confer as to what arrangements are to be in place for coffee/tea and lunches during the hearing days. In some instances there are numerous places to obtain a quick-service lunch within a couple minutes of the hearing venue, but in the majority of

cases it is more efficient to arrange for food to be delivered to the venue, allowing for a shorter lunch break.

- **Lodging**—Suitable lodging needs to be arranged within a reasonable distance of the hearing venue (preferably within easy walking distance) for out-of-town witnesses, counsel, and arbitrators. Utilizing more remote lodging invites the possibility of delays due to traffic-related and similar causes.

III. Arbitration Hearing Structure

The procedures that are utilized to manage the arbitration hearing can have a profound effect on the proceeding. For one, the procedures adopted for case presentation can influence how the arbitrators assess the merits of a party's claims or defenses. But in addition, the procedures utilized can also greatly influence the time required for and cost of the hearing. The hours spent in the hearing are without doubt the most expensive hours of the entire arbitration process, so techniques to streamline the process to ensure the hearing proceeds as efficiently and cost effectively as possible yield real value to both parties.

A. Time Management and Hearing Schedule

Time is the most important, limited resource during an arbitration hearing and accordingly must be managed carefully. The parties each need to have adequate time to present their case while still ensuring that the process proceeds efficiently.

1. Administrative Schedules

The first time-related issue that counsel and arbitrators must agree on is the schedule for the hearing day. This includes the planned start and stop times for the hearing day and the planned breaks and lunch period to be allowed during the day. For example, a common daily schedule might include a 9:00 AM start time and 5:30 PM end time, with a 10- to 15-minute morning break, a one-hour lunch break, and either one or two afternoon break(s). The hearing day schedule should be established by no later than the final prehearing conference to enable counsel to plan their schedules within the total hearing hours available.

2. Witness Lists and Detailed Daily Schedules

Advanced disclosure of the order of appearance of each party's witnesses and experts is common practice in arbitration. This enables counsel to best prepare for each day and avoids any unfair surprises. The timing of this advance disclosure varies. As one example, counsel may disclose the order of witnesses/experts approximately a week before the hearing begins, with the obligation to disclose any changes in witness order as soon as reasonably practical and a minimum of 24 hours in advance.

Arbitrators sometimes ask counsel for a more detailed daily schedule that includes the order of appearance of witnesses and experts, along with estimated (nonbinding) durations for direct and cross-examinations. Such detailed schedules can be useful in certain cases, particularly contentious multiweek hearings, because they enable counsel to better plan when their witnesses and experts must be available. The question, however, is whether the time and effort to develop such a detailed hearing schedule yields sufficient benefit to be worth the effort and the accompanying risk of prematurely disclosing a hearing strategy.

3. *Order of Presentations*

Typical U.S. arbitration practice is that followed in court proceedings—the claimant first presents all of its witness and expert evidence followed by the respondent's witnesses and experts. Time is often reserved for the claimant to put on a brief rebuttal case following the respondent's case.

The main alternative, borrowed from international arbitration practice,[2] is for the parties to first present their fact witnesses, followed by their expert witnesses, meaning (1) claimant's fact witnesses, (2) respondent's fact witnesses, (3) claimant's expert witnesses, and finally (4) respondent's expert witnesses. Some arbitrators prefer this second approach because it allows them to compare the competing fact witness and expert witness testimony closer in time, and it also allows the experts to incorporate into their testimony any new evidence from the fact witnesses that was not reflected in their written reports.

4. *Chess Clocks*

Traditionally, there are no specific time limitations imposed on a party's ability to present their case at the arbitration hearing, other than a general commitment by both sides to complete the hearing within the time that has been scheduled. This approach effectively requires counsel to overestimate the time needed to complete the hearing or risk the highly undesirable situation where

2. Int'l Bar Ass'n, *IBA Rules on the Taking of Evidence in International Arbitration*, art. 8.4 (Dec. 17, 2020) [hereinafter *IBA Rules on the Taking of Evidence*], https://www.ibanet.org/MediaHandler?id=def0807b-9fec-43ef-b624-f2cb2af7cf7b#.

the parties are unable to completely present both their cases within the allotted time. This then requires additional hearing days to be scheduled at a later time, a highly undesirable outcome that significantly increases the cost of the hearing and delays conclusion of the arbitration.

Given the practical difficulties associated with scheduling additional hearing time, counsel now frequently agree to use a "chess clock" time management practice. The chess clock approach requires counsel to agree on (or the arbitrators to decide in the absence of agreement) the allocation of the available hearing time between the parties. The available hearing time is the total amount of actual hearing time after deducting breaks and lunches and administrative time not chargeable to either party. Once a party uses all of its allocated hearing time, it has no further right to present its case. Assuming that the initial allocation of time is reasonable, the chess clock approach is effective at ensuring that the parties present their cases within the scheduled number of hearing days and requires the parties to focus their presentations on the key disputed issues.

Hearing time can be allocated based on a number of considerations. A 50/50 allocation of time between two parties is most common,[3] but other factors can affect this, such as where one party has significantly more witnesses than the other, an interpreter will be needed for some of one side's witnesses, or there is considerable background information that the claimant will need to present but the respondent can largely avoid. If counsel cannot reach agreement on the allocation of time, the arbitrators will need to make the allocation.

Once the hearing time is allocated, counsel then agree to a process for tracking each party's time usage during the hearing. Sometimes arbitrators prefer to keep track of time usage themselves, but far more commonly each party keeps a record of time usage during each day, and the parties compare their records at the end of the day to agree upon how much time each party used that day (despite the name, the actual use of a chess clock for this purpose is rare). The daily time logs can be recorded in Excel files, and by applying simple Excel formulas, the total time used and remaining time for each party can easily be calculated.

As the hearings will likely encounter disruptions related to administrative tasks, and the arbitrators are likely to ask questions of witnesses that cannot

3. Chess clock time management is also very effective in multiparty cases. However, the allocation of time among the parties is typically more complex and must be fairly apportioned based upon the respective roles of the parties involved in the arbitration.

easily be planned for, counsel must also agree to a process for handling such time. One approach is simply to agree that any administrative or arbitrator time will simply be divided evenly between the parties and charged to their time allocations. The opposite approach is to track such time but not charge it to either party. In other cases, counsel agree to set aside a certain amount of hearing time each day for administrative issues and arbitrator questions and then review how this allocation is working as the hearing progresses. In any event, keeping track of administrative and arbitrator question time is important, because it can affect the time remaining to the parties. If the arbitrators are asking lots of questions, for example, the parties may both need to adjust their remaining time to assure on-schedule completion of the hearing.

B. Bifurcation/Separate Arbitration Tracks

Bifurcation refers to dividing the arbitration into two (or potentially more) separate hearings and can be a particularly useful means of organizing some complex construction arbitrations. When used, bifurcation is typically agreed or ordered by the arbitrators very early in the arbitration, so that it can be incorporated into planning for the hearings from the outset.

Likely the most common use of bifurcation is dividing the arbitration into an initial phase dedicated to issues of liability and a second phase dedicated to issues of damages. This form of bifurcation can save considerable time and expense by eliminating the need for damages evidence on claims where no liability has been found. However, bifurcation between liability and damages phases almost necessarily extends the overall duration of the arbitration, and having two evidentiary hearings increases the costs, such that the benefits of the bifurcation can be entirely lost.

The second form of bifurcation that also is used with some frequency is bifurcating claims by subject matter or occasionally by claim value. If a large number of individual claims fall naturally into a small number of subject matters—such as electrical claims and HVAC claims—then it can make sense to hear separate groups of claims at separate hearings.[4] Similarly, hearing a small group of large-dollar-value claims first can be more efficient if the chances are strong that the remaining small claims can be settled once the major ones

---

4. A similar effect can be achieved without bifurcation if the parties structure the presentation of evidence during a single hearing around particular groups of related claims. Using this method, all of the fact and expert witnesses addressing a particular group of claims are heard, before progressing to another set of witnesses and experts on a different set of claims.

are decided. An example of where bifurcation makes sense is a case where the validity of a liquidated damages clause is the central issue, and that limited issue is heard and decided first. In the second phase, the remaining issue then will be either whether there are excusable delays that reduce liquidated damages (if the liquidated damages clause is enforceable) or the amount of actual damages incurred (if the liquidated damages clause is found to be invalid), either way eliminating issues rendered moot by the initial ruling.

C. Written Direct/Witness Statements

The use of written witness statements or affidavits to set out the direct testimony of witnesses in lieu of oral direct testimony, a technique borrowed from international arbitration,[5] has become increasingly common in recent years in complex construction arbitrations. As such, a review of the advantages and disadvantages to using witness statements is worthy of consideration.

1. Process of Using Written Witness Statements

Witness statements are typically submitted well in advance of the arbitration hearing. As a result, counsel must agree to the use of written witness statements early in the arbitration process and establish a schedule for their submission as part of the initial scheduling order.

Witness statements are a substitute for direct examination, so they are used to set out the relevant facts that support the affirmative case *based on a witness's direct personal knowledge*. Thus, while counsel commonly assists witnesses in preparing their witness statements, it is critical to ensure that the witness agrees fully with the contents and language of the statement. Witness statements containing points that the witness cannot fully support on cross-examination or must qualify significantly are likely to greatly affect the credibility and persuasiveness of the witness's entire testimony.

There are different ways to organize the submission of witness statements, but by far the most common is to provide for two rounds of witness statements. The first round serves as the witness's initial direct testimony. The second round provides witnesses the opportunity to respond to the opposing party's initial round of witness statements, where needed. This approach is effective in helping to crystalize the core issues in dispute.

Following submission of witness statements, neither party is typically allowed to present any further direct evidence from fact witnesses, other than exhibits. As a result, the hearing then focuses almost exclusively on

---

5. *E.g.*, *IBA Rules on the Taking of Evidence*, *supra* note 2, art. 4.

cross-examination and redirect. That said, witnesses are commonly allowed a few minutes to address new issues, such as new factual allegations raised in a reply witness statement, and to correct any minor errors noted in their witness statements.[6]

2. *Advantages and Disadvantages of Written Witness Statements*

The key advantages of written witness statements are:

- **Shorter Hearings**—Written witness statements can eliminate almost all oral direct examination. This significantly shortens the duration of a hearing. Hearing time is the most expensive time in arbitration, and in addition to the cost savings, a shorter hearing makes scheduling the hearing easier.
- **Focused Hearings, Particularly Cross-Examination**—Having the direct testimony in hand well in advance of the hearing aids greatly in preparing a focused cross-examination that deals with the most significant issues in the case.
- **Limited Need for Depositions**—Written witness statements should obviate the need for depositions in almost all cases. Instead of having to ask questions to draw out what the witness will say at the hearing, his or her entire testimony is placed in opposing counsel's hands well in advance of the hearing. When utilized, depositions add significant cost to the arbitration process, so this is another source of potentially significant cost savings.

However, witness statements have some drawbacks.

- **Limits Witnesses' Evidence**—The most significant limitation is that witness statements limit the ability of a witness to speak directly to the arbitrators in their own voice and "tell their story" without significant interruption. For a particularly compelling witness, written direct testimony can be a strategic disadvantage.
- **Overly Lawyered Statements**—Because most witness statements are prepared with the assistance of counsel, there is a risk that the

6. *IBA Rules on the Taking of Evidence*, *supra* note 2, art. 8.5; Int'l Bar Ass'n, *Commentary on the Revised Text of the 2020 IBA Rules on the Taking of Evidence in International Arbitration*, https://www.ibanet.org/MediaHandler?id=4F797338-693E-47C7-A92A-1509790ECC9D 27; Albert Bates, Jr. & R. Zachary Torres-Fowler, *2020 Update to the IBA Rules: Modest Changes for Challenges New and Old*, 36 MEALEY'S INT'L ARB. REP. 3, 5 (2021).

> statements do not represent the true testimony of a witness. An overly lawyered witness statement will be less convincing (since the lawyer's involvement will not be hard to discern) and often results in a less open or fair portrayal of the facts known to the witness. The net effect is to reduce the credibility of the witness. However, the aid of a lawyer in preparing the witness statement with a lighter touch preserves the witness's own story but helps the statement to be more precise and focused on the issues in dispute without wandering into unimportant areas. Witness statements prepared without assistance of counsel tend to be unfocused, to omit key supporting facts, and to inappropriately emphasize irrelevant facts.

A frequently heard complaint from counsel not used to utilizing witness statements is that preparing a good witness statement takes at least as long as preparing the witness for direct examination, so there is really no cost savings. This misses the point. The cost savings come at the hearing, where the number of hourly billers in the room is at a maximum and the hourly cost is far higher than when preparing a witness statement. The reduction in hearing hours is where the cost savings lie.

D. Expert Presentations

An increasingly common practice in complex construction arbitrations is the use of expert presentations in place of direct testimony by experts. With this approach, there is some limited introduction of the expert from counsel, but thereafter the expert is allowed a set period of time to make an oral presentation (usually with the assistance of PowerPoint slides) to explain to the arbitrators his or her opinions as set out in the expert report.

These presentations can involve some questions from counsel if desired, but the expert is largely expected to lead the presentation. Given the technical nature of many expert reports, many arbitrators find expert presentations to be a helpful way of both understanding the core opinions in the expert's report and assessing the expert's credibility.

However, counsel should carefully consider the presentation skills of the expert, the nature of the testimony, and the preferences of the arbitrators in determining whether expert presentations are appropriate for a particular case. If expert presentations are used, counsel largely cedes control of the presentation to the expert, and the pace of the presentation is largely controlled by the expert. Counsel's judgment as to whether the expert is moving too fast for the arbitrators to follow, or too slow and boring them, may be more refined than that of the expert.

E. Witness Conferencing

"Witness conferencing," sometimes colloquially referred to as "hot-tubbing" or "witness panels," has gained a good deal of attention in recent years, along with increasing use in complex construction arbitrations.[7] Conceptually, witness conferencing involves the concurrent appearance and testimony of two or more witnesses or experts. In practical terms, if the parties and arbitrators agree to utilize witness conferencing, two or more witnesses or experts will be sworn as witnesses at the same time—often physically sitting next to each other. The witnesses/experts will then answer questions from counsel or the arbitrators and have the opportunity to respond to their counterpart's responses in real time.

Witness conferencing is most commonly used with expert witnesses, and most often the arbitrators (as opposed to counsel) will initially lead the questioning. However, there are a variety of different formats for witness conferencing that are in use.[8]

- **Tribunal-Led Witness Conferencing**—In tribunal-led witness conferencing, the arbitrators take responsibility for conducting the initial witness/expert examination. While both counsel have the opportunity to ask follow-up questions subsequent to the arbitrators' questions, counsel's role naturally becomes more limited under this framework than the typical cross-examination. Tribunal-led witness conferencing involving experts generally has the arbitrators' questioning follow either presentations by each expert or direct examinations of the experts by counsel. Tribunal-led witness conferencing tends to be the most common form of expert witness conferencing. However, it requires the arbitrators to become very familiar with the reports submitted by each expert and to prepare questions for the experts in advance. If utilized with lay witnesses, it generally requires the use of

---

7. *See* Chartered Inst. of Arbs., *Guidelines for Witness Conferencing in International Arbitration* 13–14 (2019), https://www.ciarb.org/media/4595/guideline-13-witness-conferencing-april-2019pdf.pdf [hereinafter *CIArb Guidelines for Witness Conferencing*]; Int'l Chamber of Com., *ICC Commission Report: Construction Industry Arbitrations: Recommended Tools and Techniques for Effective Management, 2019 Update* 27, https://cdn.iccwbo.org/content/uploads/sites/3/2019/02/icc-arbitration-adr-commission-report-on-construction-industry-arbitrations.pdf.

8. *CIArb Guidelines for Witness Conferencing*, *supra* note 7, at 20–23 (providing detailed review of witness conferencing techniques).

witness statements that the arbitrators can study in advance in order to prepare questions.

- **Counsel-Led Witness Conferencing**—Counsel-led witness conferencing utilizes the traditional cross-examination, following initial presentations or direct testimony in the traditional manner. The unique element of this cross-examination by counsel is that the witnesses/experts can be concurrently examined. So, counsel has the option of posing traditional cross-examination questions to the opposing witness/expert but can invite their own witness/expert to respond to a particular question and answer as well, in order to highlight and clarify the differences in their respective testimony. Often, an opportunity for the arbitrators to ask questions following counsels' questions is also provided.
- **Witness-Led Witness Conferencing**—In witness-led witness conferencing, the competing witnesses or experts lead the presentation of evidence. Witness-led witness conferencing is generally viewed as appropriate only for experts with significant testimonial experience in arbitration proceedings.[9] The experts generally make presentations but then engage in a more free-flowing dialogue regarding their respective opinions, to identify their key points of disagreement. Special care must be taken in connection with a witness-led witness conferencing session to make sure the precise format and process are agreed in advance, as otherwise there is a substantial risk that one expert or the other will seek to undermine the process. Because of this risk, witness-led witness conferencing is the least-often utilized approach and should be avoided in most situations.

Witness conferencing offers a number of potential advantages. First, the simultaneous availability of the witnesses or experts for questioning greatly improves the ease of comparing the testimony or opinions of each witness or expert. Second, witness conferencing arguably improves the quality of testimony because a witness or expert may well feel more constrained to provide precise and accurate responses to questions when there is a distinct possibility of having any exaggerations or misstatements identified on the spot by the counterpart witness or expert. Third, and maybe most significant, the active role of the arbitrators in asking questions (at whatever point this occurs) allows the arbitrators to obtain direct answers almost simultaneously from both sides

9. *See id.* at 57–58.

of the dispute to the questions that most concern the arbitrators. This is not only for their benefit but also counsels' by providing insight to their concerns. Finally, presenting witnesses or experts in a witness conference format is usually a significant time-saver as compared to separate examinations.

As to disadvantages, there are a number of risks associated with witness conferencing. First, depending on the personalities and experience of the witnesses or experts, some can become overly argumentative or even hostile to one another during the witness conferencing session. This can diminish the clarity of their testimony, take away from the credibility of one or both, and perhaps complicate rather than simplify the decision-making process of the arbitrators. Second, the use of witness conferencing may in some cases have the effect of elevating the status of an expert with minimal qualifications, or whose opinions are inherently flawed or misguided, by treating him or her as equal in stature to a much more qualified opposing expert.

Witness conferencing has received a good deal of attention in recent years, but it is still the exception and not the rule in U.S. construction arbitrations. Many counsel and arbitrators are generally familiar with witness conferencing in concept but do not have direct experience with the process. Lack of familiarity turns some counsel away from trying the process and also presents some risk that inexperienced counsel will decide on an unwieldy conferencing procedure that loses much of the potential benefit of this technique.

F. Examination Practice

State and federal rules of evidence do not apply to arbitration proceedings unless application is specifically agreed. These rules generally limit the scope of cross-examination to the subject matter of the witness's direct testimony or matters affecting the witness's credibility.[10] Similarly, they restrict counsel from using leading questions during direct and redirect examination of a friendly witness.[11]

In arbitration, approaches to the conduct of examinations vary. Many times, the scope of cross-examination is not strictly limited to the subject matter of the direct testimony, and counsel can use leading questions more liberally than generally permitted in a courtroom. A rule of reason tends to apply in both cases, however. For example, the arbitrators may remind counsel who is relying on leading questions that testimony from the witness will be given more weight than testimony from the lawyer that the witness simply agrees

---

10. *E.g.*, FED. R. EVID. 611.

11. *Id.*

with. Of course, counsel are free to agree to a more court-like proceeding, but arbitrators will generally prefer a more relaxed approach.

G. Presentation of Exhibits

As arbitration rules generally do not require the parties to apply a specific set of evidentiary rules, questions concerning the authenticity, credibility, and weight of particular evidence are left to the discretion of the arbitrators.[12] There are, however, some guidelines concerning the presentation of documentary evidence of which counsel should be aware.

1. Use of Exhibits

Many arbitrators require counsel to use or otherwise reference an exhibit during the hearing if they want the arbitrators to rely on an exhibit when drafting their award. This position is largely in response to the widespread practice of listing many hundreds of documents as exhibits, knowing many are unlikely to be used during the hearing, "just in case" they may be needed at some point. When arbitrators adopt this view, they are essentially telling counsel that important documents should be brought to the attention of the arbitrators during the hearing and the arbitrators do not intend to wade through a long list of exhibits never referenced at the hearing to see if there is anything in them that may influence the award. It is accordingly good practice to obtain clarification if this standard will be applied in advance of the hearing, so that counsel can plan accordingly.

2. Use of Electronic Exhibits

Counsel commonly present exhibits to a witness or expert in electronic format (that is, on a computer monitor or TV screen). Presenting exhibits electronically can streamline the proceedings because it allows counsel to quickly direct the witness to the desired document without needing to fumble through hard-copy binders. With some exhibits, such as large Excel files, it is practically impossible to examine the witness using a hard-copy document.

However, this raises the issue of how, and to what extent, counsel can present exhibits to a witness solely in electronic format, where counsel has sole control over what is shown on the screen. It is efficient to direct the witness's attention to specific language in the document for purposes of the examination,

---

12. *E.g.*, American Arbitration Association Construction Industry Arbitration Rules and Mediation Procedures, Rule R-35 (July 1, 2015); International Centre for Dispute Resolution, International Dispute Resolution Procedures, art. 22 (Mar. 2021).

but it also limits the ability of the witness to review the entire exhibit and appreciate the document's broader context. Accordingly, it is good practice to agree in advance how to handle this, such as by providing a separate hard copy to the witness that can be reviewed or by at least allowing the witness an opportunity, if requested, to examine the entire document before responding to the question. Fairness is served by having a protocol that both parties have agreed to abide by.

3. *Additional Hearing Exhibits and Demonstrative Exhibits*

It is by no means unusual that during the course of a hearing, counsel may need to introduce new exhibits that were not previously marked. As a result, it is useful for counsel to agree in advance on a protocol for introducing new exhibits during the hearing. The arbitrators will be sensitive to the risk of prejudicing the opposing party when adding new exhibits and the need to avoid a trial-by-ambush scenario. Commonly the agreement is to permit the introduction of new exhibits only for good cause and after the introducing party provides the opposing party advance notice (e.g., 24 to 48 hours) of the new exhibit to allow time to review it and raise any appropriate objections.

If there is no such protocol in place, or it is not followed, the arbitrators may well allow the document to be used nevertheless but give the opposing party time not only to review and object to it but also for any other steps (such as introducing other new responsive documents) needed to avoid prejudicing the opposing party. This only extends the hearing needlessly and quite possibly draws the ire of the arbitrators as well.

A similar concern applies to demonstrative exhibits, such as PowerPoints, charts, photographs, and so on that compile information from documents that are already in the record. Counsel should define what constitutes a demonstrative exhibit and agree on a protocol for using demonstrative exhibits at the hearing to avoid unfair surprise. This generally involves providing the opposing party with a copy of the proposed demonstrative exhibit 24 to 48 hours in advance of its intended use. Also, to the extent parties wish to use visual aids during an opening or closing statement, it is again good practice to agree to exchange those visual aids 24 to 48 hours in advance to avoid surprise.

H. Remote Hearing Issues

As noted previously, the cost savings and logistical advantages of virtual hearings are difficult to ignore. Since they will continue to be with us, there are a few unique issues associated with remote arbitration hearings in construction cases of which counsel need to be aware.

1. Time Zones

When scheduling the hearing day, counsel must keep in mind the effect time zones can have on the reasonably available hearing time. Construction professionals routinely relocate for their next project, and especially when a hearing is taking place years after the project concluded, you can expect that the witnesses may well have scattered far and wide, including internationally. With counsel, arbitrators, witnesses, and experts scattered across multiple time zones, the window of available hearing time during the day becomes constrained, and accommodations may need to be made on particular days to allow a witness now located in the Middle East or Asia to testify at a reasonable hour in his or her time zone. All concerned, including the arbitrators, need to be flexible regarding the hearing hours and accept compromises that work best for the entire group that will be in attendance on a daily basis.

2. Exhibits

Remote hearings require careful planning by counsel to determine how witnesses and experts should be provided with copies of exhibits and other relevant documents in advance of the hearing. The simplest answer—to provide all concerned with complete access to the full set of electronic exhibits—may not always be desirable or appropriate. Indeed, as discussed previously, an overreliance on electronic documents can impair a witness's ability to fully assess a document. But providing hard copies to remote witnesses becomes a significant logistical challenge. Providing relevant subsets of exhibits electronically to each witness has its own complexities but is often the most practical solution.

If there is a concern regarding providing a remote witness in advance with the exhibits that are to be used in cross-examination, those exhibits can be sent to the witness in advance in a sealed envelope. At the start of cross-examination, the examiner can ask the witness to break the seal, remove the documents, and then proceed with cross. The use of a sealed container prevents the witness from examining the documents in advance in an effort to gain an unfair advantage.

In remote hearings, the logistical difficulties of reproducing several identical sets of hearing exhibit binders in hard copy are multiplied by the need to ship those sets of binders to multiple recipients in different locations and the added lead time and expense this involves. Even when arbitrators and counsel tend to prefer hard copies, this added complexity often tips the balance in favor of using electronic exhibits stored on a common platform accessible to all those needing access.

At the hearing, presenting exhibits to a witness through the videoconferencing platform by sharing the examiner's computer screen (i.e., the "share screen" function on Zoom) has substantial limitations. Doing so precludes the witness from reviewing other portions of the document beyond what is on the shared screen. The better practice is to utilize the common database of electronic exhibits in examining witnesses, allowing arbitrators, counsel, and the witness ready access to the entire exhibit and not just the portion on which the examining attorney wishes to focus.

3. *Witness Tampering Considerations*

It is an unfortunate reality that allowing witnesses to testify from remote locations, such as their home or office, multiplies the opportunities for improper mischief, such as receiving guidance from another person off-camera or referring to notes out of the camera's field of view. To combat this risk, many arbitrators impose rules related to a remote witness's appearance, such as having the witness confirm that he or she will not consult any documents or notes other than the exhibits presented in examination and that there are and will be no other persons present in the room with the witness. If the arbitrators fail to implement such restrictions, counsel can always agree to them as an alternative. Some arbitral institutions have provided helpful guidelines on this topic.[13] While it is difficult to impossible to fully guarantee against witness tampering when witnesses are testifying remotely, some basic precautions along these lines can effectively minimize the risk.

4. *Logistical Requirements*

Whenever witnesses or experts will be testifying remotely, it is important not to overlook the logistical requirements associated with their appearance. This includes technical requirements such as ensuring the witness has a robust internet connection, a high-quality video camera, computer monitor, microphone, and speakers, as well as issues such as an appropriate setting, good

---

13. Int'l Chamber of Com., *ICC Guidance Note on Possible Measures Aimed at Mitigating the Effects of the COVID-19 Pandemic* (Apr. 9, 2020), https://iccwbo.org/news-publications/arbitration-adr-rules-and-tools/icc-guidance-note-on-possible-measures-aimed-at-mitigating-the-effects-of-the-covid-19-pandemic/; Am. Arb. Ass'n & Int'l Ctr. for Disp. Resol., *AAA-ICDR® Virtual Hearing Guide for Arbitrators and Parties* (2021), https://go.adr.org/rs/294-SFS-516/images/AAA268_AAA%20Virtual%20Hearing%20Guide%20for%20Arbitrators%20and%20Parties.pdf; *IBA Rules on the Taking of Evidence*, *supra* note 2, art. 8.2.

lighting, and limited ambient noise. Failing to verify that the right logistical requirements are in place in advance of the witness's appearance risks interruptions and delays to the proceedings, creating a significant distraction that makes focusing on the testimony difficult or in the worst case renders the testimony almost wholly ineffective. This is a basic responsibility of all counsel when planning to present testimony from a witness from another location.

I. Witness Sequestration

Witness sequestration rules applied in arbitration proceedings vary more than those applied in court proceedings. Three approaches to witness sequestration are commonly seen. The first is that witnesses are entirely precluded from entering the hearing room before testifying, until the witness is called.[14] The second is that witnesses and experts can be in the hearing room and listen to the testimony of other witnesses but cannot speak to counsel, witnesses, or corporate representatives during the course of testimony. The third is that no form of witness sequestration applies.

That said, the rules applying to experts and corporate representatives are often different. Indeed, it is relatively common that experts are permitted to attend the entire hearing, so that their opinions can be fully informed by the hearing testimony. Alternatively, experts are sometimes only allowed to attend when the opposing expert is testifying. As to corporate representatives, it is common to allow one corporate representative to be present at all times, sometimes even if the representative is expected to testify at the hearing.

The applicable witness sequestration rules depend on the preferences of the arbitrators, in the first instance, and secondarily on the views of counsel. The issue of witness sequestration typically comes down to balancing the needs of counsel to communicate with a key witness or corporate representative during the hearing with the need to ensure that witnesses provide complete and honest testimony, not influenced by what prior witnesses have said.

It is not uncommon for one party to act in accordance with its own understanding of the "usual rules" applying to sequestration, only to find out mid-hearing that the other party has a very different idea of what limitations should apply. So, it is good practice to establish the applicable ground rules in advance of the hearing.

---

14. Often party witnesses are permitted to attend the hearing following the completion of their testimony, but usually with the limitation that they are not subject to recall as a rebuttal witness. As with other aspects of this topic, the ground rules should be discussed and established for each arbitration.

A related and potentially more important issue is when counsel may confer with a witness while the witness is giving testimony. Practices tend to differ a bit among different court jurisdictions, so again this is an area where misunderstandings that do not surface until mid-hearing are not uncommon. The most stringent rule is that witnesses may not confer with counsel at all once they are called to testify. The less stringent version is that this bar on conferring goes into effect only at the point when the witness is turned over for cross-examination. And some counsel may assume that if the issue has not been clarified in advance, given the relaxation of the usual court rules in arbitration, there is no bar at all on conferring with a witness while he or she is testifying. Again, a discussion and clarification of the applicable ground rules in advance of the hearing usually obviates problems in this area as well.

J. Corporate Representatives

There is general consensus that nonwitness corporate representatives (in-house counsel, corporate executives, or other relevant members of the client team) should be permitted to attend the hearing. The more common issue relates to *how many* corporate representatives may attend. The answer is most often dictated by the amount of available physical space in the hearing room. If the parties are proposing to bring more corporate representatives than can fit comfortably in the hearing room, the arbitrators are likely to impose an equal limit on both parties. This consideration of course disappears in a remote proceeding, although there may still be issues, rooted in the confidential nature of arbitration proceedings, if one side or the other asks to have an inordinate number of attendees compared to what can reasonably be justified.

IV. Posthearing Considerations

Following the close of the arbitration hearing, there is an important posthearing phase of the proceedings. Generally, the parties are given an opportunity to marshal the evidence presented during the hearing in a final effort to lay out their case to the arbitrators. This most often takes the form of one or more rounds of posthearing briefing, but other formats are frequently seen as well.

In complex construction arbitrations, both the number of claims and the volume of evidence as to each claim can be quite daunting, and the posthearing brief is counsel's best opportunity to put all the pieces together to demonstrate what has been proven or disproven by the totality of the evidence, often including statements from witnesses and excerpts from exhibits that were referenced many days or weeks apart during the course of a long hearing.

Structuring the posthearing phase presents the question of how best to balance the need to present a final summary of the evidence against the time and cost involved in elaborate posthearing submissions. Preparing detailed posthearing briefs with extensive citations (or links) to pertinent testimony and exhibits is both quite time consuming and expensive. Moreover, the length of the schedule for posthearing submissions directly affects the date when the award will be rendered, as the arbitrators will generally await the receipt of all posthearing submissions before commencing final deliberations and award drafting. However, few construction arbitrations present simple enough issues for decision that the posthearing phase can be skipped altogether, settling instead for final arguments following immediately after close of evidence at the hearing. The challenge is to find a balance that is appropriate for the size and complexity of the case.

When the structure of the posthearing phase is determined varies significantly, depending in large part on the preferences of the arbitrators. The nature and timing of the posthearing submissions are sometimes set out in the initial scheduling order. More commonly, structuring the posthearing phase is deferred until the final prehearing conference shortly before the hearing, decided at some point during the course of the hearing, or deferred until the close of the evidence. Counsel generally defer to the preferences of the arbitrators, but there is some logic to the view that counsel can best make decisions regarding the presentation of evidence at the hearing when the posthearing phase has been defined ahead of the hearing. Arbitrators tend in general to defer the issue, waiting to see how the hearing unfolds so they can best assess the complexity of the issues to be determined before fixing the extent of the posthearing submissions and schedule.

A. Posthearing Formats

There is a wide variety of possibilities for structuring the posthearing phase. The key distinctions tend to be written vs. oral submissions and the level of detail and number of opportunities that counsel will have to address the issues.

1. Posthearing Briefs

When posthearing briefs are to be utilized, the options and issues for consideration include:

- **Number of Briefs**—The issue here is whether each side will submit a single posthearing brief or alternatively whether there will be an opportunity for a reply brief following the initial round. A closely related issue is whether the submissions will be simultaneous or sequential. Sequential briefing is generally disfavored because it almost always lengthens the overall briefing schedule and because at this late stage of the proceeding, the respondent generally has no need to review the claimant's brief before preparing its own—the issues are already well known. The norm is thus a simultaneous exchange of initial briefs, followed (if desired) by a simultaneous exchange of reply briefs.

- **Page Length**—Page limits are common for posthearing briefs, with a shorter page limit for reply briefs, when used. This is an attempt to keep the parties on a relatively even footing and signals to counsel how much detail the arbitrators believe is reasonably necessary for their purposes in writing the award.

  A driver in setting page lengths is also the form of award that is to be rendered by the arbitrators. If the award requested is to be in an abbreviated form, shorter posthearing briefs are likely appropriate as compared to when a detailed award will be prepared. If findings of fact and conclusions of law are to be provided, either posthearing briefs will need to be more extensive or the parties may well be requested to submit proposed findings of fact and conclusions of law, either instead of or accompanied by shorter posthearing briefs focusing more on legal issues and only the most contentious factual issues.
- **Deadlines**—The deadlines for submitting posthearing briefs and reply briefs vary depending on the complexity of the dispute and the schedules and preferences of counsel. Where there is a transcript, the timing of receiving the final transcript from the court reporter is often a driver of the schedule, at least where transcript citations are to be included. In general terms, however, a deadline 30 days from either the close of the hearing or receipt of the full transcript for the initial briefs, and two weeks for reply briefs, is probably most common.
- **Claim Schedules**—For construction cases involving a multiplicity of claims, such as a long list of disputed change orders, arbitrators sometimes request, or counsel can propose, the use of a claim schedule to serve as a quick reference guide for the arbitrators, detailing each individual claim and where the arbitrators can locate the relevant evidence and testimony associated with that claim. Claim schedules (sometimes referred to as "Scott schedules") can be appended to each party's posthearing brief, submitted in lieu of a posthearing brief, or submitted on a joint basis with input from both parties, depending on preference and the needs of the case.

Claim schedules are essentially tables or charts that summarize the parties' positions and provide references to the available testimony and evidence in connection with each individual claim in the arbitration.[15] There is a row for each individual claim. The parties then add information in various columns for each claim. This generally includes (1) the amount of the claim, (2) claimant's position, (3) respondent's position, (4) relevant exhibits, (5) relevant testimony, and (6) relevant expert evidence.

2. *Oral Closing Presentations*

Oral closing presentations, typically held at a separate session a few weeks after the close of the evidentiary hearing, are a commonly used alternative for avoiding some of the cost and time required for preparing detailed posthearing briefs.

At oral closings, each party is given a set amount of time to lay out its summary of the evidence, argue the case, and respond to the opposing party's arguments. Typically, either separate time limits will be set for a short reply (and often a sur-reply) or some of the total time allocation may be reserved by counsel for this purpose. Oral closings are often transcribed for the arbitrators' reference in drafting the award, which obviates the need for the arbitrators to take accurate notes of transcript references and exhibit cites mentioned during the presentations.

Oral closing presentations are reliably less time consuming and costly than submitting posthearing briefs. Careful preparation of the presentation is still required, but there is a significant savings in avoiding the drafting of a formal written brief. Further, counsel can respond to the opposing side's position in real time and have an opportunity to directly address arbitrator questions, which will tend to focus on the issues that the arbitrator considers most significant.

That said, in a large, complex construction arbitration, an oral presentation, even if it lasts two hours or more, cannot address all the issues with as much precision and detail as a posthearing brief. References to the record, essentially unlimited in a written brief, must be used more conservatively because they tend to break up the flow of the presentation. Further, the disadvantage

15. Neil Wittmann, Q.C., *Using a "Scott Schedule" in Arbitration*, ADR INST. OF CAN., https://adric.ca/using-a-scott-schedule-in-arbitration/ (last visited Apr. 21, 2023).

of real-time replies is that they are necessarily more off the cuff, do not allow for careful analysis and a detailed response, and can inadvertently overlook key points.

3. *Hybrid Structures*

It is also not at all uncommon for counsel and arbitrators to adopt a hybrid structure for the posthearing phase, utilizing aspects of both written briefs and oral presentations, in order to address the issues in a more efficient fashion than two rounds of full briefing. Examples include:

- Initial posthearing briefs from each party followed by an opportunity for oral presentations and arbitrator questions in lieu of reply briefs
- Initial posthearing briefs from each party followed by the arbitrators posing a list of written questions for the parties to address orally in a separate session in lieu of reply briefs
- Initial posthearing briefs from each party followed by the arbitrators posing a list of written questions for the parties to address in writing in lieu of reply briefs

V. Conclusion

There is no one-size-fits-all approach to structuring the arbitration hearing for a complex construction case, and counsel should take advantage of the flexibility afforded by arbitration to propose procedures to most effectively and efficiently resolve the dispute. The most common practices covered in this chapter are only a guide. Moreover, arbitration procedures continue to evolve and adapt to implement successful innovations, so staying on top of recent developments and new ideas is imperative.

CHAPTER 8

Strategy and Tactics During the Hearing

ADRIAN L. BASTIANELLI, III
JENNIFER L. HARRIS

There are countless books and articles on trial strategy and tactics in jury trials, bench trials, and arbitrations that are more detailed and comprehensive than this chapter. Instead of applying a broad brush, this chapter focuses on the strategy and tactics that are most applicable in a complex construction arbitration and provides practical advice to those involved in such an arbitration.

I. The Arbitrators

Know your audience. Before choosing a presentation strategy for an arbitration, prudent lawyers should first seek to understand who the arbitrators are, and their level of knowledge and expertise in construction claims and disputes, in order to tailor the arbitration presentation to those arbitrators. Arbitrators are not a jury or judge, and deciding on a presentation style specifically for the arbitrators in your case is one of the most important and difficult tasks facing the advocate in a complex construction arbitration.

Most construction arbitrators are either veteran construction lawyers who have tried many issues similar to those being presented in your case or are construction professionals who have been involved in related issues throughout their career. Construction arbitrators generally have an in-depth knowledge of both the law and types of claims involved in the case and usually even understand the technical issues well. That is often why they were selected as the arbitrators for your dispute in the first place. However, this experience may also bring with it biases regarding the law, particular types of claims, and technical issues. Therefore, the first thing you need to investigate and consider in developing your hearing strategy is understanding the breadth and depth of the arbitrators' knowledge and biases.

A. Design Your Presentation for Your Audience: The Arbitrators

After you understand your audience, you need to walk a fine line in deciding on the complexity of the presentation. For example, you should not use the Thanksgiving dinner or house construction example to explain how a critical path method (CPM) schedule works to knowledgeable construction arbitrators, as you might to a jury or judge. It is a waste of precious hearing time and risks offending the arbitrators' intelligence. However, assuming too much knowledge or sophistication on the part of the arbitrators can be even more disastrous. While the arbitrators should, and often do, speak up and admit that they do not understand a point being made by a lawyer, expert, or fact witness, it is difficult for many to acknowledge a lack of understanding on a topic that it has been erroneously assumed the arbitrator already understands. That lack of understanding can undermine your entire case if you fail to recognize and plan for it.

Thus, when there is reason for doubt, you should err on the side of being too basic and take a reasonable chance that the arbitrators will be offended. The arbitrators are more likely to tell you that the presentation is too basic, maybe even with pride, than admit that they do not understand a concept that possibly everyone else in the room understands. You can also ask nicely if you are being too basic. With a "yes" answer, you can then safely shorten explanations and ratchet up the sophistication of the presentation. Comparatively, little is lost with a presentation that is too basic, but if the presentation is beyond the arbitrators' level of knowledge, then much can and most likely will be lost.

Counsel's judgments prior to the hearing regarding the arbitrators' sophistication and knowledge of the subject matter are just a start, to be adjusted based on the arbitrators' actions and questions during the hearing. Counsel should constantly ask themselves: Are the arbitrators bored or attentive, and what issues seem to up their attention level? Be ready to adjust your presentation based on these signs.

An arbitrator's questions are usually the best source of hints regarding what the arbitrator believes is important, as well as how to address those issues. Too often the lawyer and witness treat the arbitrators' questions as they would opposing counsel's cross-examination, meaning they attempt to dodge or evade tough questions. By dodging a question, you may think you have avoided acknowledging weakness on a difficult issue. But to the contrary, the arbitrator is more likely to conclude that the failure to answer the question means that the witness has no good answer, which is not a good outcome for your client. In addition, when the arbitrator is drafting the award, he or she is likely to remember those key questions and the witness's failure to respond to them.

As trial counsel, you cannot afford to become so enveloped in your case that you lose focus on what is most important—to convince the arbitrators to find in your client's favor. As best you can, you need to see your presentation from the viewpoint of the arbitrators. Take a step back and ask yourself. If I were an arbitrator, what would I make of the case at the outset, what would be important for me to find out, and what would convince me to decide the case in a favorable way? A frank and honest evaluation might well change your approach to the hearing and result in a more convincing presentation. A passionate, fanatical, and extreme justification of every aspect of your client's position normally is not the right decision.

Another way to get valuable input on the effectiveness of your presentation is to enlist a different lawyer in your firm to act as a mock arbitrator, listen to an abbreviated version of the case, and provide advice on what works and what does not. This process can be as detailed or streamlined as the case justifies. The resulting advice is often to simplify, by abbreviating explanations and leaving out unnecessary technical details that the arbitrators can ask about if desired but otherwise can be omitted.

B. The Theme

Every trial lawyer understands the importance of a theme in a jury or bench trial. It is no less important, and may be even more important, in the complex construction arbitration where there are multiple claims each involving a multiplicity of factual, technical, and legal issues.

The theme should be short and simple, fully supported by the facts and law, and repeated over and over from the opening brief to the closing brief. The arbitrators should be able to repeat the theme before the end of the opening statement. The big picture is particularly important in cases where the arbitrators can easily get lost in the countless facts and details that are typical of a complex construction arbitration. Do not let that happen to you—develop your theme and stick to it.

II. The Chess Clock

Without restraint and a firm arbitrator hand, counsel often overrun the time allotted for arbitration because of poor estimating on the front end and the inability to restrain themselves from offering every piece of evidence they have and cross-examining a witness on every point. The extended time typically results in a poorer presentation and adds substantially to the cost of the arbitration. In addition, trying to find additional time at the end of the scheduled hearings, given busy arbitrator, trial counsel, and witness schedules, can be very difficult. One solution to this problem is the use of a so-called chess clock.

In the chess clock approach, the estimated hearing time is divided between the parties. The arbitrators or another person tracks the time spent by each party in the proceeding, and when the party uses up its allotted time, it is done; no further direct, cross, or argument is permitted by that party.[1] The approach is very successful because it forces counsel to refrain from offering testimony, cross-examination, or argument that really is not necessary. The extraneous and irrelevant is deleted to stay within the allotted time.

For the lawyers, the first key step is making an accurate estimate of the time needed for the hearing. Underestimating the time will mean that key pieces of the case cannot be presented. In most cases, the time is divided 50/50; however, that is not always appropriate. The claimant must spend time putting on basic information about the project and contract, which gives the respondent a natural advantage. In addition, one party's case may not require as much evidence as compared to the other party. Thus, counsel should make a fair allocation of the time, not just default to an automatic 50/50 split.

III. The Timeline

Complex construction disputes are fact intensive and often include many claims and defenses, complex technical issues, and multiple parties and require substantial hearing time to try. Many counsel use a shotgun approach for their hearing tactics, hoping one of the buckshot will hit the target. Seldom is this approach successful.

1. In a case large enough that counsel each have a paralegal attending the hearing, an effective approach is to have a paralegal on each side track the time used each day and then agree on the final time allocation right after the hearing adjourns for the day.

Instead of the shotgun, use the rifle; find your best theory for each claim or defense and stick with it. In some cases, you may have a backup theory or two, but they should be severely limited. Multiple theories of liability or defenses detract from your presentation and make it less effective. If you cannot win on your strongest theory, then you seldom will prevail on a weaker backup theory.

Similarly, some counsel often present a multitude of facts and jump around the timeline of the project in a disjointed and confusing manner. Arbitrators have limited ability to absorb information and follow such presentations—it is far more difficult to process information that is not presented in a logical order. Normally, it is better to present the facts in a chronological manner to explain what happened on the project. You can then summarize the facts relevant to each claim as you present the claim. And, unless you have a bad case, narrow the facts that you present to those that are truly relevant and necessary.

In a complex arbitration involving many relevant events, you should consider providing the arbitration panel a written timeline or chronology of the major events in your opening argument or attaching it to your opening brief. The arbitrators may keep it by their side throughout the hearing and, hopefully, will refer to it regularly during the testimony to put the facts in chronological context. It can be invaluable to the arbitrators and, therefore, to your chances of prevailing.

The timeline should be simple and should not include irrelevant events; however, the timeline should not exclude key events just because they do not support your case. The events that do not support your position will most likely come into evidence anyway and may become even more important or visible because you left them out.

IV. Opening Brief, Opening Statement, or Both

Do not skip any opportunity at the beginning of the arbitration to tell the arbitrators your big-picture story and theme of the case. That means you should ask for the right to provide both an opening (prehearing) brief and opening statement if allowed by the panel. In addition, some arbitrators do better with the written word, some with a verbal presentation, and the purpose of each is a little different. If you have the opportunity to impress your theme upon the arbitrators more than once, take it—at the beginning of the case, the arbitrators' minds are a blank slate on which you are writing. After the initial impression is made, every piece of information provided thereafter simply confirms the first impression you made or—the more difficult task—changes it.

A. Opening Brief

What is the key to drafting an opening brief in a complex construction arbitration? There obviously is no one size that fits all; however, there are a few key points that should appear in most briefs. Before you begin presenting the intricacies of your case and arguing the issues, tell the arbitrators about the construction project itself, particularly the parts that are involved in the case. As stated before, the arbitrators start with a blank slate, even about something as basic as the project.

As soon as practicable, define the dispute and establish your theme. Then tell the "Reader's Digest" version of your story, including the key facts and arguments. You need to tell the story simply and credibly, and it needs to be a story you can and will prove. Overstatement and hyperbole will have an adverse effect on the outcome.

Finally, you should conclude with a discussion of damages. During the hearing, not only will the arbitrators be listening to the detailed factual testimony for its impact on liability, but also, if the claimant (or counterclaimant) prevails on liability, the panel will be judging the extent of the damages that have been proven. The panel wants to know the elements of damage and the amount the claiming party is seeking before the hearing commences. Too many lawyers focus on liability to the detriment of damages, even in the opening brief, which is generally a mistake.

B. Opening Statement

You almost always should request an opening statement, even if you wrote an opening brief. There are many purposes for the opening statement, including but not limited to (1) developing your credibility and connecting with the arbitrators, (2) implanting your theme in the arbitrators' minds, and (3) educating the arbitrators about the case by telling your story with broad brushstrokes. The opening statement should be upbeat and short. Limited graphics, photographs, and exhibits often are a good way to engage the arbitrators' interest and tell your story. Your presentation should not be a lecture but more a conversation with the arbitrators.

One effective step in commencing the opening statement is to tell the arbitrators a little about the project and the technical issues involved in the case. Most construction arbitrators are in the business because they like construction. The arbitrators probably will be interested in the building of the project and any unique technical challenges of the project. Even if the information does not relate directly to the critical issues in the case, take a few minutes to draw the arbitrators into the project and educate them. Use it to start developing your credibility and rapport with them.

It is important, however, to find a balance. Do not get lost in the details during the opening statement. Simplify, simplify, simplify. Lodge your theme and a few key dates in the arbitrators' minds. There will be plenty of time for the details and nuances.

The credibility of the lawyer is always critical, so you should never over-promise in your opening presentation and always prove what you say you are going to prove. Once you lose credibility in the arbitrators' eyes, you may be in a hole from which you cannot extricate yourself. That should be at the forefront of your mind throughout the hearing.

Everyone understands that the statements made by counsel in the opening are not evidence. However, the statements become lodged in the arbitrators' minds, only to be removed or dislodged by future evidence or actions of counsel or the parties. Thus, the opening statement is far more important than some lawyers treat it.

V. Direct Examination

Like opening briefs and statements, no single approach to direct examination fits every complex construction arbitration; however, there are some general principles that apply to most such arbitrations. Generally, direct examination is story time. You need to put together your direct case in a manner that best tells your story to the arbitrators and maintains their attention and interest. Remember that most complex construction arbitrations are long and most often boring, at least some of the time. If you see your arbitrators having a hard time keeping their eyes open, then you are not doing your job.

A. Witness Selection and Order

The selection of your first witness is critical. The first witness sets the tone for the rest of the arbitration and should be articulate but more importantly must be credible. If, after the direct of your first witness, the arbitrators do not feel you have a winning case, then you made a mistake in your selection of the leadoff batter.

If you have a credible witness who can tell the story from the beginning to the end, it normally is preferable to start with that witness rather than put the case on through numerous storytellers. When separate witnesses, whose testimony is split by cross-examination, are used to present pieces of the case chronology, it is hard to communicate the story as a whole to the arbitrators. The panel often is left trying to figure out how the pieces fit together in the end.[2]

The best first witness, however, is not always the person who knows the most facts or knows the job from start to finish. If you have a powerful witness who can win a critical issue, establish the theme of your case, or present a great overview, you may want to start with that individual.

The last witness is also important. You should close with a strong witness that can sum up your case or drive home a critical point. You need to send the arbitrators home with a feeling that you won the case. However, always remember the game may be over by the time the last witness testifies. A strong finish alone is not going to turn around a weak case, so in such cases the strong witness is better used when you are still in the game and the scales can still be tipped in your direction.

Where do you put the company executive who is articulate and persuasive but has little firsthand knowledge about the project? This witness is normally offered to provide an overview of your case and argue the issues. The tendency is to make the executive the last witness so the witness can leave the arbitrator with a good feeling about your case and client, which is important. However, as just indicated, keep in mind that by the end of the case, the arbitrators probably have (at least in large part) a pretty good idea as to which party will prevail, and if the company executive witness is exceptional, you may have wasted the benefit of that testimony. Where the executive is very persuasive and articulate, you should always consider the opening slot to set the tone and paint the big picture.

Other witnesses that you must not forget are the dirt-on-their-boots job-site workers including the superintendents, foremen, or craft laborers. They can be extremely persuasive because their testimony is often forthright, and they are not seen as having a vested interest in the outcome. However, for just that reason, they can be devastating if not fully vetted and prepared. So, more preparation time should be spent with them.

---

2. One way to avoid this is by presenting the timeline via a panel of those witnesses needed to cover the entire timeline (with the arbitrators' permission). If, for example, your client had three different project managers who did not overlap much, they can far more easily present the overall story by testifying in a panel format, getting the full timeline before the arbitrators before they are cross-examined.

B. Objections

How often should you object to testimony in a construction arbitration? The answer is: seldom. Regular objections may antagonize the arbitrators and generally serve no useful purpose. Most construction arbitrators admit almost all testimony and give it the weight it deserves. Many lawyers do not understand that the arbitrators often mean what they say, and factual testimony that is admitted into evidence in an arbitration may receive little or no weight because it deserves none. For example, hearsay almost always comes into evidence, but arbitrators understand the untrustworthiness of secondhand testimony that cannot be cross-examined and seldom will give it much, if any, weight in reaching a decision on a critical fact.

There may be instances, however, where an objection is warranted. If the testimony is very prejudicial and has no evidentiary value, you should object, unless the objection highlights the issue to your detriment. In limited cases, you may want to make a hearsay objection just to remind the arbitrators that they should be aware that this is untrustworthy hearsay evidence, particularly when it is double or triple hearsay. In addition, an objection to a leading question may be effective in some circumstances, particularly when your adversary is testifying through leading questions, the subject matter goes to the heart of the dispute, and the witness does not have much independent recollection or is a poor witness.

The bottom line is that peppering the proceeding with objections in a complex construction arbitration diminishes the value of the valid and helpful objections, antagonizes the arbitrators, and is almost always a mistake. Objections should be limited to instances where they will advance your case in the eyes of the arbitrators.

C. Arbitrators' Questions

Arbitrators can be active questioners of witnesses, more so than the judge in a nonjury trial. How should your witnesses respond to an arbitrator's question? Your witnesses must remember that the arbitrators are not opposing counsel and are not the witness's adversary, and the questions by the arbitrators are not cross-examination where some obfuscation and evasiveness may be acceptable. The witnesses should try to bond with the arbitrators and convince them of the witness's knowledge and credibility. The witnesses, therefore, should not avoid, obfuscate, or use technical jargon to evade questions from the arbitrators. The arbitrators want an answer, and witnesses are fooling themselves if they believe that any good can come from avoiding a question. Witnesses should be educated that an arbitrator question should be viewed as an opportunity—a chance to clarify something where an arbitrator needs a bit of assistance and always a chance to speak directly and frankly to the panel and enhance their credibility.

D. Witness Statements

Written witness statements that are used in lieu of direct testimony are a staple of international construction arbitration proceedings. The statements are submitted under oath prior to the hearing, and the witness is allowed a brief opportunity by way of direct testimony to introduce him- or herself, become acclimated to testifying, and address any new issues that may have arisen in the arbitration. The statements shorten the hearing time, result in more articulate testimony, and give the opposing party the ability to prepare more directed cross-examination.

Drafting a witness statement is an art. If the statement is too summarized, the arbitrators may reject it or give it little weight. If it is too dense, the arbitrators may not get through it. The witness and lawyer must strike a delicate balance between the two extremes and make the statements interesting and easy to read, yet complete enough to stand as the witness's direct testimony.

The witness, not the lawyer, must write the statement, although the lawyer can help edit and correct it. The first question for the witness is always: What part did you write? In addition, it is normally obvious to the arbitrators if a statement was written by the lawyer, and the witness seldom holds up under cross-examination when asked to defend the lawyer's words.

VI. Exhibits

A. Control the Documents

The complex construction case normally involves an overwhelming quantity of documents that *can* be included as hearing exhibits. In the past, and sometimes even today, the lawyers used to place copies of all the documents that are related in any way to the dispute into large three-ring notebooks that were so big that the arbitrators could not even pick them up. Each binder was so stuffed with documents that the arbitrators could not navigate through the notebook to find individual exhibits, the rings became misaligned, and the documents fell out. The unwieldy notebooks were then placed in bookshelves behind the arbitrators, witnesses, and all counsel to be used during the hearings. This was a disservice to the arbitrators, the witnesses, your client, and yourself.

If you are going to keep with the tradition of providing hard copies of exhibits rather than move entirely into the era of electronic exhibits, then be sure each notebook is of reasonable size and weight and is user friendly. An electronic index of exhibits showing the date, author, recipient, and subject matter summary in a searchable format is critical for the arbitrators to use during the award-writing phase as well as during the hearing. A paper version of the index may be more readily referred to during the hearing day. This advice is so basic that it may seem too elementary to mention; however, too many lawyers fail to pay attention to such obvious fundamentals.

Today, the norm is an electronic courtroom or hearing room, and yet, many construction arbitrators, often seasoned veterans who were raised on paper copies of exhibits, still prefer the hard copy so they can make notes on the documents and hold them in their hands. And, some arbitrators are simply uncomfortable with electronic exhibits. You need to determine what your arbitrators prefer and cater to their preferences. You do not want to teach the old-timer new tricks in your case. Let someone else do that and wait for the next generation of arbitrators to come along.

If you have a paperless hearing, then you need to make sure that at the end of the hearing, the arbitrators are provided a final electronic copy of all exhibits, including those first offered and admitted at the hearing, in a format with which each arbitrator is comfortable. As with the paper exhibits, a good, easily searchable electronic index is a must.

Unless there is a good reason to sort the exhibits by subject matter, exhibits normally should be in chronological order. When the arbitrators are in the award-drafting phase and are looking for a particular exhibit, it may be easier to find it if the exhibits are in date order. In addition, the arbitrators may want to review all correspondence occurring in a critical time period. Leafing through exhibits in chronological order, rather than jumping around, is more convenient, even if the exhibits are in an electronic format. Always look to make life easier for your arbitration panel.

A contrary piece of advice, because it often cuts against numbering the exhibits in date order, is to assign an exhibit number when the exhibit is first used in the case and then stick with that same number throughout. This becomes more important in cases where there are depositions taken (and thus deposition exhibits) and expert witness reports. It becomes a significant source of time-wasting confusion for all concerned when hearing exhibit 42 in other contexts is referenced as deposition exhibit 192, exhibit 27 in claimant's expert report, and exhibit 279 in respondent's expert report. In short, this is a subject well worth some thought at the outset of the case and, if the right course for the case is not clear, worth raising at the initial scheduling conference with the arbitrators for their guidance.

While there may be thousands of exhibits in a complex construction arbitration, in most arbitrations, only a small number of documents are controlling, and they are typically referred to over and over throughout the hearing. You should consider a separate notebook, even in an electronic hearing, with those documents that will be referred to repeatedly and are the foundation on which your case rests. At a minimum, when a key exhibit is presented, you should refer to the exhibit in a way that causes the arbitrator to remember it and possibly tag or mark it for future reference.

It is typical to admit all exhibits at the commencement of the hearing to avoid wasting the time to follow normal court evidentiary procedures for admission of exhibits, since in an arbitration hearing, almost every exhibit will be admitted and given the weight it deserves. The problem with this process arises when there is an exhibit that is never mentioned in the hearing testimony and is then cited as a key or controlling document in the briefing phase. Some arbitrators will give exhibits that are not mentioned in the hearing little or no weight since, by definition, an exhibit not mentioned in the hearing cannot be important. The way to avoid this problem is to admit only exhibits that are mentioned in the hearing and delete from the record those that were never referenced.

B. Using the Exhibits at the Hearing

Handling the multitude of exhibits smoothly at the hearing is critical. You must have command of your exhibits, know each one, and understand the purpose of each. A lawyer who constantly is searching for an exhibit; asking the second chair, paralegal, or assistant for help; hunting for a critical paragraph in an email; or having problems with the technology may lose the arbitrators' attention and, even worse, lose credibility and trust. It effectively transmits the message "I am not really prepared." The flow of the testimony and hearing becomes disjointed and difficult to follow. However, the first chair also needs an assistant who knows the exhibits thoroughly and understands and is proficient with the technology in use.

In direct examination, some lawyers skip all over the timeline of the project with no effort to tell a coherent and cohesive story from the beginning of the job to the end. They pick and choose their best exhibits and present them more or less randomly. This approach often makes it very difficult for an arbitrator to follow and understand the presentation. There usually is a beginning, middle, and end to every story, and that is normally, but not always, the way to tell it.

However, the mistake made by more lead counsel in a complex construction arbitration is to march through the project, day by day, referring to seemingly every email and letter written on the job. This most often assures that the arbitrators lose interest long before the end of the testimony. In addition, in this type of presentation, the arbitrators see only the trees and not the forest. There is no coherent or cohesive story.

In a complex construction arbitration, it is important to elicit direct testimony on all key emails and correspondence. As a general rule, a witness's testimony must be supported by contemporaneous documents to be believed. Arbitrators seldom trust a witness's recollection from years before without a contemporaneous written document to confirm that recollection. Some arbitrators go so far as to believe that if there is no written record anywhere at least partially corroborating a key event or discussion, it probably did not happen. The documents should be used to lead the witness through the job and as triggers for the witness's memory.

While you must rely on and use a significant number of documents in a complex construction arbitration, you must avoid the monotonous slog through interminable emails and correspondence with no break for more interesting evidence. You must find ways to break up the direct testimony to maintain the panel's interest and attention. Some ways include (1) summarizing testimony about the prior exhibits at each logical break point in the testimony; (2) referencing a chart (such as a CPM printout in a delay case), summary, graph, video, photograph, or piece of physical evidence; and (3) getting the witness out of the chair to make a sketch or perform a calculation. In the absence of any other mechanism, you can at least alert the arbitrators when a particularly significant email or letter is coming up next by simply saying as much and pausing for a dramatic moment.

C. Demonstrative Exhibits

Demonstrative exhibits can be powerful tools in making your points, engaging the arbitrators, and breaking up the mundane. Photographs can be extremely valuable in a complex construction arbitration. First, they can be used to show what happened on a particular day or in a particular time period. Second, they can help the arbitrator visualize what is shown on a drawing or described in testimony. Regardless of how vivid the picture is in your mind, the arbitrators may not be able to visualize the construction as well as you do or may visualize it incorrectly. Often, the picture in the arbitrators' minds does not match reality until a photograph is seen.

There also are special procedures that can be used with photographs. An aerial photo can be magnified to show incredible detail, such as whether the rebar was tied or installed on that particular day. Satellite imagery from Google Earth may be able to show the overall status of construction on a particular day. Time-lapse photography can show construction as it is proceeding. Use your imagination to help the arbitrators see the picture.

When you use a photograph, take your time to put it in perspective; identify the date, location, and relevance and either note that information on the photograph or have the witness so identify it. If it is an important photograph, enlarge it, put it on an easel or a display screen, and use a pointer to show the arbitrators the relevant information. Too often words are not sufficient to enable the arbitrators to appreciate the key feature of the photograph, even if they have it on the desk in front of them. Putting an arrow on the photograph pointing to the relevant part also may help. Remember, the arbitrators are not only looking at a photograph during the testimony but also often viewing it after the hearing during the award-writing phase, and you do not want to force them to search for the relevant information in the photograph.

In addition to photographs, counsel should consider using tangible objects or demonstrations as possible demonstrative exhibits or presentations. This could be a light fixture, a defective weld, a failed pipe connection, or a showing of how different soils react to water. A physical object or demonstration can be even more effective than a photograph. And, it is often more fun for the arbitrators to put their hands on the object or see the problem play out. Touching the evidence likely will make a longer-lasting impression, and the evidence will go home with the arbitrator.

Physical and computer models can also be very effective. They have become more economically viable and often can convey the story better than any other approach. Arbitrators are more likely to overlook proof problems that a lawyer might encounter with such an exhibit when in court. However, you must make sure the model accurately depicts what it is offered to show, or your credibility could be destroyed. Arbitrators will have little forgiveness if they think the model is intended to deceive.

But with the new, do not forget the old-style trial board with a photograph, map, or other information on it that you put on an easel in front of the arbitrators. It may not be as exciting as a video animation, but it can be very effective. You may be able to leave it up in front of the panel throughout the proceedings, so they see it constantly, and it becomes indelibly imprinted. Even if you cannot leave it up, you can use it constantly with different witnesses. At the end of the day, the board goes home to one of the arbitrators' offices where it sits, possibly in front of the arbitrator, until the award is written.

Videos can be helpful to show the progression of an activity. However, videos do not work well when you are showing just a single frame. The photo of the frame should be pulled from the video so the arbitrators can see it for an extended time and have it available during award writing. If you use a video, make it as short as possible to keep the arbitrators' attention—a half hour of watching brick layers is not scintillating. And, keep in mind that arbitrators are not going to watch videos in their office for an extended time as they work on the award.

Because construction arbitrations often involve a substantial amount of data, summaries, graphs, and other charts can be invaluable to summarize and portray your big picture and as a source of data to support your client's position. When the arbitrators do not buy your complete story, argument, or damages, the data may also provide them with information to use in the award writing to reach a partial award of what you are seeking.

D. Site Visits

Site visits can also be useful. It is sometimes hard for arbitrators to put the size, location, interrelationships, and other physical factors of the project into perspective from testimony or even drawings and photographs. A site visit may solve this problem. The site visit, however, should occur after the opening statements or later in the hearings. Much of the benefit of a site visit is lost if it occurs before the arbitrators understand the issues in dispute. The site visit should be free from advocacy, and there should be strict rules as to what can be said and by whom.

VII. Experts

The selection of the right expert for a construction arbitration is critical and can mean the difference between winning and losing. Many attorneys select the same expert for both litigation and arbitration matters. That can be a mistake. In construction arbitration, the arbitrators are usually experts in construction claims and may have in-depth knowledge of the technical issues. The arbitrators may have used your expert in the past or at least know the expert's reputation. In any event, once the expert begins testifying, seasoned construction arbitrators will know quickly whether the testifier is a real or faux expert. As a result, the minimum criterion for selection of an expert in a complex construction arbitration is someone who knows more about the subject on which the expert is testifying than the arbitrators. In addition, you want a witness the arbitrators respect and who is a good teacher, thorough and credible, as opposed to a slick testifier full of technical jargon. An expert with a long list of credentials who will support your position to the bitter end and never admit even the most obvious defects in your case will not serve your client well.

What are the requirements of an expert report in a complex construction arbitration? Neither Rule 26 of the Federal Rules of Civil Procedure nor similar state court rules apply to the contents of the expert report in an arbitration absent a contract provision, scheduling order, or other agreement that makes them applicable. If there is no applicable rule or agreement, then you need early on to seek a written agreement with opposing counsel or an order from the arbitrators regarding the minimum contents of the report, or you may find yourself in a dispute when the expert testifies.

Some lawyers and experts try to hide the reasoning of the expert by including minimal information and conclusory opinions in the expert report, believing that this will make it harder for the opposing counsel to effectively depose and cross-examine the expert. This is generally a mistake in a complex construction arbitration. When an objection is made at the hearing that the testimony goes beyond the expert's report and therefore should be excluded, the objection probably will not be sustained and the testimony likely will be admitted, but the arbitrators will not be pleased with the expert who was not open in the report, and the expert will lose some of his or her ever-important credibility. Further, the arbitrators likely will grant the objecting party any remedy reasonably requested that will help cure the failure of the other party to fully and fairly disclose the facts upon which the expert relied and the opinions expressed. In addition, there is always the chance that the arbitrators may exclude the opinion. So, don't gamble with the report.

The expert report first and foremost should fully provide the expert's reasoning and argument to support the ultimate conclusions. It must be simple enough for the arbitrators to understand. However, if it is superficial and conclusory, the arbitrators will readily notice that and may reject the opinions as a result. If the report is too detailed and complex, with a multitude of technical terms and jargon, the arbitrators may not understand it and reject the opinion for that reason. An appropriate balance must be struck between these two extremes.

Counsel sometime forget that the expert report may be the key document used by the arbitrators to write the award, particularly where there is no transcript. A well-written expert report can be a perfect road map and source for the arbitrators in the award-drafting phase. It can only help your cause if your expert's report is so useful that it can be utilized in this manner. As a result, the expert and lawyer should work to produce a report that will benefit the arbitrators after the hearing is over, instead of attempting to hide or disguise the basis of the expert's opinion.

There should be numerous headings in the expert report with an index that can be used effectively by the arbitrators. The supporting exhibits and backup documents should be identified by hearing exhibit and page number (not a separate numbering system adopted by the expert). Attaching the important exhibits or providing hyperlinks to the key documents can be invaluable to the arbitrators. Calculations should be laid out in detail so the arbitrators can follow them (and, if necessary, modify them readily to fit their factual findings). In other words, sufficient information should be supplied so the arbitrators can do their own calculations or analysis if they do not accept the expert's testimony in total. The use of rhetoric, overstatement, undue repetition, and confusing technical jargon is a mistake. The report should attack head on the other expert's primary arguments and provide the expert's best response to those arguments.

Credibility is a key in construction arbitration for the fact witnesses and lawyers. But it is even more important for the expert. Many construction arbitrators believe that construction experts are nothing more than hired guns or lawyers in disguise, for example, claimant's damages expert will calculate the highest dollar amount possible and defend the client's position to the bitter end. Such arbitrators may give the expert's testimony very little credence, unless the credibility of the report and testimony is sufficient to overcome the arbitrators' initial bias. As a result, your expert's report needs to disabuse the arbitrators of their inherent biases by being a credible report that references and is supported by the evidence and does not overreach.

An honest and credible expert makes a huge difference. That is particularly true in the area of damages. The goal is not to inflate the damages as high as possible and hope for a 50 percent recovery but instead to calculate the damages in a logical manner that is supported by the evidence. The first step many construction arbitrators take is to perform a sanity check of the damages claimed, and if the damages do not pass that analysis, the expert's credibility will be significantly diminished. This can result in the expert's testimony being rejected in total.

In an inaccurate belief that experts need to protect their client's position at all costs, many experts refuse to admit even the most obvious and fundamental defect, error, or fact that harms the client's position. The expert may receive great praise from the client for "hanging tough," but the expert's credibility can be significantly diminished, if not destroyed, by this. This is particularly true when the expert takes the same tack in responding to an arbitrator's questions. The ability to gracefully concede a point that will not be won and smoothly move on should be seen as a necessary capability when selecting your experts. Practice with your expert as needed to eliminate the tendency to deny the obvious and fail to exhibit honesty. Frankness and honesty are far more convincing to the arbitrator than just about anything else the expert says on the stand.

The expert often is the most articulate witness in your stable. Do not waste the expert's talent by providing summary, overreaching, or boring testimony or simply having the expert repeat facts already in evidence through other testimony. The expert is often your best chance to have an articulate storyteller pull together your case in a cohesive and coherent manner and move the arbitrators to find in your client's favor. Use the expert correctly and effectively.

A time-saving technique used frequently is to let experts testify by way of a PowerPoint presentation instead of a traditional direct examination (remaining subject to a traditional cross-examination). This can be very effective in that it can let an experienced expert move smoothly through a planned presentation rather than having to respond to a long series of rehearsed questions. If used, however, be sure to give the arbitrators a hard copy of the presentation in advance so that they can take notes directly on the slides for future reference. Also keep in mind that listening to one person talk on a technical subject for an extended time can be both boring and difficult to follow. So even where the "presentation in lieu of direct examination" concept is adopted, occasional questions from counsel can effectively be used to break up the testimony, such as when changing topics or summarizing the key opinion on a topic, and makes for a more interesting and understandable presentation.

Finally, "simplify" is again the watchword. The expert's conclusions must be stated in a fashion that the arbitrators understand. For example, the scheduling expert may provide many pages of electronic CPM schedules and other documents to support the opinions regarding delays, and those documents should be made part of the record in evidence. However, the expert needs to have summary documents that simplify the expert's conclusions, for example, X delay days for delay no. 1, Y days for delay no. 2, and so forth. If the arbitrators are not clear on the bottom-line opinions and do not understand the bases for them, the arbitrators are likely to reject the testimony. Unlike a jury or a judge with no technical background, most arbitrators will not select one expert's opinion over another simply because the expert is a better testifier. Most arbitrators need to understand the basis of the expert's opinion and agree with it before they will adopt it as the basis for the award.

A. "Hot-Tubbing" or Joint Testimony of Opposing Experts

In a lengthy arbitration hearing, days, weeks, or even months may pass in between competing experts' testimony. The opposing experts' testimony may or may not address all the issues raised by the other expert, although both are addressing the same subject matter, such as delays or damages. This gap in time can make it very difficult for arbitrators to put the opposing experts' views together and compare and contrast their approaches to what is often a multiplicity of technical issues. One solution to this problem that is being adopted more often in recent years utilizes arbitration's flexibility to fashion a procedure to fit the situation, via joint testimony by the opposing experts on the same subject matter, sometimes colloquially referred to as "hot-tubbing."

In practice, there are many versions of hot-tubbing. The one common element to all is for the experts to testify in the same time frame, usually after all fact witness testimony is completed. Depending on the procedure adopted, there will be expert reports in the record and direct examination of (or a presentation from) each expert, followed by seriatim cross-examination of each expert.

A key component in the process is an opportunity for questions from the arbitration panel that are posed to one or both experts, with an opportunity for the other expert to address the same question or reply. This provides a great opportunity for the arbitrators to raise the issues that seem most significant to them and obtain some "give and take" between the experts that allows the arbitrators to compare and contrast their respective opinions directly. There is a significant benefit for the arbitrators to see the experts at the same time and have each expert confront the points made by the other expert just a few moments before. With this process, the experts cannot effectively dodge issues raised by the other, and it is easier to judge the validity of each expert's arguments. For counsel, it also provides valuable insight as to which issues the panel is most concerned about, allowing them to be further addressed during the remainder of the hearing as needed.

VIII. Specific Issues in Construction Arbitrations

A. Damages

Many arbitrators believe that the weakest part of most hearing presentations in a complex construction arbitration is the damages. Counsel typically concentrate on the liability portion of their case and make a very good presentation on that part but then fall flat on damages. Construction damages often are imprecise and hard to prove, particularly demonstrating the cause and effect between the entitlement and the incurred damages. Rather than devoting more time, effort, and ingenuity to the challenge, claimant's counsel tends to offer an expert's broad-brush opinion, concluding with an outlandishly high number that does not address the cause and effect of each claim. Respondent's counsel then does the same in the other direction, leaving the arbitrators to figure out a reasonable answer.

Counsel should not leave the arbitrators in this position. An outlandish damages claim by the claimant is unlikely to increase the amount the panel actually awards the claimant. To the contrary, it more likely will cause the claimant to lose credibility and result in a reduction of the award. The amount of damages claimed should be rational, reasonable, and provable. A sanity check should always be performed because the arbitrators will doubtless perform one.

The respondent should do the same from the other side. Many respondent's lawyers simply snipe at the claimant's damages calculation, pointing out that it is exaggerated, that there is a lack of proof to support it, and that it uses an invalid theory of damages or contains other errors. However, if the arbitrators find for the claimant on liability, they probably will not award zero dollars. Thus, the respondent is generally well advised to offer its alternative calculation of damages, assuming it does not prevail on liability. Many lawyers feel this may be perceived by the arbitrators as an admission or a sign of weakness, so they elect not to offer an alternative to the arbitrators. This may be true in a jury trial but is often an error in arbitration. The typical construction arbitrator is sophisticated enough to understand that providing an alternative calculation is an effort to help the arbitrators and not an admission of weak entitlement. The alternative calculation will not affect the arbitrators' ruling on liability but may result in a lower award if liability is found.

Both parties should consider what the arbitrators will do if they do not find 100 percent for either party or reject both damages calculations and should provide sufficient, detailed information that will allow the panel to calculate damages in a different amount. The more you facilitate the arbitrators in doing this, the better off your client is likely to be.

B. The Total Cost Approach

One damages theory that is utilized all too often in construction cases is the total cost approach or a variation of the total cost approach (such as modified total cost). While the total cost approach is uniformly disfavored in the law (which treats it as a "last resort" method), some form of it can be helpful in a construction arbitration, particularly if there is no better approach available. The first step to acceptance of a total cost approach by the arbitrators is to apply it to the smallest activity possible. For example, limiting a total cost claim to the overrun in excavation costs in an impacted area, or the cost overrun on the particular type of pipe that is impacted, will be more easily accepted than claiming the total overrun on the entire project or even the entire overrun on excavation or piping. The second step is to consider seriously whether to convert to a modified total cost approach by removing identified errors in the bid and contractor-caused inefficiencies. There are almost always some errors or inefficiencies, or that is likely to be the arbitrators' view, so taking the initiative to identify and quantify them yourself is often advantageous as compared to leaving the arbitrators to figure it out. Finally, provide some other alternative approach, such as an independent estimate, to provide as much support as possible for the modified total cost approach.

If there is a better approach than total cost that is practicable, use it. The total cost approach has such negative connotations with most arbitrators (who are well aware of its disfavored place under the law), it is most often best utilized to provide backup and supplementation of some other form of damages analysis. There *is* an advantage to showing that your client actually incurred losses on the impacted activities. This prompts the arbitrators to ask themselves in deliberations just what caused those losses, other than the claimed events, and how the arbitrators should quantify them.

C. Lost Productivity

Lost productivity is a frequently seen part of the claimant's damages in a complex construction arbitration. Counsel frequently do an even poorer job proving this element of damages than the other portions. In part, this is because these damages are inherently hard to prove. Typical means of proof are an analysis by a construction claims consultant that uses the total cost approach, published lost productivity rates, estimates, or a measured mile analysis that seldom compares apples to apples.

Expert testimony is almost always necessary for proving loss of productivity, but the proof of lost productivity should not depend solely on an expert's cold calculations. The arbitrators understand that the expert can make the numbers come out just about anywhere they want and so often do not trust them. The fact witnesses must make the arbitrators feel the lost productivity before the expert takes the stand. If the arbitrators have concluded that the claimant has been significantly impacted, then they are just looking for help from the expert to establish the amount of lost productivity.

The fact witness evidence may involve the witness walking through repetitive instances of problems explaining how each instance impacted the work activities affected. Superintendents, foremen, or craft laborers who were close to the actual activity involved make the best witnesses for this. Make the arbitrators feel the workers' pain in the field. This approach almost unavoidably involves repetitious testimony, reciting similar event after similar event, so it has some risk of aggravating the arbitrators. But taking that risk may be necessary to maximize the recovery. Use reasonable judgment to determine when to switch from detailed descriptions of each instance of disruption to a more summary presentation of how widespread the problem was.

Conversely, from the respondent's side, the respondent must paint the picture as best as possible that this is a type of problem that is encountered regularly on every job, is already included in the contract price, was of negligible scope and reach on this project, or is otherwise just the claimant blowing smoke.

D. Delay Analysis and Delay Damages

Damages for delay are another typical component of damages claims in a complex construction arbitration. The legal principles and practicalities of proving delays and delay damages are addressed in numerous books and articles, so the discussion here is limited to a few thoughts with particular application to proving delay and delay damages in a complex construction arbitration.

Delay claims are complicated, and juries and judges without prior experience in delay cases often do not understand a complex delay analysis. As a result, they most often default to adopting the presentation of the most credible expert. As discussed earlier, construction arbitrators are less likely to take that approach. Construction arbitrators almost always have had experience with numerous delay claims and understand what CPM and time impact analyses are and how they work. They often will not just accept either expert's position in full but be more inclined to do some rudimentary analysis of their own, generally borrowing from both side's experts. At the least, they may do enough of their own assessment to feel comfortable that the experts' analyses reflect the real delays to the project.

As a result, a delay presentation to seasoned construction arbitrators is different from what would be presented in court. In all venues, you must prove that your expert is the most credible by demonstrating that the expert performed a thorough analysis and considered all relevant facts, and you must assist the expert in making an excellent presentation on the witness stand. In a complex construction arbitration, however, the expert must go further and summarize the analysis in a form that the panel can use in making their own decisions regarding what caused a particular delay to the critical path, the extent of that delay, and the impact of any concurrent delays.

Concurrent delay is a particularly complex concept and quite often presents a difficult issue in delay claims. In a complex construction arbitration, the delay expert should (1) explain his or her definition of the term "concurrent delay," for this differs significantly among experts, lawyers, and arbitrators; (2) identify the concurrent delays in the schedule and why the expert considers them to be concurrent delays; and (3) explain how the expert treated the concurrent delay in the analysis and how this affects the final opinion as to the cause of the delay in completion of the project.

Many delay experts tend to speak quickly and move through their analysis hurriedly. This in part seems to be a reaction to being told in the past that delay analysis presentations are boring when too much detail is presented. Additionally, the expert knows the facts and the analysis and tends to assume the arbitrators are keeping up. However, when construction arbitrators are trying to understand the analysis presented deeply enough to perform their own assessment and do not know the facts as well as the expert, a rapid presentation can be a serious mistake. Instead, slow down your delay expert and make sure your arbitrators are following the analysis.

As with other technical testimony that can quickly become dry and boring, try to make the delay analysis come to life. An expert walking through schedule after schedule pointing to activity bars and reading names, nodes, and dates from CPM charts becomes an invitation for attention to wander. Photographs, plan views of the construction site, charts, labor plots, and other demonstrative exhibits can make the delay presentation become real and much more interesting. Break up the expert's testimony to eliminate the boredom.

A sanity check of any delay analysis, as with the damages analysis, is a must. An analysis showing the contractor completing before it actually started or a critical path that runs through a $1,000 activity for a year is a dead giveaway to construction arbitrators that the expert is overreaching and the analysis is not credible.

Finally, always remember that when the award is being written, the arbitrators will be sitting in a room by themselves assessing the delay issues. So, leave the arbitrators with an expert report and analysis that they can follow and use in reaching their decision.

IX. Cross-Examination

Like the opening statement and direct examination, the key to effective cross-examination in a complex construction arbitration starts with an appreciation of the audience. Construction arbitrators understand the games played in cross-examination and can see through superficial cross-examination tactics that try to make a witness look bad, without providing information that will aid the arbitrators in deciding the key issues. The arbitrators may appreciate your court-honed cross-examination skills, and your client may shower you with praise for your artful performance; the question, however, is whether the cross-examination moved the arbitrators closer to a favorable award for your client. Construction arbitrators want cross-examinations to focus on demonstrating the truth or falsity of the critical factual assertions, not dazzle them with fancy footwork on irrelevant points. In selecting areas for cross-examination, prudent lawyers should ask themselves whether a successful cross on a point will move the needle in their direction. If not, that point is likely not a good one for cross-examination and should be dropped.

Cross-examination should not be long and drawn out, a point made in every article on the subject that is just as applicable in arbitration as it is in court. A good cross-examination is usually short and successfully attacks on the relevant issues. Make your important points and sit down.

Some cross-examiners take their notes from direct examination and go back through every point addressed on direct, one by one, trying to score as many points as they can, both major and minor. Even if the cross-examiner is successful on many issues, the cross-examination will almost always be boring, lose its punch, mix the relevant testimony with irrelevant, and fail to move the needle. An arbitration is not a basketball game where the team with the most points wins.

Good cross-examination attacks the issues on which the case turns, the ones that the arbitrator must decide in your favor for you to prevail. The experienced arbitrator understands what cross is relevant to the decision and what is extraneous, irrelevant, and mainly for show or client relations. The latter portion may help you with a jury or make your client feel good about your abilities, but seldom will it advance the likelihood that your client will prevail. It may instead have a negative effect on the outcome of the case.

Effective cross-examination in arbitration is not about browbeating an honest and sympathetic witness into a bloody pulp to try to force them to agree with you. Arbitrators generally have seen this done many times and indeed may even have done this in their own past cross-examinations. While you are attacking the sympathetic witness, the arbitrators probably are thinking how they would answer the questions and put you in your place. Normally, you should attack only the witness who appears arrogant, boastful, a liar, or otherwise unsympathetic or who must be destroyed for you to prevail. Otherwise, obtain the agreements you can get from the witness, succinctly make the points that you can, and move on to the next witness.

A construction arbitration generally involves countless facts, as the events in dispute often unfolded over a period of months or even years. Many witnesses remember all the facts on direct but cannot remember a single fact on cross-examination. The arbitrator understands what is happening. In those instances, attacking the witness's bias by demonstrating that the witness no longer has a memory is fair game. However, once you have made your point, sit down.

It is almost too basic to say that you should be prepared with a document to refresh the witness's memory where the witness claims a lack of knowledge on cross-examination. Refreshing the witness's recollection on several occasions will have a favorable impact on the arbitrators. In addition, after you have done this several times, you may have trained the witness to believe you have a document to support every question you ask. This sometimes causes the witness to cave and agree with you on an important question where the supporting document does not exist. This is particularly true of witnesses whose direct examination consisted largely of leading questions, where the witness just confirmed the lawyer's statements without demonstrating any independent recollection.

No witness in a complex construction dispute has personal knowledge of all the facts, but many testify as if they do. Arbitrators generally are not rigorous in limiting witnesses to testifying to events clearly within their personal knowledge. It is usually worthwhile in cross-examination to distinguish those facts of which the witness has personal knowledge from those the witness has only heard from the lawyer or others.

If you can, make the other party's witness your witness by getting the witness to agree with you where there are points of agreement. However, this is valuable only if the agreed facts are important facts. Getting a witness to agree with you on numerous irrelevant facts may perversely build the witness's credibility, without gaining any ground for you in proving your case.

X. Transcript

Do you want a hearing transcript? Many construction lawyers opt out of a transcript because the ability to appeal the award is very limited in arbitration and the cost is significant, so the lawyer believes there is no need for a transcript. That decision may be regretted in retrospect. The lack of a transcript will almost assuredly eliminate whatever ability might otherwise exist to successfully appeal an egregious award, should that be the outcome.

The primary value of a transcript, however, is not for an appeal but for the arbitrators to use in drafting the award. Generally, the award is completed more than 60 days after the testimony and sometimes much longer.[3] The arbitrators' memory may have faded by the time the award is drafted, or the arbitrators may have missed a key point or nuance in the testimony. Some arbitrators take almost verbatim notes, while others take few notes and rely on their memory and the documents in evidence. The longer the hearing, the harder it is to precisely recall all the testimony and the more a transcript is valuable to the arbitrators.

Regardless of the arbitrators' notetaking style and ability, they may have trouble deciding a critical factual issue without a transcript by the time the award is actually being written and recollection of the testimony is no longer fresh. If the parties want a reasoned award, particularly a detailed one with findings of fact, a transcript is imperative. That said, economics may dictate this decision. If the cost of the transcript is significant in comparison to the amount in dispute, the answer may be obvious. In any event, do not automatically default to not having a transcript just because you are in arbitration.

XI. Closing Briefs, Closing Arguments, or a Hybrid

A. Closing Arguments

While complex construction arbitrations are fact and document intensive, by the end of the hearing, the arbitrators have heard, often over and over, and fully understand each party's big-picture positions and themes of the case. Another repetition in a closing argument, even with increased passion and intense rhetoric, seldom helps the arbitrators decide the dispute. Much more often, the answers for the arbitrators are buried in the myriad of details, which are not easily conveyed in a closing argument. As a result, many arbitrators prefer not to have closing arguments at the end of the hearing. They want to get back to their office and dig into the details that will actually decide the case.

---

3. The AAA Construction Industry Rules, among others, require the award to be issued within 30 days after the record is closed, absent an agreed extension. But in most cases the record is not closed immediately after the hearing but left open to accommodate various types of posthearing submissions and briefing.

If closing arguments are allowed, however, how should you handle this? Remember your audience is not a jury, and the arbitrators are not looking for the black hat—they know that all parties in a complex construction arbitration are usually wearing hats in shades of gray. The arbitrators are looking for your most persuasive arguments on the difficult issues in the case, not rhetoric, passion, outrage, repeating the obvious, or answering the easy or irrelevant questions. In fact, rhetoric, passion, and outrage can easily backfire on you, unless there is a real basis for it. Construction arbitrations are about contract disputes where both parties usually have legitimate positions. People may have made mistakes in the course of project execution, but they are usually honest mistakes. Seldom do cases involve intentional misconduct or bad faith that would justify passionate emotions, and when they do, both parties are often worthy of such emotions. So, leave the outrage behind and rely on common sense and logic to make your case.

Do not rely solely on your verbal skills in your closing. Take advantage of the exhibits, particularly the demonstrative exhibits. Use the key photographs, charts, and graphs to make your points. Do not read verbatim what the correspondence says. Instead, show the arbitrators on a screen or board the key phrases from the correspondence that prove your case. Make your closing argument interesting and compelling, not "here we go again" with the same old rhetoric.

One advantage of having closing arguments is the opportunity for the arbitrators to ask questions and seek to clarify issues and facts that they do not understand or possibly test tentative findings that they are considering. But the arbitrators generally need to think through the key decisions to be made before the oral argument and come prepared with questions to make closing argument effective. That is a tough ask at the conclusion of a long hearing.

When an arbitrator asks a question in closing argument, it normally is because the arbitrator genuinely wants to know the answer. So, answer the question head on as best you can. Treat the question as an opportunity to move the needle in your favor. Do not be evasive and confusing, even if your answer to the question is not great.

B. Closing Briefs

Complex construction arbitrations generally involve significant factual disputes, scheduling issues, damages issues, and legal issues. In such cases the parties should almost always opt for written posthearing briefs, and most arbitrators will demand them. The briefs should have a fact section. You should provide citations to the record to support every fact mentioned except the obvious or clearly undisputed facts. Never force the arbitrators to search for an exhibit to support your argument or asserted fact. Hyperlinks in the brief can be very helpful to the arbitrators in this regard, if they take the arbitrators directly to the document being referenced. A Word version of the brief should be provided so the arbitrators can borrow from it when writing the award. The more headings, the better, and a table of contents is valuable to provide the arbitrators a road map for locating particular findings and arguments when drafting the award or deliberating with the panel.

Do not ignore the difficult issues or bad facts. The other party will highlight them, and they will not go away. The arbitrators need to hear your best argument in response.

Construction arbitrators generally know the basic principles of construction law, and legal citations to commonly accepted principles are unnecessary. However, if you have a case directly on point, the case law is not well settled, or the applicable law is significantly different from that of other jurisdictions, you need to provide citations and legal analysis to the arbitrators. At least a one-line summary of every case cited should be included. The case cites in the brief should be hyperlinked, or electronic or hard copies should be provided to the arbitrators (in accordance with their preferences). Many arbitrators do not have easy access to a law library or the likes of Lexis, nor do they have the desire to search for the cases.

Generally, you should seek an opportunity for a reply brief, even a very short one, to answer issues raised by the other party but not anticipated by you. The purpose of your reply brief is not to repeat what you said in your closing brief. Doing so will only result in the arbitrators possibly missing the key points of your reply brief.

C. Hybrid Closings

There are several hybrid approaches to closing the arbitration. The arbitrators may have firm preferences as to what will work best for them or may give counsel an opportunity to suggest an approach that best fits the case.

At the end of the hearing, the arbitrators sometimes provide questions to be briefed. However, the arbitrators often do not know what questions to ask until they have spent some time in deliberations or begin drafting the award. A better approach is for the questions to come after the closing briefs and after the arbitrators have a sense of where the award is likely going. The questions can be responded to in the reply brief, but often a more productive approach is to have closing oral arguments focused on the issues raised in the arbitrators' questions. This allows the parties an opportunity to directly address the issues the arbitrators find important and allows the arbitrators to fully explore those issues with counsel. In any event, an oral argument that is focused on the arbitrators' questions is likely to be much more efficient and useful to the arbitrators than simply giving each side an hour or so for closing arguments at the conclusion of the evidence.

Remember always that construction arbitration is a form of alternative dispute resolution, and while usually governed by a set of arbitration rules, those rules are intentionally flexible and can be readily adapted to the circumstances of the case. The arbitrators and parties are not stuck with much in the way of mandatory rules and can use the inherent flexibility of arbitration to design a closing that is most effective for the case.

CHAPTER 9

Appeals from Arbitration Awards

KATHLEEN OLDEN BARNES[1]

This chapter addresses the potential ways a litigant can challenge an arbitration award. In some cases, where the rules so provide, the award may be challenged by way of a formal appeal to an appellate arbitration panel. In all other cases, the only means available for challenging the award is to do so *collaterally*, by attacking the award in courts through a motion to vacate or modify the award. This chapter addresses each of these methods.

When reading this chapter, it is important to keep in mind that the law actively discourages courts from reviewing and second-guessing the merits of an arbitral award. This is true for the Federal Arbitration Act, as well as the Uniform Arbitration Act, on which many state arbitration acts are based, and the New York Convention on the Enforcement of Foreign Arbitral Awards, which governs many international awards.

The U.S. Supreme Court, in *Stolt-Nielsen S.A. v. AnimalFeeds International Corp.*, acknowledged that parties waive "the procedural rigor and appellate review of the courts in order to realize the benefits of private dispute resolution: lower costs, greater efficiency and speed, and the ability to choose expert adjudicators to resolve specialized disputes."[2] In other words, when parties choose arbitration for the resolution of disputes, they also are choosing the arbitrator as the final finder of fact and law for the dispute.

---

1. The author thanks Brittney Weisner for her invaluable contribution to the research and drafting of this chapter.

2. Stolt-Nielsen S.A. v. AnimalFeeds Int'l Corp., 559 U.S. 662, 681–82, 685 (2010).

The intent of the Federal Arbitration Act (FAA) is to avoid a full "on the merits" judicial review of an arbitration award. Any litigant who undertakes a campaign to reverse, vacate, or modify an award faces long odds.[3]

I. Appellate Arbitration Panels

It has become increasingly common for arbitral bodies to offer an optional procedure for an appellate-type review by a separate panel of arbitrators.[4] For example, both the American Arbitration Association (AAA)[5] and JAMS[6] offer optional sets of appellate rules. Similarly, the CPR International Institute for Conflict Prevention & Resolution (CPR) has promulgated a set of rules called the CPR Appellate Arbitration Procedure, which parties may adopt at any time by written agreement without regard to whether the arbitration was administered by the CPR.[7] A table summarizing the key differences between the optional appellate rules promulgated by AAA, JAMS, and CPR is set forth in an appendix to this chapter.

Such appellate arbitration panels, sometimes called "nonjudicial appeals,"[8] are an exception to the general rule that arbitration awards are not subject to further review on the merits. Like arbitration itself, the appellate panels are a creature of contract. They do not come into play unless the parties have agreed, either in advance of or during the arbitration, that the award will be subject to review by an appellate panel of arbitrators. This is typically accomplished by

---

3. *See* David A. Senter & Andrew L. Chapin, *Statutory Grounds for Challenging Arbitration Awards*, 19 Constr. Law. 30 (1999) (summarizing the low success rates that litigants face when challenging awards).

4. John W. Hinchey & Troy L. Harris, 1 International Construction Arbitration Handbook 735, § 12.2 (Thomson Reuters 2018); Mauro Rubino-Sammartano, *The Fall of a Taboo: Review of the Merits of an Award by an Appellate Arbitration Panel and a Proposal for an International Appellate Court*, 20(4) J. Int'l Arb. 387 (2003).

5. American Arbitration Association Optional Appellate Rules (Nov. 1, 2013) [hereinafter AAA Appellate Rules].

6. JAMS Optional Arbitration Appeal Procedures (June 2003) [hereinafter JAMS Appellate Procedures].

7. CPR Appellate Arbitration Procedure, Rule 1.1, https://drs.cpradr.org/rules/arbitration/appellate-arbitration-procedure.

8. Brent O.E. Clinkscale et al., *Nonjudicial Appeals of Arbitral Awards*, 63 Fed. Law. 36 (2016).

incorporating one of the optional sets of the appellate arbitration rules just discussed.[9]

The appellate arbitration rules are designed to provide an expedited appellate review, as opposed to the lengthy process for appeal of the judgments of most state and federal courts. For example, the AAA Appellate Rules require a notice of appeal to be filed within 30 days from the date of the underlying award, with the appellant's initial brief due no later than 21 days after the notice of appeal.[10] Appellee's answering brief is due in another 21 days, and appellant's reply brief, if any, is due ten days later.[11] Other than one seven-day extension "for good cause shown," extensions will be permitted only "in extraordinary circumstances."[12] The decision of the appellate panel is due 30 days from the date of the last brief.[13] The JAMS Appellate Procedures are even more expedited, providing that the entire process, "absent any cause for delay, will be completed in 21 days."[14]

Both major sets of appellate arbitration rules set forth procedures for selecting and appointing the appellate panel. Under the AAA Appellate Rules, the panel is made up of three arbitrators selected using the same strike-list method used by the AAA for the selection of arbitrators, unless the parties have already agreed on the tribunal.[15] Under the JAMS Appellate Procedures, the case manager will seek the agreement of the parties as to the selection of the panel, and if the parties cannot agree, the case manager "will appoint an Appeal Panel."[16]

Regarding the grounds for the appeal, the AAA Appellate Rules permit a party to "appeal on the grounds that the Underlying Award is based upon: (1) an error of law that is material and prejudicial; or (2) determinations of fact that are clearly erroneous."[17] The JAMS Appellate Procedures provide that "[t]he Appeal Panel will apply the same standard of review that the first-level

---

9. *Id.* at 39. *See also* AAA Appellate Rules, *supra* note 5, Rule A-1; JAMS Appellate Procedures, *supra* note 6, Procedure (a).

10. AAA Appellate Rules, *supra* note 5, Rules A-3, A-17(a).

11. *Id.* Rule A-17(b), (d).

12. *Id.* Rule A-17(g).

13. *Id.* Rule A-19(a).

14. JAMS Appellate Procedures, *supra* note 6, Optional Arbitration Appeal Overview.

15. AAA Appellate Rules, *supra* note 5, Rule A-5.

16. JAMS Appellate Procedures, *supra* note 6, Procedure (a).

17. AAA Appellate Rules, *supra* note 5, Rule A-10.

appellate court in the jurisdiction would apply to an appeal from the trial court decision."[18]

At least one U.S. district court has upheld a ruling by an appellate arbitration panel acting under the AAA Appellate Rules. In *Hamilton v. Navient Solutions, LLC*, the District Court for the Southern District of New York refused to vacate an award issued by an appellate panel that had reversed the original award.[19] The court upheld the award using the traditional standards under the FAA for confirming or vacating an award, noting that the "court's role in reviewing an arbitral award is 'narrowly limited,' and requires 'great deference' to the arbitrators' determination."

II. FAA Grounds for Vacating an Arbitration Award

The starting point in discussing appellate review of arbitration awards is that parties cannot contractually expand the scope of *judicial* (as opposed to *non-judicial*) review of an arbitration award. In *Hall Street Associates LLC v. Mattel Inc.*, the U.S. Supreme Court held that the grounds enumerated in the FAA for vacating and modifying an arbitral award are exclusive and cannot be expanded through contractual agreement.[20]

The FAA provides four statutory grounds for vacating an arbitral award: (1) where the award was procured by corruption, fraud, or undue means; (2) where there was evident partiality or corruption; (3) where the arbitrators were guilty of misconduct in refusing to postpone the arbitration hearing or in refusing to hear material evidence; and (4) where the arbitrators exceeded or imperfectly executed their powers.[21] While this chapter focuses on the statutory grounds set forth in the FAA, it is worth noting that most, if not all, states have enacted their own arbitration laws that may provide somewhat differing grounds for vacating an award.[22]

---

18. JAMS Appellate Procedures, *supra* note 6, Procedure (d).

19. Hamilton v. Navient Sols., LLC, No. 18 Civ. 5432 PAC, 2019 WL 633066, at *3 (S.D.N.Y. Feb. 14, 2019).

20. Hall Street Assocs. LLC v. Mattel Inc., 552 U.S. 576 (2008).

21. 9 U.S.C. § 10(a).

22. For a discussion of obtaining a review on the merits of an arbitration award under certain state arbitration laws, see Conna A. Weiner, *Getting the Arbitration That You Want: Appeals? Really? Tips for Post-Arbitration Review*, ABA Prac. Points (June 8, 2018), https://www.americanbar.org/groups/litigation/committees/commercial-business/practice/2018/getting-the-arbitration-you-want-appeals-really/.

Courts apply a limited standard of review when hearing a motion to vacate an arbitration award, regardless of the ground that is being alleged as the basis for vacatur.[23] Some courts have gone as far as to describe the standard of review as "severely limited,"[24] and the U.S. Supreme Court has said that courts may vacate an arbitrator's decision "only in very unusual circumstances."[25] The purpose of this very limited review is to "maintain arbitration's essential virtue of resolving disputes straightaway" and to prevent a "cumbersome and time-consuming judicial review process."[26]

The limited review is "confined to determining whether or not one of the [four] grounds specified in 9 U.S.C.A. § 10 for vacating an award exists."[27] A mere mistake of law or fact or the arbitrator's failure to correctly apply the law to the facts is insufficient to vacate an arbitration award.[28] Rather, an award may be set aside only if the party bringing the motion can make a clear showing that one of the four grounds enumerated in section 10 of the FAA exists. In addition to facing a limited review, the party bringing a motion to vacate faces a heavy burden as all presumptions will be in favor of enforcing the award.[29]

Because of the limited scope of review and the moving party's burden, the decision to incur the costs for a transcript of the hearings and to request that the arbitrator issue a reasoned award is critical. In the absence of a transcript of the arbitration hearing and a reasoned award, a court is likely to be unable to determine the basis for the arbitrator's award, making even the very limited appellate review under the FAA impracticable.[30]

A. Corruption, Fraud, or Undue Means

The first statutory ground for vacatur (section 10(a)(1)) is where the award was procured by corruption, fraud, or undue means.[31] The terms "fraud" and "corruption" describe dishonest, illegal, and deceptive conduct. The term "undue

---

23. Major League Baseball Players Ass'n v. Garvey, 532 U.S. 504, 509 (2001).

24. Off. of Supply Gov't of Rep. of Korea v. N.Y. Nav. Co., Inc., 469 F.2d 377, 379 (2nd Cir. 1972).

25. First Options of Chi., Inc. v. Kaplan, 514 U.S. 938, 942 (1995).

26. Hall Street Assocs. LLC v. Mattel, Inc., 552 U.S. 576, 588 (2008).

27. *Id.*

28. Kergosien v. Ocean Energy, Inc., 390 F.3d 346, 352 (5th Cir. 2004); Federated Dep't Stores, Inc. v. J.V.B. Indus., Inc., 894 F.2d 862, 866 (6th Cir. 1990).

29. *See* Oxford Health Plans LLC v. Sutter, 569 U.S. 564, 568–69 (2013) ("A party seeking relief under [section 10(a)(4)] bears a heavy burden.").

30. *E.g.*, *Federated Dep't Stores*, 894 F.2d at 868.

31. 9 U.S.C. § 10(a)(1).

means" is interpreted in conjunction with the words "fraud" and "corruption."[32] Courts generally require "proof of intentional misconduct" or "bad faith" or "behavior that is immoral if not illegal" to support a finding of undue means.[33]

Section 10(a)(1) is invoked much less frequently than the other grounds available under the FAA. Of course, this is a good thing. Section 10(a) provides a necessary guardrail for reviewing courts that have been directed by Congress to give unusual deference and a hands-off approach to arbitration awards. Section 10(a)(1) permits courts to ensure that parties who consent to arbitration are not deprived of their right to a full and fair hearing before an impartial finder of fact and law.

Generally, reviewing courts have applied the following test to determine whether an arbitration award should be vacated due to fraud or corruption: (1) "the movant must establish the fraud by clear and convincing evidence"; (2) "the fraud must not have been discoverable upon the exercise of due diligence prior to or during the arbitration"; and (3) "the person seeking to vacate the award must demonstrate that the fraud materially related to an issue in the arbitration."[34]

Finally, FAA § 10(a)(1) provides that the award must be *procured* by corruption, fraud, or undue means. The circuits are split as to the interpretation of this statutory language. Some circuits require the moving party to establish that the corruption, fraud, or undue means "caused the award to be given."[35] Others require the moving party to show a "nexus" between the conduct and the award.[36] The movant need not, however, "establish that the result of the proceedings would have been different had the fraud not occurred."[37]

---

32. PaineWebber Grp., Inc. v. Zinsmeyer Trusts P'ship, 187 F.3d 988, 991 (8th Cir. 1999).

33. *Id.*

34. Bonar v. Dean Witter Reynolds, Inc., 835 F.2d 1378, 1383 (11th Cir. 1988); *see also* Int'l Bhd. of Teamsters, Local 519 v. United Parcel Serv., Inc., 335 F.3d 497, 503 (6th Cir. 2003); Renard v. Ameriprise Fin. Servs., Inc., 778 F.3d 563, 569 (7th Cir. 2015); MCI Constructors, LLC v. City of Greensboro, 610 F.3d 849, 858 (4th Cir. 2010); A.G. Edwards & Sons, Inc. v. McCollough, 967 F.2d 1401, 1404 (9th Cir. 1992).

35. *See PaineWebber*, 187 F.3d at 994 ("there must be some causal relation between the undue means and the arbitration award"); *A.G. Edwards & Sons*, 967 F.2d at 1403 ("the statute requires a showing that the undue means caused the award to be given").

36. Forsythe Int'l, S.A. v. Gibbs Oil Co. of Tex., 915 F.2d 1017, 1022 (5th Cir. 1990) (the phrase "procured by fraud" to be read as "requiring a nexus between the alleged fraud and the basis for the panel's decision").

37. *See* Odeon Cap. Grp. LLC v. Ackerman, 864 F.3d 191, 196 (2d Cir. 2017); *Bonar*, 835 F.2d at 1383.

B. Evident Partiality

The second statutory ground for vacating an arbitration award (section 10(a)(2)) is "where there was evident partiality or corruption in the arbitrators."[38] As a practical matter, evident partiality generally arises from the arbitrator's failure to disclose a relationship with one of the parties. The seminal case is *Commonwealth Coatings Corp. v. Continental Casualty Co.*,[39] where the U.S. Supreme Court determined that evident partiality existed where one of the arbitrators had a previous financial relationship with a party that was not disclosed during the arbitration.[40] The Court did not find evidence of actual bias on the part of the arbitrator. Rather, the Court's decision was based on the need to prevent any appearance or impression of bias. Justice Black, writing for the Court in a plurality decision, explained that arbitrators "not only must be unbiased but also must avoid even the appearance of bias in order to maintain confidence in the arbitration system." Justice Black's opinion stressed the importance of mandatory disclosures, which would avoid a perception of bias: "[W]e can perceive no way in which the effectiveness of the arbitration process will be hampered by the simple requirement that arbitrators disclose to the parties any dealings that might create an impression of possible bias."[41]

A concurring opinion by Justice White, which was joined by Justice Marshall, suggested that some undisclosed relationships might be so "trivial" or "too insubstantial" to merit a finding of evident partiality.[42] Justice White stated, however, that arbitrators are not Article III judges and should not be held to the same standards as Article III judges.[43]

A split has developed in the circuits regarding the standard articulated by the Supreme Court in *Commonwealth Coatings*. A majority of circuits require parties seeking to vacate an arbitration award to establish that "a reasonable person would have to conclude that an arbitrator was partial to one party to the arbitration."[44] For example, the Fifth Circuit addressed the role of disclosure in

---

38. 9 U.S.C. § 10(a)(2).

39. Commw. Coatings Corp. v. Cont'l Cas. Co., 393 U.S. 145 (1968).

40. *Id.* at 146–48.

41. *Id.* at 149.

42. *Id.* at 150–52.

43. *Id.* at 150–51 (White, J., concurring).

44. Morelite Constr. Corp. v. N.Y.C. Dist. Council Carpenters Benefit Funds, 748 F.2d 79, 83–84 (2d Cir. 1984); *see also* Cooper v. WestEnd Cap. Mgmt., L.L.C., 832 F.3d 534, 545 (5th Cir. 2016); Freeman v. Pittsburgh Glass Works, LLC, 709 F.3d 240, 253 (3d Cir. 2013); JCI Commc'ns, Inc. v. Int'l Bhd. of Elec. Workers, Local 103, 324 F.3d 42, 51 (1st Cir. 2003); ANR Coal Co. v. Cogentrix of N.C., Inc., 173 F.3d 493, 500

vacating awards for "evident partiality" in *Positive Software Solutions, Inc. v. New Century Mortgage Corp.*[45] In that case, the sole arbitrator and his former law firm had previously served as co-counsel with the law firm and one of the primary lawyers who represented New Century in a protracted and significant litigation that lasted over a period of years. The arbitrator, along with 12 other attorneys, entered an appearance in cases on which New Century's counsel worked. Although their names appeared together on pleadings, the arbitrator never attended or participated in any meetings, telephone calls, hearings, depositions, or trials with New Century's counsel. After losing the arbitration, Positive Software moved to vacate the award on the basis that, among other things, despite the lack of contact between the arbitrator and New Century's counsel, the arbitrator had been biased, as evidenced by his failure to disclose the past connection. The district court vacated the award, finding that the arbitrator failed to disclose "a significant prior relationship with New Century's counsel," thus creating an appearance of partiality requiring vacatur.[46]

In an en banc decision, the Fifth Circuit reversed the district court's vacatur of the award, holding that the former business relationship involving the arbitrator and counsel for New Century was so trivial that the standard of evident partiality was not met and, therefore, did not require the award to be vacated. The court held that the FAA "does not mandate the extreme remedy of vacatur for nondisclosure of a trivial past association."[47] The Fifth Circuit then articulated a standard that is more akin to Justice White's concurrence in *Commonwealth Coatings*. The resulting standard is that in nondisclosure cases, an award may not be vacated because of a trivial or insubstantial prior relationship between the arbitrator and the parties to the proceeding. The "reasonable impression of bias" standard is thus interpreted practically rather than with utmost rigor.[48]

(4th Cir. 1999) (noting that courts have given Justice White's "concurrence particular weight" and holding that "an arbitrator's failure to reveal facts may be relevant in determining evident partiality under 9 U.S.C. § 10(a)(2), but that mere nondisclosure does not in itself justify vacatur"); Andersons, Inc. v. Horton Farms, Inc., 166 F.3d 308, 328 (6th Cir. 1998).

45. Positive Software Sols., Inc. v. New Century Mortg. Corp., 476 F.3d 278 (5th Cir. 2007).

46. Positive Software Sols., Inc. v. New Century Mortg. Corp., 337 F. Supp. 2d 862, 865 (N.D. Tex. 2004).

47. *Positive Software*, 476 F.3d at 283.

48. *Id.*

On the other hand, the Ninth and Eleventh Circuits appear to have adopted Justice Black's more rigid standard that authorizes vacatur where there is a "reasonable impression of partiality."[49] The key difference between the standards is the likelihood of the bias: whether a reasonable person must believe that the arbitrator actually was biased (majority) or if the mere possibility that the arbitrator was biased is sufficient to require vacatur of an arbitration award.

C. Misconduct in Refusing to Postpone the Hearing or Refusing to Hear Evidence

The third statutory basis for vacatur (section 10(a)(3)) is "where the arbitrators were guilty of misconduct in refusing to postpone the hearing, upon sufficient cause shown, or in refusing to hear evidence that is pertinent and material to the controversy; or of any other misbehavior by which the rights of any party have been prejudiced."[50] This reflects the principle that "[a]lthough an arbitrator need not follow all the niceties observed in court proceedings, the arbitrator must grant the parties a fundamentally fair hearing."[51] Arbitrators are not required to hear all the evidence proffered by a party; however, an arbitrator "must give each of the parties to the dispute an adequate opportunity to present its evidence and argument."[52] Courts reviewing motions to vacate an award based on allegations of misconduct are restricted to determining whether the procedure was fundamentally unfair.[53] In addition, the alleged misconduct

---

49. Schmitz v. Zilveti, 20 F.3d 1043, 1046–47 (9th Cir. 1994) (adopting the "reasonable impression of partiality" standard; to establish evident partiality, actual bias need not be demonstrated if there was an appearance of impropriety); Middlesex Mut. Ins. Co. v. Levine, 675 F.2d 1197, 1201 (11th Cir. 1982); Monster Energy Co. v. City Beverages, LLC, 940 F.3d 1130, 1138 (9th Cir. 2019) (finding that the arbitrator's failure to disclose his ownership interest in JAMS, given its nontrivial business relations with Monster, created a reasonable impression of bias that supports vacatur of the arbitration award).

50. 9 U.S.C. § 10(a)(3).

51. Bell Aerospace Co. Div. of Textron v. Local 516, 500 F.2d 921, 923 (1974).

52. Hoteles Condado Beach v. Union de Tronquistas Local 901, 763 F.2d 34, 39 (1st Cir. 1985).

53. *See* Teamsters, Local Union 657 v. Stanley Structures, Inc., 735 F.2d 903, 906 (5th Cir. 1984); *accord* Concourse Beauty Sch., Inc. v. Polakov, 685 F. Supp. 1311, 1318 (S.D.N.Y. 1988) ("The misconduct must amount to a denial of fundamental fairness of the arbitration proceeding in order to warrant vacating the award.") (quoting Transit Cas. Co. v. Trenwick Reins. Co., 659 F. Supp. 1346, 1354 (S.D.N.Y. 1987), *aff'd mem.* 841 F.2d 1117 (2d Cir. 1988)).

must have involved a matter material to the outcome, resulting in prejudice to the challenging party.[54]

D. Arbitrator Exceeds His or Her Powers

Arbitration is a creature of contract. The power and jurisdiction of the arbitrator are limited to only those matters the parties have specifically contracted to submit to arbitration. Therefore, an arbitrator has no power to rule on issues except for those expressly assigned in the arbitration agreement. An arbitrator's failure to observe this fundamental limitation is the fourth statutory basis for vacating an arbitral award (section 10(a)(4)).[55] When a court considers whether an arbitrator has exceeded his or her powers, the court must ask whether the arbitrator extended his or her decision to a matter over which he or she did not have authority, not whether the arbitrator's decision was correct.[56] Specifically "convincing a court of an arbitrator's error, even his grave error, is not enough. So long as the arbitrator was 'arguably construing' the contract . . . a court may not correct his mistakes . . . . The arbitrator's construction holds, however good, bad, or ugly."[57]

In *Stolt-Nielsen S.A. v. AnimalFeeds International Corp.*,[58] the U.S. Supreme Court held that arbitrators exceed their powers if they stray from the interpretation and application of the agreement, substituting their "own brand of industrial justice" for the parties' agreement. Under this standard, the court may vacate an award where there is no arguable basis on which to conclude that the arbitrator construed or applied the parties' agreement.[59] Similarly, in *Oxford Health Plans LLC v. Sutter*, the Supreme Court stated that a party seeking relief under section 10(a)(4) bears a heavy burden: "It is not enough . . . to show that the [arbitrator] committed an error—or even a serious error." Because the parties "bargained for the arbitrator's construction of their agreement," an arbitral decision "even arguably construing or applying the contract" must stand, regardless of a court's view of its (de)merits.[60] The Supreme Court's most oft-quoted guidance is "if the arbitrator's award 'draws

---

54. 9 U.S.C. § 10(a)(3).
55. *Id.* § 10(a)(4).
56. *See* Landmark Ventures, Inc. v. InSightec, 63 F. Supp. 3d 343, 357 (S.D.N.Y. 2014).
57. Oxford Health Plans LLC v. Sutter, 569 U.S. 564, 571–73 (2013).
58. Stolt-Nielsen S.A. v. AnimalFeeds Int'l Corp., 559 U.S. 662 (2010).
59. *Id.* at 668–72.
60. *Oxford Health*, 569 U.S. at 571–73.

its essence from the . . . agreement,' and is not merely the arbitrator's 'own brand of industrial justice,' the award is legitimate."[61] Thus, the sole question on judicial review is whether the arbitrator interpreted the parties' contract, not whether he or she construed it correctly.

III. Manifest Disregard of the Law as a Basis for Vacatur of Arbitral Awards

The FAA does not include the phrase "manifest disregard of the law." Yet, a number of courts have determined that the Supreme Court's use of the phrase "manifest disregard" in 1953 in *Wilko v. Swan*[62] signaled the judicial creation of a ground for vacatur in addition to those included in the FAA. In *Wilko*, the Supreme Court invalidated agreements to arbitrate future disputes between securities brokers and investors. First, the Court determined that "the protective provisions of the Securities Act require the exercise of judicial discretion to fairly assure their effectiveness." Then, the Court reasoned that Congress must have intended section 14 of the Securities Act to prohibit a waiver of judicial trial and appeal.[63] Finally, the Court reviewed the arbitration agreements at issue and held that they constituted an invalid waiver of the investors' right to select a judicial forum under the Securities Act.

In his opinion for the majority, Justice Reed acknowledged the lower court's assumption that an arbitrator's failure to "decide in accordance with the provisions of the Securities Act would constitute grounds for vacating the award pursuant to section 10 of the Federal Arbitration Act."[64] Justice Reed noted, however, that an improper arbitration award should be subject to vacatur only in cases where the arbitrator's failure to accurately interpret the Securities Act was obvious:

> In unrestricted submission, such as the present margin agreements envisage, **the interpretations of the law by the arbitrators in contrast to manifest disregard are not subject, in the federal courts, to judicial review for error in interpretation.**[65]

---

61. United Steelworkers of Am. v. Enter. Wheel & Car Co., 363 U.S. 593, 597 (1960) (internal citations omitted).

62. Wilko v. Swan, 346 U.S. 427 (1953).

63. *Id.* at 436.

64. *Id.*

65. *Id.* at 436–37 (emphasis added).

With these words, the Court opened a debate over whether manifest disregard is grounds for vacating an arbitration award, in addition to the limited grounds for vacatur set forth in the FAA.

The Supreme Court revisited *Wilko*'s language regarding manifest disregard in *Hall Street Associates v. Mattel, Inc.*[66] That case involved the question of whether a court may vacate an arbitration award based on a ground that is not in sections 10 and 11 of the FAA, where the parties contractually agreed to that ground in their arbitration agreement. The appellant, seeking vacatur, relied on *Wilko* and argued that "if judges can add grounds to vacate (or modify) [arbitral awards], so can contracting parties."[67] Appellant argued further that the *Wilko* Court's language regarding "manifest disregard" should be interpreted as an addition to the grounds for vacatur set forth in the FAA.[68] The Supreme Court rejected that argument and held that sections 10 and 11 of the FAA set forth the *exclusive* bases for vacatur of an arbitration award.[69]

In holding that the FAA provided the exclusive grounds for vacating an arbitration award, the *Hall Street* Court rejected the argument that manifest disregard is an independent basis for vacatur. Rather, the Court theorized that *Wilko*'s use of the term "manifest disregard" could have referred to one or more of the grounds enumerated in the FAA: "Maybe the term 'manifest disregard' was meant to name a new ground for review, but maybe it merely referred to the § 10 grounds collectively, rather than adding to them. Or, as some courts have thought, 'manifest disregard' may have been shorthand for § 10(a)(3) or § 10(a)(4), the paragraphs authorizing vacatur when the arbitrators were guilty of misconduct or exceeded their powers."[70] Thus, the *Hall Street* Court was able to avoid eliminating manifest disregard as a ground for vacatur by showing that it could be interpreted in a way that is consistent with the Court's holding that sections 10 and 11 of the FAA provide the exclusive grounds for vacating an award.

The *Hall Street* decision has, however, led to disagreement among the circuits about the extent to which the manifest disregard doctrine remains a viable ground for vacatur of an arbitral award. One group of circuits has held that the doctrine remains a valid basis for vacatur, including the Second,[71]

66. Hall Street Assocs. v. Mattel, Inc., 552 U.S. 576 (2008).

67. *Id.* at 585.

68. *Id.*

69. *Id.* at 578.

70. *Id.*

71. *See* Stolt-Nielsen S.A. v. AnimalFeeds Int'l Corp., 548 F.3d 85, 95 (2nd Cir. 2008), *rev'd on different grounds*, 559 U.S. 662 (2010). In that case, the Second Circuit

Fourth,[72] Sixth,[73] and Ninth[74] Circuits. Another group has held that the doctrine is not an independent basis for vacatur of arbitral awards after *Hall Street*, including the Fifth,[75] Seventh,[76] Eighth,[77] and Eleventh[78] Circuits. Finally,

---

upheld the use of the manifest disregard standard, stating that "the 'manifest disregard' doctrine survives *Hall Street*" and "[w]e view the manifest disregard doctrine, and the FAA itself, as a mechanism to enforce the parties' agreements to arbitrate rather than as judicial review of the arbitrators' decision." After laying out the standard, the Second Circuit went on to find that the arbitrators had not manifestly disregarded the law. *Stolt-Nielsen S.A.*, 548 F.3d at 95. The Supreme Court reversed the Second Circuit's decision on the merits by ruling that the award should have been vacated under section 10 of the FAA because the arbitrators had exceeded their authority. *Stolt-Nielsen S.A.*, 559 U.S. at 685–87. However, the Supreme Court expressly declined to "decide whether 'manifest disregard' survives our decision in *Hall Street Associates, L.L.C. v. Mattel, Inc.*, as an independent ground for review or as a judicial gloss on the enumerated grounds for vacatur set forth at 9 U.S.C. § 10." *Id.* at n.3.

72. In *Wachovia Securities v. Brand*, 671 F.3d 472, 480 (4th Cir. 2012), the Fourth Circuit expressly held that manifest disregard survived *Hall Street* as an independent ground for vacatur of an arbitration award.

73. In *Coffee Beanery v. WW*, 300 F. App'x 415, 419 (6th Cir. 2008), the Sixth Circuit determined that "[i]n light of the Supreme Court's hesitation to reject the 'manifest disregard' doctrine . . . we believe it would be imprudent to cease employing such a universally recognized principle." Accordingly, the court chose to follow "its well-established precedent" and continue to employ the manifest disregard doctrine. *Id.*

74. Finally, in *Comedy Club, Inc. v. Improv West Associates*, 553 F.3d 1277, 1281 (9th Cir. 2009), the Ninth Circuit held that "an arbitrator's manifest disregard of the law remains a valid ground for vacatur of an arbitration award under § 10(a)(4) of the Federal Arbitration Act."

75. In *Citigroup Global Markets, Inc. v. Bacon*, 562 F.3d 349, 350 (5th Cir. 2009), the Fifth Circuit held that "*Hall Street* restricts the grounds for vacatur to those set forth in § 10 of the Federal Arbitration Act . . . and consequently, manifest disregard of the law is no longer an independent ground for vacating arbitration awards under the FAA."

76. The Seventh Circuit, in *Affymax, Inc. v. Ortho-McNeil-Janssen Pharmaceuticals, Inc.*, 660 F.3d 281, 284 (7th Cir. 2011), concluded that section 10 of the FAA is an exclusive list and "neither judges nor contracting parties can expand it. Disregard of the law is not on the statutory list."

77. In *Medicine Shoppe International, Inc. v. Turner*, 614 F.3d 485, 489 (8th Cir. 2010), the Eighth Circuit held that "the claim that the arbitrator disregarded the law [is] not included among those specifically enumerated in § 10 [of the FAA] and [is] therefore not cognizable."

78. In *Frazier v. CitiFinancial Corp.*, 604 F.3d 1313, 1324 (11th Cir. 2010), the Eleventh Circuit held that "our judicially-created bases for vacatur [including that

there is a group of circuits that have acknowledged *Hall Street*'s impact on the manifest disregard doctrine but have not decided finally whether the doctrine remains viable. This last group includes the First,[79] Third,[80] Tenth,[81] D.C.,[82] and Federal[83] Circuits.

Those circuits that continue to recognize the manifest disregard doctrine use varying tests to determine whether an arbitrator has manifestly disregarded the law. In *Stolt-Nielsen*, the Second Circuit Court of Appeals held that courts must consider three factors when deciding whether an award may be vacated for manifest disregard of the law: (1) "whether the law that was allegedly ignored was clear, and in fact explicitly applicable to the matter before the arbitrators"; (2) "whether the law was in fact improperly applied, leading to an erroneous outcome"; and (3) the arbitrator knew the law existed and applied to the issue and intentionally disregarded it.[84] To determine if the arbitrator knew of the law, the court should "impute knowledge of governing law identified by the parties to the arbitration."[85] The Third Circuit has also applied the Second Circuit's test from *Stolt-Nielsen*.[86]

---

manifest disregard doctrine] are no longer valid in light of *Hall Street*."

79. *See* Mountain Valley Prop., Inc. v. Applied Risk Servs., Inc., 863 F.3d 90, 95 (1st Cir. 2017) ("[T]his court has yet to decide [post-*Hall Street*] whether manifest disregard of the law remains as a ground for vacatur of arbitration awards, and no manifest disregard of the law occurred in the present case. We can therefore assume the validity of the doctrine and proceed to apply it.").

80. Paul Green Sch. of Rock Music Franchising v. Smith, 389 F. App'x 172, 175–76 (3d Cir. 2010) (finding that the facts of the case did not warrant a decision on "whether manifest disregard of the law remains, after *Hall Street*, a valid ground for vacatur" because "the arbitrator did not manifestly disregard the law").

81. THI of N.M. at Vida Encantada v. Lovato, 864 F.3d 1080, 1088 (10th Cir. 2017) ("We assume (without deciding) the viability of [the manifest disregard of the law] exception.").

82. Affinity Fin. Corp. v. AARP Fin., Inc., 468 F. App'x 4, 5 (D.C. Cir. 2012) (deciding the case by "[a]ssuming without deciding that the 'manifest disregard of the law' standard still exists" after *Hall Street*).

83. Bayer CropSci. AG v. Dow Agroscis., 680 F. App'x 985, 992–93, 997 (Fed. Cir. 2017) (holding that the arbitrators in this case did not manifestly disregard the law but acknowledging that other circuits have found the "manifest disregard" doctrine to still be viable).

84. Stolt-Nielsen S.A. v. AnimalFeeds Int'l Corp., 548 F.3d 85, 93 (2nd Cir. 2008).

85. *Id.*

86. In *Paul Green School of Rock Music Franchising v. Smith*, 389 F. App'x 172, 179 (3d Cir. 2010), the Third Circuit affirmed a district court's decision to confirm an

In *Wachovia Securities v. Brand*, the Fourth Circuit announced a two-part test for courts to determine if an arbitrator manifestly disregarded the law.[87] Under that test, the party seeking vacatur must show "(1) the applicable legal principle is clearly defined and not subject to reasonable debate; and (2) the arbitrators refused to heed that legal principle."[88] The Sixth Circuit quoted and applied the *Wachovia Securities* test in *Coffee Beanery v. WW*.[89] The Federal Circuit also quoted and applied this test in *Bayer CropScience AG v. Dow Agrosciences*.[90] The D.C. Circuit has announced a very similar two-part test in *Affinity Financial Corp. v. AARP Financial, Inc.*[91]

The Ninth Circuit applies a different standard. In *Comedy Club, Inc. v. Improv West Associates*, the Ninth Circuit Court of Appeals held that "for an arbitrator's award to be in manifest disregard of the law, '[i]t must be clear from the record that the arbitrator . . . recognized the applicable law and then ignored it."[92] The Ninth Circuit has held that "[m]anifest disregard of the facts [alone] is not an independent ground for vacatur in this circuit."[93]

The First Circuit applied yet another test in *Mountain Valley Property, Inc. v. Applied Risk Services Inc.*[94] In that case, the court held that for an award

---

arbitration award, finding that "[i]t is enough for a court to determine that, as was true in this case, an arbitrator's decision was not a willful flouting of known, governing law."

87. Wachovia Secs. v. Brand, 671 F.3d 472, 483 (4th Cir. 2012).

88. *Id.*

89. Coffee Beanery v. WW, 300 F. App'x 415, 418 (6th Cir. 2008).

90. Bayer CropSci. AG v. Dow Agroscis., 680 F. App'x 985, 993 (Fed. Cir. 2017).

91. Affinity Fin. Corp. v. AARP Fin., Inc., 468 F. App'x 4, 5 (D.C. Cir. 2012) (stating that the court should consider whether "(1) the arbitrators knew of a governing legal principle yet refused to apply it or ignored it altogether and (2) the law ignored by the arbitrators was well defined, explicit, and clearly applicable to the case").

92. Comedy Club, Inc. v. Improv West Assocs., 553 F.3d 1277, 1290 (9th Cir. 2009) (quoting Mich. Mut. Ins. Co. v. Unigard Sec. Ins. Co., 44 F.3d 826, 832 (9th Cir. 1995)).

93. Coutee v. Barington Cap. Grp., L.P., 336 F.3d 1128, 1133 (9th Cir. 2003).

94. Mountain Valley Prop., Inc. v. Applied Risk Servs., Inc., 863 F.3d 90, 95 (1st Cir. 2017) (quoting McCarthy v. CitiGroup Glob. Mkts., Inc., 463 F.3d 87, 91 (1st Cir. 2006)). *See also* Raymond James Fin. Servs., Inc. v. Fenyk, 780 F.3d 59, 64 (1st Cir. 2015) ("We have invoked that standard primarily for cases where the award contradicted unambiguous contract language or 'the arbitrator recognized the applicable law but ignored it.'") (quoting Gupta v. Cisco Sys., Inc., 274 F.3d 1, 3 (1st Cir. 2001)). Stolt-Nielsen S.A. v. AnimalFeeds Int'l Corp., 559 U.S. 662, 672 n.3 (2010) (noting party's description of the standard as "requiring a showing that the arbitrators knew of the relevant [legal] principle, appreciated that this principle controlled the outcome of

to be vacated for manifest disregard of the law, the party seeking vacatur must show that the arbitral award was "(1) unfounded in reason and fact; (2) based on reasoning so palpably faulty that no judge, or group of judges, ever could conceivably have made such a ruling; or (3) mistakenly based on a crucial assumption that is concededly a non-fact."[95] The Tenth Circuit has held that, "[t]o warrant setting aside an arbitration award based on manifest disregard of the law, the record must show that the arbitrators knew the law and explicitly disregarded it."[96]

IV. Modification of an Arbitration Award

Section 11 of the FAA permits a reviewing court to correct or modify an award in the following circumstances:

> (a) Where there was an evident material miscalculation of figures or an evident material mistake;
>
> (b) Where the arbitrators have awarded upon a matter not submitted to them; and
>
> (c) Where the award is imperfect in matter of form not affecting the merits of the controversy.[97]

As a practical matter, a request to modify the award will often be raised first with the arbitrator, since most arbitral bodies have rules that expressly permit a party to seek modification of the award.[98] If the party does not obtain the modification requested from the arbitrator, or if the party believes that raising the matter with the arbitrator would be disadvantageous, that party may bring a motion with the district court in the district wherein the award was made pursuant to section 11 of the FAA.

---

the disputed issue, and nonetheless willfully flouted the governing law by refusing to apply it" (alteration in original) (internal quotation marks omitted)).

95. *Mountain Valley Prop.*, 863 F.3d at 95.

96. THI of N.M. at Vida Encantada v. Lovato, 864 F.3d 1080, 1085 (10th Cir. 2017) (internal quotations omitted).

97. 9 U.S.C. § 11.

98. *E.g.*, American Arbitration Association Construction Industry Arbitration Rules (July 1, 2015), Rule R-51; JAMS Engineering and Construction Arbitration Rules and Procedures (June 1, 2021), Rule 24(j).

The most common basis for seeking modification of an award is for a material miscalculation or misdescription under subdivision (a) of section 11. In such cases, the majority view is that the miscalculation or misdescription must appear "on the face of the arbitration award," or the error may not be corrected.[99] In other words, the majority of circuits have held that section 11 of the FAA does not permit the court to search the underlying arbitration record to discern the arbitrator's error. For example, in *Mid-Atlantic Capital Corp. v. Bien*, the losing party argued that the arbitrators improperly had granted a double recovery to the claimant by awarding both sets of damages that had been requested in the alternative. The court found the arbitration award "disturbing" and acknowledged that the award of both "net out-of-pocket losses" and "market-adjusted damages" amounted to a double recovery. However, the court declined to correct the arbitration award, finding that section 11 of the FAA authorizes a court to correct "an evident material miscalculation of figures" only if the miscalculation appeared "on the face of the award." The court confirmed the award because the double counting could be identified only upon a review of the record of the arbitration.[100] In contrast, the Fifth and Seventh Circuits will permit consideration of the underlying arbitration record to identify material miscalculations.[101]

V. Procedures for Modification or Vacatur of an Arbitration Award under the FAA

The procedure for applying to vacate or modify an arbitration award under the FAA can be briefly summarized. Typically, the party whom the award favors is applying to confirm the award at the same time the party opposing the award is applying to have it vacated, with the party opposed to confirmation of the award relying on the same grounds raised in the application or motion to vacate or modify the award. This chapter does not address the complexities

---

99. Mid-Atl. Cap. Corp. v. Bien, 956 F.3d 1182 (10th Cir. 2020). The Fourth, Sixth, and Eleventh Circuits also follow the "on the face of the award" rule. *See also* Grain v. Trinity Health, Mercy Health Servs., Inc., 551 F.3d 374 (6th Cir. 2008); AIG Baker Sterling Heights LLC v. Am. Multi-Cinema, Inc., 508 F.3d 995 (11th Cir. 2007); Apex Plumbing Supply, Inc. v. U.S. Supply Co., 142 F.3d 188 (4th Cir. 1998).

100. *Mid-Atl. Cap. Corp.*, 956 F.3d 1182, 1185 (10th Cir. 2020).

101. Eljer Mfg., Inc. v. Kowin Dev. Corp., 14 F.3d 1250 (7th Cir. 1994); Valentine Sugars, Inc. v. Donau Corp., 981 F.2d 210 (5th Cir. 1993).

that can arise in cross-border cases where the application to confirm and the application to vacate are brought in different countries.[102]

A. Timing of the Application to Vacate or Modify

In section 12, the FAA provides that if a party wishes to apply to vacate, modify, or correct an arbitral award, that party must serve the adverse party with notice of the application within three months after the award is filed or delivered. Note that "three months" in this section of the FAA is not the same as 90 days. Rather, the Ninth Circuit Court of Appeals, in *Stevens v. Jiffy Lube International, Inc.*, held that Federal Rule of Civil Procedure 6(a) governs the calculation of the three-month period for filing a motion to **vacate or modify** an arbitration award.[103] The *Jiffy Lube* court stated that calculation of the filing deadline requires three steps. First, exclude the day the award was delivered. Second, calculate three months: "The first month began September 15 and concluded October 14; the second month began October 15 and concluded November 14; and the third month began November 15 and concluded December 14." It does not matter whether you are counting a 28-day or a 31-day month. What matters is the day of the month the award was delivered. The third and final step, if the end of that three-month period is a weekend or holiday, is to extend the period to the next business day.[104]

B. Venue for the Application

When an application to vacate or modify an award is brought under the FAA, venue is proper in "the United States court in and for the district wherein the award was made."[105] There used to be a split in the circuits as to whether the FAA's venue provisions were mandatory or permissive, but that split was settled by the Supreme Court in *Cortez Byrd Chips, Inc. v. Bill Harbert Construction Co.*, which found that the FAA's venue provisions are permissive, meaning that a motion to confirm, vacate, or modify **may** be brought either

---

102. *E.g.*, *In re* Arb. between Int'l Bechtel Co., Ltd. & Dep't Civ. Aviation of the Gov't of Dubai, 360 F. Supp. 2d 136 (D.C. Dist. 2005); *In re* Arb. of Certain Controversies between Chromalloy Aeroservs. & Arab Repub. of Egypt, 939 F. Supp. 907 (D.C. Dist. 1996).

103. Stevens v. Jiffy Lube Int'l, Inc., 911 F.3d 1249 (9th Cir. 2018).

104. *Id.*

105. 9 U.S.C. §§ 10(a), 11.

in the district where the award was made or in any district proper under the general venue statute.[106]

C. Form of the Application

The application to vacate or modify an award is "made and heard in the manner provided by law for the making and hearing of motions."[107] It must be accompanied by the following papers:

> (a) The [arbitration] agreement; the selection or appointment, if any, of an additional arbitrator or umpire; and each written extension of the time, if any, within which to make the award.
>
> (b) The award.
>
> (c) Each notice, affidavit, or other paper used upon an application to confirm, modify, or correct the award, and a copy of each order of the court upon such an application.[108]

An order vacating or modifying an arbitration award is immediately appealable.[109] An order denying an application to vacate or modify an award is appealable only to the extent that it is a final decision with respect to the arbitration at issue.[110]

---

106. Cortez Byrd Chips, Inc. v. Bill Harbert Constr. Co., 529 U.S. 193, 197–98 (2000).

107. 9 U.S.C. § 6.

108. 9 U.S.C. § 13.

109. *Id.* at § 16(a)(1)(E).

110. *Id.* at § 16(a)(3).

Appendix to Chapter 9

Comparison of Optional Appellate Arbitration Rules

Organization	Time for Filing	Briefing Available	Oral Argument	Standard of Review	Time to Decision	Required Vote of the Panel	Assessment of Appeal Costs and Fees
AAA Appellate Rules	30 days from receipt of original award. Cross-appeal may be filed within seven days of Notice of Appeal.	Yes, appellant may file an initial brief and reply brief. Appellee may file an answering brief. Same briefing for cross-appeal.	No, unless panel determines oral argument is necessary or if panel approves request of a party.	Material and prejudicial error of law or clearly erroneous finding of facts.	Within 30 days of submission of final brief. May be extended for good cause shown.	Majority	Unsuccessful appellant assessed costs and attorneys' fees of appellee, if required by statute or contract. Nonrefundable $6,000 administrative fee paid by appellant.
JAMS Appellate Procedures	14 days from date the award becomes final. Cross-appeal filed within seven days of service of the appeal.	Parties may agree to rely on briefs in original arbitration. If no agreement, only initial briefs by both parties.	Yes, if requested by all parties or by panel in complex cases.	Same standard of review that the first-level appellate court would apply to the trial court decision.	Within 14 days of oral argument or submission of the final brief.	Majority	No specific rule—parties may address in the contract.
CPR Appellate Arbitration Procedure	30 days from receipt of original award. Cross-appeal within 14 days of Notice of Appeal.	Yes, appellant may file an initial brief and reply brief. Appellee may file an answering brief. Same briefing for cross-appeal.	Yes, if any party requests oral argument.	Material and prejudicial errors of law or clearly unsupported factual findings or may be vacated on one or more of the FAA § 10 grounds.	Appeal must be concluded within six months of filing.	Majority	Unsuccessful appellant bears 100 percent of appellee's appeal attorneys' fees and costs, unless panel determines otherwise.

CHAPTER 10

Navigating an International Construction Arbitration

ANDREW D. NESS

I. Introduction: The Distinctive Features of International Construction Arbitrations

Handling an international construction arbitration requires learning a good deal of new terminology and adapting your skills, gained from handling state and federal court litigation and domestic arbitrations, to a different procedural regime. Much about the international arbitration process will be familiar, but there are a number of significant differences, some obvious and some subtle. It can seem daunting at the outset, but rest assured, your advocacy skills will largely carry over, and with some adjustments you can quickly become as effective in the international arbitration arena as you are domestically. This chapter is intended to be a guide to the international arbitration process, as it is experienced in a substantial construction dispute, focusing on what you need to know to get up to speed quickly and be successful.

The great majority of international construction arbitrations are, as with domestic arbitrations, contract disputes where the parties have expressly agreed to arbitration as their chosen method of dispute resolution. These fall within the realm of international commercial arbitration and are the focus of this chapter. International investment arbitration, alternatively known as "investor-state," "treaty," or ICSID arbitration, is a separate category, with quite different rules and norms. Investment arbitrations are treaty based and involve claimed violations of the terms of a bilateral or multilateral investment treaty. There are some situations in which owner–contractor construction disputes can be appropriately addressed via an investment arbitration, but investment arbitration is beyond the scope of this chapter.

Before getting into specific elements of the international commercial arbitration process, how in general terms does international arbitration differ from U.S. domestic arbitrations of construction disputes? Because international arbitrations can be set anywhere in the world and involve parties from different countries, they are subject to very considerable variation. Arbitrations can take place in well over 100 countries, each with its own distinctive culture and legal system that can influence the process, making it inherently difficult to offer statements of general applicability.

International commercial arbitration is a meld of practices and procedures taken from both the common and civil law, but how these different influences interact in a specific case can vary widely. Nevertheless, there are a number of general differences that you are likely to experience in an international construction arbitration.

A. They Are Significantly More Expensive

This starts with the fees charged by international arbitral institutions, which generally include both the fees for administering the arbitration and the fees and expenses of the arbitrators. For a domestic case involving $10 million in dispute that is filed under the AAA Construction Industry Arbitration Rules, the AAA currently charges an initial filing fee of $11,000 and a subsequent fee of $13,750, for a total administrative fee of $24,750.[1] By comparison, a dispute with the same $10 million in controversy filed at the International Chamber of Commerce (ICC) Court of Arbitration under the ICC Arbitration Rules will incur an administrative fee of $57,515.[2] In both cases, these amounts do not include arbitrator fees. Where the arbitrators are paid on the basis of hourly rates, they will generally be significantly higher for international arbitrators. In an ICC Rules arbitration, however, arbitrator fees are determined by the size

---

1. AAA Construction Industry Arbitration Rules and Mediation Procedures, Administrative Fee Schedules (May 1, 2022).

2. *See Costs Calculator*, INT'L CHAMBER OF COM., https://iccwbo.org/dispute-resolution-services/arbitration/costs-and-payments/cost-calculator/ (last visited Apr. 25, 2023). Fee schedules at other international arbitral institutions vary—generally less than ICC but significantly more than a domestic AAA arbitration.

of the dispute and not the time expended.[3] For the $10 million case, the parties will be billed near the outset of the case for $339,852 for the three arbitrators' fees (split between the parties), although the final fees may be up to a total of $562,200. Arbitrator expenses are in addition to this and based on a generous daily rate.

Then of course you need to figure in the added cost of bringing counsel, experts, and witnesses to the hearing, which frequently is held in a high-cost city such as London, New York, Paris, Geneva, or Singapore. Voluminous written submissions may regularly need to be sent out to far-flung locations by FedEx or other express delivery service (notwithstanding parallel electronic submissions). The costs add up fast. In a 2019 survey conducted by Queen Mary School of International Arbitration at the University of London,[4] in-house counsel most often said that "over $10 million" was the minimum amount in dispute that would justify undertaking the cost of an international arbitration.

B. You Might Recover Your Attorney's Fees, or You Might End Up Paying the Other Side's Fees

Most international arbitration rules expressly provide for fee and cost shifting, including attorney's and experts' fees, based on the English rule of "loser pays." Such fee-shifting awards are regularly issued. If you are deemed the prevailing party, you can expect to recover at least some of your arbitration and attorney's fees. But if you are not, you will very likely have an award entered against you that includes some or all of the other side's fees and costs.

C. They Take Longer to Reach Completion

Meaningful statistics for construction arbitrations are hard to come by, but experience generally is that an international arbitration will move more slowly than the domestic U.S. equivalent. The several required prehearing

3. Setting arbitrator fees based on the amount in dispute is also the practice of several other of the major international arbitral institutions, including the Hong Kong International Arbitration Centre (HKIAC), Singapore International Arbitration Centre (SIAC), and Stockholm Chamber of Commerce (SCC).

4. Queen Mary Univ. of London & Pinsent Masons, *International Arbitration Survey—Driving Efficiency in International Construction Disputes* (Nov. 2019), https://www.pinsentmasons.com/thinking/special-reports/international-arbitration-survey. A key finding was that 43 percent of in-house counsel surveyed believed that construction disputes need to be valued between $11 million and $25 million to make the claims worth pursuing in arbitration.

submissions of the parties (discussed later) are generally done sequentially, not simultaneously, leading to an extended prehearing process. After the hearing, there are few effective deadlines for issuing the award, and because the awards are generally lengthy and the arbitrators often separated by several time zones, they can take considerable time to issue. In recent years several sets of international arbitration rules have been amended to add aggressive targets for resolving cases. Article 31(1) of the ICC Rules states that the arbitral tribunal must render its award within six months from signing the Terms of Reference (a step near the outset of proceedings in ICC cases, discussed later), but this seems to be routinely extended in any reasonably complex case.[5] Per the ICC 2020 Statistics, the average time from Request for Arbitration to award was 26 months.[6] As a rough guess, you should expect an international arbitration will likely require 50 percent longer than a comparable domestic arbitration, on average.

D. They Are Considerably More Paper Intensive

The international arbitration process generally involves extensive written submissions by the parties and in general is conducted much more on paper with less done orally than domestic arbitrations, making the entire process more paper intensive from start to finish. While many arbitrators now prefer electronic submissions, paper copies of filings are generally also required.

E. The Governing Arbitration Rules Are Usually Less Specific, Leaving More Room for Variations in Procedure

International arbitration rules are generally intended for use in a wide variety of cases and jurisdictions, with quite different legal systems, and as a result tend to be somewhat more general in nature than U.S. counterparts like the AAA or JAMS Rules. For example, they usually provide that a hearing will be held if requested by any party or the tribunal but say almost nothing about how

---

5. The International Centre for Dispute Resolution (ICDR) Rules similarly contain an aggressive timetable of 60 days from closing the hearing to issue the award, but again this is frequently extended.

6. *ICC Dispute Resolution Statistics: 2020* (Aug. 3, 2021), https://iccwbo.org/publication/icc-dispute-resolution-statistics-2020/ [hereinafter *ICC 2020 Statistics*]. The London Court of International Arbitration (LCIA) reported that for the period 2013–2016, the median duration was 16 months and for disputes between $10 million and $100 million, 18 months. London Ct. Int'l Arb., *Facts and Figures: Costs and Duration: 2013–2016* (Oct. 3, 2017), https://www.lcia.org/News/lcia-releases-updated-costs-and-duration-analysis.aspx. The median duration at ICC was 22 months. *ICC 2020 Statistics*, *supra*.

the hearing will be conducted. This leaves a lot of room for interpretation and significant variation from one case to the next. The chair of the arbitral tribunal generally decides the specifics of the hearing procedure utilized, and it is a maxim of international arbitration that the specific procedure often depends significantly on the home country of the chair. An UNCITRAL[7] Rules hearing chaired by a U.S. national is likely to be conducted in general accordance with U.S. norms. A hearing under the same rules chaired by a Swiss national may proceed quite differently, influenced more by the civil law tradition as used in Switzerland. When uncertain as to the specific procedure that will be utilized, you are well advised to raise this subject at the initial procedural hearing so you can start planning for the tribunal's preferred method of proceeding.

F. Secondary Sources (Guidelines, Reports, and Rules) Have Outsized Influence

As a result of both the general nature of institutional rules and wide variations in practice around the world, recent years have seen a number of supplementary resources published by the likes of the International Bar Association (IBA), the Chartered Institute of Arbitrators (CIArb), and the ICC. These resources, generally titled as supplementary rules, guidelines, or reports, seek to establish common standards for conducting international arbitrations or at least to provide practical guidance to tribunals and practitioners. None of these is binding or will automatically apply to your arbitration, but they are frequently referenced, expressly adopted, or relied upon by tribunals. It is important to have a working knowledge of the most significant of these resources, and tribunals will frequently assume that counsel are familiar with them. Many of these resources are identified in the notes to this chapter, but new ones (and revisions to the existing ones) are published all the time.

G. They Are Conducted in a More Formal Manner, with a Greater Emphasis on Politeness and Civil Conduct

Some U.S. arbitrators in recent years have taken to addressing counsel by first names and welcome being called by their first names in response. This would definitely not be advisable in international arbitration, as formal means of address (and dress) are the norm. Similarly, international arbitrators expect that opposing counsel will address each other politely at all times and without raising their voice or showing any of the rough edges that might exist in their relationship. The same holds true when cross-examining witnesses. The

---

7. UNCITRAL is the United Nations Commission on International Trade Law.

aggressive style some litigators use with witnesses before a U.S. jury almost certainly will not play well before international arbitrators and may frankly appall non-U.S. arbitrators used to much more deferential treatment of opposing witnesses.

H. Starting with the End in Mind Is Even More Important Than in a U.S. Arbitration

It is certainly good practice before commencing any litigation or arbitration to consider whether the prospective defendant/respondent has the assets to pay the hoped-for judgment or award. In international arbitration, there are more layers to consider than simply solvency of the respondent. Some basic additional questions to consider are: Where are the respondent's assets (particularly liquid assets such as bank accounts) located, and are they reachable by the courts in those countries? Are those countries signatories to the NY Convention that governs enforcing international arbitration awards, and what is the track record of courts in those countries in terms of the ease or difficulty of enforcing such awards against businesses located there? The rudiments of an effective enforcement strategy should be in place even before initiating the arbitration process, or you risk large expenditures of time and money to obtain an award that will be difficult and perhaps next to impossible to enforce.

II. International Arbitral Institutions and Jurisdiction

There are numerous international arbitral institutions, some with a worldwide focus and many others with a regional focus. Typically, each institution has its own set of rules, although there is general consistency among most sets of rules, with relatively modest variations in specifics of procedure and level of detail. There are three U.S.-based organizations with international rules: the AAA International Centre for Dispute Resolution (ICDR), JAMS, and the International Institute for Conflict Prevention & Resolution (CPR). None, however, is a major player in the field. The institution with the largest number of filed cases by far is the ICC, headquartered in Paris. Other arbitral institutions that see substantial numbers of construction cases include the London Court of International Arbitration (LCIA), the Dubai International Arbitration Center (DIAC), and the Hong Kong and Singapore International Arbitration Centres (HKIAC and SIAC).

ICC publishes an annual set of statistics that provide significant insight into the nature and breadth of international construction arbitrations. In 2020, 929 ICC Rules cases were filed, and construction cases comprised the largest share, at 194 cases (21 percent).[8] For all ICC cases, parties came from 145 countries (9 percent from the United States and 40 percent from Europe), arbitrators came from 92 jurisdictions (10 percent U.S., 14 percent U.K., and 57 percent Europe), and arbitral seats were located in 113 cities in 65 countries (but 45 percent of cases were seated in one of five cities: London, Paris, Geneva, New York, and Zurich).

The most important distinction is between administered and nonadministered arbitration rules. The rules of a particular arbitral institution generally provide for administration of the arbitration proceeding along the same lines as AAA administration of U.S.-based arbitrations. It assesses and collects the administrative fees and arbitrator fees and expenses, assists in arbitrator selection when needed, and has a procedure for challenging the appointment of individual arbitrators and appointing replacement arbitrators when needed. Notably, ICC actively reviews the substance of the draft award submitted by the arbitral tribunal in detail for completeness and quality, but without impinging on the tribunal's authority to determine the merits of the case.

The leading set of nonadministered arbitration rules is published by the United Nations Commission on International Trade Law (UNCITRAL) and contemplates an arbitration process administered entirely by the arbitration tribunal, with no institution standing behind it, other than an "appointing authority."[9] The appointing authority's role is generally limited to resolving impasses over the selection or removal of arbitrators, actions requiring an administrative authority apart from the tribunal to resolve the issue. Many arbitral institutions, including ICC, LCIA, and CPR, allow that institution to be designated as an appointing authority for these purposes without otherwise invoking the institution's own rules.

Hopefully your case arises under an arbitration provision that includes all of the important requirements. These include (1) the basic agreement to submit disputes to binding arbitration; (2) an applicable set of arbitration rules; (3) if nonadministered arbitration rules such as the UNCITRAL Rules are specified, designation of an appointing authority; (4) the place or "seat" of the

---

8. *ICC 2020 Statistics*, *supra* note 6. By comparison, LCIA reported a total of 407 cases filed under the LCIA Rules in 2020, of which 5 percent were classified as Construction/Infrastructure. London Ct. Int'l Arb., *2020 Annual Casework Report* (May 17, 2021), https://www.lcia.org/News/lcia-news-annual-casework-report-2020-and-changes-to-the-lcia-c.aspx.

9. UNCITRAL Arbitration Rules (rev. 2010), https://uncitral.un.org/sites/uncitral.un.org/files/media-documents/uncitral/en/arb-rules-revised-2010-e.pdf.

arbitration (usually specified as a particular city); (5) the governing law; and (6) the language of the arbitration. That said, so long as there is the basic agreement to arbitrate and an applicable set of rules is identified, the tribunal, once appointed, has the power to set any of the other missing elements, but this will require either additional agreements between the parties or added proceedings before the tribunal.

The governing law that is designated applies to the substantive legal aspects of the dispute. The law applicable at the seat applies to any procedural issues not covered by the applicable rules. As the national arbitration law of different countries can vary significantly, particularly as to how much the local courts can get involved in issues such as the arbitrability of particular claims, the selection of the seat is important. That said, it is entirely possible for the tribunal to conduct the hearing at a more convenient location than the designated seat, while still retaining the designated seat location and the applicable national arbitration law of that seat to govern procedural matters.

III. Arbitrator Selection

Most international arbitration rules provide for appointing a single arbitrator or a panel of three, deferring in the first instance to the choice of the parties and leaving it to the arbitral institution to decide if the parties cannot agree. If a three-arbitrator tribunal is chosen, the usual default means of arbitrator selection is that each party selects one arbitrator (the "party-appointed" or "wing" arbitrators), and then the two wing arbitrators confer and agree on selection of the tribunal chair. Other methods agreed by the parties (such as the increasingly popular choice of the parties agreeing on all three arbitrators) will generally be respected as well. All sets of rules also provide for the appointment of the chair by the arbitral institution if the parties are unable to agree on the chair selection. Deadlines for the wings to agree on the chair are generally fairly short, often 30 days, but this period is frequently extended in practice.

It is commonplace for parties to interview prospective candidates for their wing arbitrator selection, so long as the interview is confined to questions of availability, willingness to serve, and potential conflicts.[10] In the process of appointing the chair, it is generally considered acceptable to confer with your appointed wing about the chair candidates he or she would recommend, any suggestions you wish to make, and the candidates suggested by the other wing

10. International Arbitration Practice Guideline on Interviews for Prospective Arbitrators (Chartered Institute of Arbitrators 2015).

(this is the only time after appointment that you are permitted to have an ex parte conversation with your wing appointee). It is, however, good practice first to confirm with opposing counsel that each side can do this, as it is not a universal practice with clear rules.

Some rules (including the ICC and LCIA Rules) expressly provide that the arbitral institution will not appoint a chair who is from the country of either party and instead will select only an arbitrator from a third country. Most other institutions seem to follow this rule in practice even if not expressly provided. The practical effect of this is that you are free to reject any proposed chair candidate who is from the same country as the opposing party, on that basis alone, and you should expect that any candidates you suggest from your client's country are subject to being similarly rejected. There are occasional exceptions, generally limited to candidates who are so highly respected that they are trusted to rise above any considerations of nationality in their rulings.

Experienced practitioners in domestic arbitrations generally concur that arbitrator selection is one of the most important steps in the entire process, and this is doubly true in international arbitrations. As noted, brief interviews of potential wing arbitrator appointees are a common practice, and there is a useful set of guidelines published by CIArb that cover what can and cannot be covered in such interviews.[11] The guidelines additionally cover interviews of chair candidates (which should be done only jointly by both parties) and conferring with your chosen wing regarding potential chair candidates.[12]

It is worth expending considerable effort to find out as much as possible about the candidates for your wing appointment as well as the prospective candidates for chair. That said, this is easier said than done. You may well find yourself trying to gather information on a proposed chair candidate from Egypt or another far-flung country, and you need to be creative in finding and tapping as many sources of information as you can. There is little in the way of published information about arbitrators available, although the ICC now does make available information on how many appointments to ICC cases a particular individual has had.

Every candidate is likely to have an impressive resume, but this tells you little about what kind of arbitrator he or she will be in the context of your

---

11. *Id.*

12. *See* ICC Note to Parties and Arbitral Tribunals on the Conduct of the Arbitration under the ICC Rules of Arbitration ¶ 68 (2021) (specifying that communications with the wings about chair candidates should occur only "[t]o the extent that the parties so agree").

dispute. International arbitration practitioners are generally used to and comfortable with receiving emails or calls asking about arbitrator candidates, even from lawyers they do not know, but you should not expect a high degree of candor in the comments you obtain from lawyers you do not know well. They will likely be quite circumspect about offering any negative comments, and you will need to read between the lines a good deal when the endorsement of the candidate you are calling about seems unenthusiastic or carefully worded.

Most sets of arbitration rules now provide expressly that the appointed arbitrators must all be independent and impartial, but if there is any question whatever about this, it is good practice to confirm it expressly with the tribunal at an early point. The *IBA Guidelines on Conflicts of Interest in International Arbitration*[13] provide generally well received and sound guidance on arbitrator conflicts and disclosures, but the standard of disclosure is not as aggressive as has become the norm in U.S. arbitrations. The practice of having "party arbitrators" as the wings (as opposed to "party-appointed"), who are permitted and expected to advocate for the positions of the party who appointed them, was frequently seen in some parts of the world. But that practice has been in steady decline in recent years.

IV. Initial Pleadings: Request for Arbitration and Answer; Counterclaims

An international arbitration is generally commenced by a Request for Arbitration that is the rough equivalent of the complaint in U.S. litigation. Arbitration rules are typically specific about administrative requirements like identifying the parties and counsel, providing contact information, and providing a copy of the arbitration agreement, but the substance of what is required to be included in the Request for Arbitration and answer often is only generally stated. For example, ICC Article 4 sets out only two substantive requirements for the request: "a description of the nature and circumstances of the dispute giving rise to the claims and of the basis upon which the claims are made" and "a statement of the relief sought, together with the amounts of any quantified claims and, to the extent possible, an estimate of the monetary value of any other claims."

The difference is more in the typical practice. The ICC Rules also provide that a party "may submit such other documents or information with the

13. IBA Guidelines on Conflicts of Interest in International Arbitration (Oct. 23, 2014), https://www.ibanet.org/MediaHandler?id=e2fe5e72-eb14-4bba-b10d-d33dafee8918.

[request, answer, or counterclaim] as it considered appropriate or as may contribute to the efficient resolution of the dispute." While this may seem to be an inconsequential provision, it is not. Requests for Arbitration, answers, and counterclaims all tend to be considerably more extensive and detailed than, for example, a federal court complaint. Pleadings that run 40 to 80 pages with 20 to 30 exhibits are frequently seen. The rationales most often heard for this are, first, that counsel want to get their side of the story out early and forcefully, so as to (hopefully) predispose the tribunal a bit in their favor. A second rationale is that since document exchange will be narrow and limited, elaborating on the case in the initial pleading can be helpful in providing context as to why a particular document request is justified. A third likely reason why this practice is fairly common is that in both civil law practice and English court practice, the U.S. standard of "notice pleading" is not followed, and much more detailed "fact pleading" is the norm.

The problem with the first rationale is that the great majority of arbitrators are experienced enough that they are unlikely to be swayed one iota by the story told by either side at this early stage. Moreover, the arbitrators may well actually pay little attention to the specifics at this stage, knowing that considerably more detailed memorials will be filed setting out each side's case soon enough.

As to the second rationale, if document exchange is likely to occur before the first memorials are filed (as discussed later), there is something to the idea that you need to lay out the key issues in sufficient detail to support the rationale for your document requests. But this can generally be accomplished effectively and concisely without providing a 50-page encyclopedic description of your case. That said, simple notice pleading, such as alleging a breach of contract without specifying what the breaches are, is probably best avoided, as the expectation of greater detail is well embedded in international arbitration practice.

There is also a real risk of a too-detailed initial pleading having the opposite effect from what is intended. Unless you have thoroughly investigated your client's case before preparing your initial pleading, it is a frequent occurrence that your arguments and take on the facts will evolve to a greater or lesser degree as you become more knowledgeable about your case. American lawyers, judges, and arbitrators generally understand this and are not taken aback when a party's case changes significantly between the initial pleadings and the evidence at the hearing or trial. Many non-U.S. arbitrators, on the other hand, come from legal cultures where it is expected that the issues in the case as initially put by each party will have been thoroughly worked out in advance and will not change during the course of the proceeding. If they have diligently read your extensive and detailed initial pleading, they may well view evolutionary changes in your arguments as later presented in your memorials and posthearing arguments as an indication of either a weak case in search of a theory or, equally as bad, counsel's lack of credibility.

V. The ICC Terms of Reference and Statement of Issues to Be Determined

A feature unique to ICC Rules arbitrations, the Terms of Reference, is worth mentioning given the prominent role of the ICC Court of Arbitration in international arbitration.[14] In a manner similar to U.S. arbitration, once the initial pleadings have been filed and the tribunal fully constituted, the next order of business in an international arbitration is normally the initial case management conference. This serves much the same purposes as the scheduling conference in a domestic AAA or JAMS arbitration and results in a procedural order and procedural timetable setting out the prehearing deadlines and hearing dates. In an ICC proceeding, however, finalizing and signing the Terms of Reference is usually the first item on the agenda at this initial conference.

As set out in Article 23 of the ICC Rules, the Terms of Reference is a document signed by counsel and the tribunal that is to be prepared, in the first instance, by the tribunal. It is required to include essentially all of the administrative information about the parties, counsel, and tribunal that is in the pleadings; the applicable procedural rules; the place of arbitration; "a summary of the parties' respective claims and of the relief sought by each party"; and, perhaps most importantly, "a list of issues to be determined."

The need for the time and significant effort to prepare and agree upon the Terms of Reference (a substantial document frequently running 20 to 30 pages or more) tends to escape most American practitioners. Its primary effect, per the ICC Rules, is that once the Terms of Reference is signed, "no party shall make new claims which fall outside the limits of the Terms of Reference unless it has been authorized to do so by the arbitral tribunal."[15] This means that both the summary of your client's claims and, in particular, the list of issues to be determined as set out in the Terms of Reference should be

---

14. Also found in the SIAC Rules.

15. Most international rules expressly allow for amendments to the basic pleadings but often indicate that they should be made near the outset of the case and are allowed at the discretion of the tribunal. In practice the standard is less liberal than the federal court standard that leave to amend should be "freely granted."

carefully reviewed to be sure that the issues are worded broadly enough to cover any foreseeable modifications in the specifics of your claims. Other than that, the practical effect of the Terms of Reference is that it consolidates the basic information about the case in one place, defines the scope of the arbitration, and thus defines the tribunal's jurisdiction, and the tribunal will tend to reference the Terms of Reference in lieu of the initial pleadings as needed going forward.

Under most other sets of international arbitration rules, no Terms of Reference are provided for, but tribunals nevertheless frequently request that the parties submit at a relatively early date an agreed statement of the issues to be determined. As this document will naturally be referenced if there is a later claim of inappropriate addition of a new claim or issue in a proposed amendment, it is also well worth taking care to be sure the list of issues is accurately but inclusively worded to allow room for alternate arguments.

International arbitration rules generally provide that the tribunal is empowered to determine issues of its own jurisdiction (subject to any limits in the applicable national arbitration law). Jurisdictional issues must typically be raised with your first submission to the tribunal (usually the answer) and generally will be ruled upon separately as an initial matter.

As with domestic U.S. arbitration rules, most international rules include provisions for amending claims, for cases with more than two parties, for adding additional parties, for consolidating related arbitrations, for bifurcating hearings as may seem efficient, and for granting preaward relief when called for ("interim measures" or "measures for protection" in most international rules). Typically, the substance of these rules is not markedly different from their U.S. counterparts, but like most aspects of international arbitration, there are often more complexities in practice than might appear from the rules.

VI. Document Exchange (Disclosure) and Discovery Generally

You can be assured that the discovery process in an international arbitration will be considerably more limited even than the usual practice in most U.S. arbitrations, much less what is widely available in a U.S. court proceeding. Of the discovery tools available under the Federal Rules of Civil Procedure, for example, you can safely assume that there will not be any interrogatories, requests for admissions, or depositions. There will very likely be only a limited opportunity for document requests and production (called "disclosure" more often than document exchange) and, in some cases, a site visit. The wide-ranging scope of discovery available under the Federal Rules is generally considered both unnecessary and overly expensive. Broad, U.S.-style discovery, you will quickly learn, has a very poor reputation in the international arbitration community.

U.S. counsel often tend to file broad claims in general terms, planning to flesh out the specifics of their case largely through documents and depositions obtained in discovery, making discovery a central part of the process. In international arbitration, disclosure is more viewed as a limited opportunity to fill in specific gaps in your proof and so plays a far less central role.

The term "discovery," in fact, will not be found in international arbitration rules. Some rules do address document production specifically, but others do not. Often all you have to work with is a general power of the tribunal to direct parties to submit evidence, such as found in Article 25(4) of the ICC Rules: "At any time during the proceedings, the arbitral tribunal may summon any party to provide additional evidence."

Notwithstanding the lack of specific guidance in most sets of rules, it is a fair general statement that there has emerged a consensus—part of the melding of common law and civil law traditions that characterizes international arbitration—that a reasonable amount of disclosure (i.e., document exchange) should be permitted, but subject to limitations much stricter than what U.S. lawyers are used to.

Of the previously mentioned secondary sources that are important in international arbitration, probably the most significant is the IBA Rules on the Taking of Evidence in International Arbitration (IBA Rules; originally issued in 1999, revised most recently in 2020).[16] The IBA Rules have achieved wide acceptance and, even when not specifically adopted in a particular arbitration, are still likely to be referenced and influential as issues arise. While there are many possible permutations, the requirements of the IBA Rules for document production requests well illustrate the standard that is likely to be applied in disclosure.[17] Per Article 3(3), each request to produce documents must state

a. a description of each requested document sufficient to identify it, or a description in sufficient detail of a narrow and specific requested category of documents that are reasonably believed to exist;

16. IBA Rules on the Taking of Evidence in International Arbitration (Dec. 17, 2020), https://www.ibanet.org/MediaHandler?id=def0807b-9fec-43ef-b624-f2cb2af7cf7b.

17. *See also* ICDR Guidelines for Arbitrators Concerning Exchanges of Information (July 2012).

b. a statement as to how the documents requested are relevant to the case and material to its outcome;
c. a statement that the documents requested are not in the possession, custody, or control of the requesting party; and
d. a statement of the reasons why the requesting party assumes the documents requested are in the possession, custody, or control of the other party.

The difference between requirements similar to this and what U.S. practitioners are accustomed to is stark and ignored at your peril. Under Rule 26 of the Federal Rules of Civil Procedure, the basic standard for discoverability is "relevant to any party's claim or defense and proportional to the needs of the case," although the information sought need not be admissible in evidence. That may not sound much different from "relevant to the case and material to its outcome," as stated in the IBA Rules, but in practice it certainly is. If the relevance of a particular request is only generally described, it is likely to be denied; providing specificity is well advised.

Just as important is how the document request is phrased. As described in the JAMS equivalent to the IBA Rules,[18] document requests

- should be limited to documents that are directly relevant to significant issues in the case or to the case's outcome;
- should be restricted in terms of time frame, subject matter and persons or entities to which the requests pertain; and
- should *not include broad phraseology* such as "all documents directly or indirectly related to."[19]

If you submit a document request using typical U.S. phrasing like "all documents relating or pertaining in any manner to," you can expect that it will reflexively draw an objection characterizing it as a "fishing expedition" and, almost as reflexively, the request will be denied. In short, document requests need to be carefully thought through and narrowly worded to identify a specific and narrow category of readily discernable documents, with a clear and concise description of the importance of the requested documents to your case.

---

18. JAMS Efficiency Guidelines for the Pre-Hearing Phase of International Arbitrations (2011), https://www.jamsadr.com/international-arbitration-guidelines/.

19. Emphasis added.

In many cases, the tribunal will request that each party's document requests be set out in a "Redfern schedule."[20] This is really nothing more than a spreadsheet. The requests are numbered, and each is on a separate line. Initially, there is generally a column for setting out each request, a column for the statement of how each request is relevant and material, and a column for the response (whether an objection or agreement to produce the documents). Additional columns are then added as needed, including a column for the requesting party to respond to an objection and, at the far right, a column for the tribunal to state its ruling on the objection. Rulings will be based on the entries in the schedule (with reference back to the statement of issues, Terms of Reference, or prior pleadings and memorials as needed); there is very rarely any opportunity for oral argument.

The idea behind the Redfern schedule is to make it simple and straightforward to see in one place all the information that the tribunal needs to consider in ruling on objections to document requests and to insert the ruling itself. In practice, Redfern schedules in construction cases tend to become unwieldly documents that are a challenge to print in a reasonable-size font and cumbersome even to read on a computer screen. Especially if there are likely to be multiple objections that the tribunal will need to rule upon, the arbitrators will appreciate brevity in your additions to the schedule, avoiding the boilerplate language typically included in U.S. discovery responses and the needless repetition of objections and other statements that can greatly increase the page count (instead, state a general objection once and just reference it when appropriate, rather than repeating it).

There will also be limited or no ability to obtain documents and testimony from third parties unless they are produced voluntarily. The IBA Rules include a provision allowing a party to request the tribunal to take whatever steps are legally available in the jurisdiction to obtain relevant documents from a third party or alternatively ask for leave to do so itself. If the arbitration is seated in the United States, section 7 of the Federal Arbitration Act will apply to the same extent as it would in a domestic arbitration, giving the tribunal limited subpoena power. But for arbitrations seated elsewhere it is likely a different story.

---

20. Named for Alan Redfern, KC, a prominent London barrister and arbitrator who popularized its use.

The UNCITRAL Model Law on International Commercial Arbitration[21] in Article 27 does provide that "[t]he arbitral tribunal or a party with the approval of the arbitral tribunal may request from a competent court of this State assistance in taking evidence. The court may execute the request within its competence and according to its rules on taking evidence." While the UNCITRAL Model Law has been influential in drafting or revising the national arbitration law in many countries, it is generally not adopted wholesale, and this provision may well have been dropped or modified. In any event, resorting to the local courts to obtain evidence from a third party is likely to entail a lengthy and uncertain process at best, so third-party discovery as a practical matter is rarely pursued unless absolutely critical to the case and no alternative means of obtaining the evidence is possible.

American lawyers naturally assume that disclosure will logically take place before they have to lay out their case in detail in a Statement of Claim or Defense. But this is not how many tribunals view it, on the theory that they need to have these initial memorials in hand in order to be in a position to rule on what documents are sufficiently relevant and material to require their production. So do not be surprised if disclosure is scheduled to take place only *after* the initial exchange of memorials.

VII. Memorials: Statements of Claim, Defense, Reply, and Rebuttal

The most important written submissions in the case are the memorials, a term that includes the Statement of Claim or Case, Statement of Defense, Reply to the Statement of Defense, and (often, but not always) a Rebuttal or Rejoinder to the Reply (that is, two memorials per side). The norm is that these are sequential submissions, not simultaneous. If there is a counterclaim, it likely will be the subject of the same three or four submissions, with the dates usually being coordinated. That is, the Statement of Counterclaim will be submitted at the same time as the Statement of Defense, the Defense to the Counterclaim will be submitted with the Reply to the Claim, and so on.

Preparing and submitting the memorials in sequence consumes a considerable amount of time. In a simple case, the submissions may be separated by

21. UNCITRAL Model Law on International Commercial Arbitration (1985, amended 2006).

only 30 days, but in more complex cases it is not unusual to allow 60 days or 90 days for each submission.[22] If, for example, the agreed procedural timetable allows 90 days between each submission and there is a counterclaim, then from the filing of the Statement of Claim to the filing of the Rebuttal to the Reply to the Counterclaim will require 360 days, a full year.

There is no counterpart to these memorials in U.S. litigation or arbitrations (they are more characteristic of civil law practice), and the most important thing to appreciate about them is that they are quite substantial and labor-intensive documents (hence the need for 60 or 90 days between filings). Essentially the Statement of Claim and Statement of Defense are intended to be where you set out in detail your entire case. This means a detailed statement of each claim and the evidence supporting (or refuting) it; a detailed statement of the relief sought or defenses asserted, including the specific amounts sought for each portion of the claim; and the legal authorities relied upon in support of your positions as well as the legal arguments for or against each part of the claim. The use of numbered paragraphs to set all this out in a clear fashion is highly advisable, if not required, so that subsequent submissions can refer back to specific points by paragraph number.

What is more, unless the parties and tribunal have agreed otherwise, accompanying each memorial should be all the documentary evidence that is relied upon to support the facts and damages asserted, copies of the legal authorities cited, the witness statements of the fact witnesses with their testimony in support of the facts asserted, and any expert reports in support of your positions. The facts stated in the memorial all need to be supported by one or more witness statements or documents, and the sources should be referenced in footnotes so that they can be easily found by the tribunal.

In short, preparing the memorials in a complex construction case is a massive undertaking, and the needed time and effort can easily be underestimated by the uninitiated. The reply and rebuttal submissions in theory should be briefer and confined to responding to the other side's preceding submission. But when the second memorial is the first to have the benefit of documents

---

22. A number of international arbitration rules expressly permit a party to designate its Request for Arbitration to also serve as its Statement of Claim or designate that its Answer may also serve as its Statement of Defense (*e.g.*, LCIA Rules, art. 15.2; UNCITRAL Arbitration Rules, *supra* note 9, art. 20(1)). This can shorten the timeline to resolution of the case significantly but requires that counsel have conducted a thorough investigation of the facts before preparing the Request for Arbitration or Answer. It is generally practical only in less complex disputes.

produced by the other side, this can lead to the second submission being as long as the first. In any event, the tribunal will generally appreciate your keeping the amount of duplication from your prior memorial to a bare minimum.

There does appear to be an emerging trend of attempting to reduce the burden of producing the traditional fully supported memorials and instead allowing documentary exhibits, witness statements, and expert witness reports to be submitted at a somewhat later point, rather than accompanying the memorials. However, this is very much a discretionary decision by the tribunal, and unless you know in advance that the preferred practice of the tribunal chair is otherwise, it is best to anticipate that the traditional method will be required.

VIII. Fact Witness Statements

Written witness statements from all fact witnesses are the norm in international arbitration practice, although this is not generally apparent from the institutional rules. In fact, there will often be two witness statements from important witnesses—one submitted with the Statement of Case or Defense, and a second submitted with the Reply or Rebuttal. The witness statement *is* the direct testimony of the witness, not an outline or starting point for more detailed oral testimony. Whatever evidence needs to come from the witness needs to be set out, in numbered paragraphs, with as much detail and specifics as you would want the witness to describe in oral testimony. For a major witness, this can easily lead to a 40- to 60-page (or even longer) witness statement, which may seem cumbersome. It is somewhat cumbersome, but if broken up by topic headings and kept concise, a long statement can still read well and smoothly. It is always better if the witness statement tells a chronological story and contains other "story-like" elements, but the key is to get all the facts and evidence into the record, clearly but succinctly.

A strong witness statement is factual and specific. Unsupported opinions and generalizations are not going to carry much, if any, weight. If you include generalizations, back them up with multiple specific examples. If, for example, the intended point is that the contractor deluged the architect with Requests for Information (RFIs) asking for basic information readily obtained from the drawings and specifications, an appropriate generalization after giving examples might be: "This pattern of unnecessary RFIs recurred frequently during the period of [date] to [date]." The conclusion should follow clearly from the examples and be as specific as practicable (i.e., not "The contractor was always asking ridiculous questions").

Whenever talking about something that was documented in the record, always include a reference to the document, including date, type of document (letter, email, meeting minutes, etc.), and exhibit number. It will not do you much good for the witness to say that something is documented if you do not provide the tribunal an easy way to find the document being referenced. Using just the exhibit number as the reference is less helpful to the tribunal than including enough identifying information to avoid having to look up exhibits that the tribunal is already familiar with.

At the outset of an initial witness statement, the witness should say enough about his or her involvement in the project and the issues addressed in the statement to provide a basis for the testimony. A short summary of relevant background and experience that the witness brought to the events being described is often also needed. But prior work experience and education can often be shortened to a one- or two-paragraph summary, supplemented by reference to an attached detailed resume or CV.

It is likely apparent from the preceding that it will be a rare witness indeed who is able to produce an effective witness statement entirely on his or her own, without assistance from counsel. Providing such assistance is generally acceptable but must be done with considerable care.[23] The cardinal, inviolable rule is that everything in the witness statement must be facts that the witness knows, can testify to, and will readily confirm on cross-examination.

The most critical step is going through the draft with the witness, preferably in person, on a paragraph-by-paragraph, often line-by-line, basis. Do not just email an edited, proposed draft of the statement, asking the witness to review and approve it! Left to their own devices, many witnesses will say that the proposed version looks fine and will be ready to sign it with a tweak or two. But they will not actually have closely read it all and so may not really subscribe to each and every statement and phrase it contains. This can easily lead to major embarrassment and significant damage to the credibility of your witness, if not your entire case, when something that is stated inaccurately gets

---

23. Guideline 20 of the *IBA Guidelines on Party Representation in International Arbitration* (2013), frequently adopted by many tribunals in the first procedural order, specifies that counsel may assist witnesses in the preparation of their witness statements and experts in the preparation of their reports, subject to important limitations like not encouraging or soliciting false statements. Keep in mind that in many legal systems, it is not considered ethical to meet with or interview fact witnesses in advance of their testimony. As the *IBA Guidelines on Party Representation* and the ICC Rules (art. 4(3)) provide, this is not the norm in international arbitration.

highlighted on cross-examination at the hearing. So, while time-consuming, it is a vital step to go through the statement with the witness in detail and make sure everything is consistent with his or her recollection and the relevant documents.

It is increasingly popular to paste the relevant snippets from key documents into the body of the witness statement. This can be particularly helpful and effective when the witness is adding context to or elaborating on an exhibit, such as describing what a drawing is showing. This should be reserved for key documents, however, as it can easily be overdone and can add unduly to the length of the statement. Another recent innovation is to add a picture of the witness on the cover sheet of the statement. After the hearing, this can help tribunal members who recall faces better than names to quickly reorient themselves to the witness's live testimony.

Repetition is the bane of witness statements. Just because a point is important does not mean it needs to be restated several times or repeated verbatim in multiple witness statements. Saying it once and clearly is usually far preferable; a repetitive witness statement invites the reader to skim rather than read closely. If it is necessary to refer back to a key point when it ties into later testimony, a brief mention to refresh recollection (and a reference to the applicable paragraphs earlier in the statement) is all that is necessary. The tribunal likely has a large pile of witness statements and exhibits to review and will respect clear and concise witness statements that are focused, without repetition.

This is doubly true with Reply or Rebuttal witness statements. There is a temptation to repeat information that was in the original statement before adding the new information. Resist this. Repetition in a Reply or Rebuttal statement just leaves the impression that counsel thought the witness should submit something in response to contrary testimony from the opposing party but really has very little to add. More importantly, it risks burying the truly new and important testimony that the witness can add by way of reply or rebuttal.

IX. Exhibits and Bundles

Documentary exhibits can be submitted either as freestanding exhibits accompanying one of your two memorials or as exhibits to a witness statement or expert report (where the witness provides foundation or context respecting the document or offers testimony related to the document). Every exhibit you want to have in the record should be submitted in connection with either your first or second memorial, unless otherwise specifically permitted. Procedural orders typically allow for the possibility of adding exhibits at the hearing, but only where good cause can be shown as to why they could not have been submitted earlier. You should expect that this requirement will be assiduously enforced by the tribunal, and be assured that it is not in your interest for the tribunal to perceive that you are attempting to gain advantage by withholding exhibits until the hearing.

For ease of future reference and to avoid confusion, you should plan from the outset how you are going to number exhibits. Often exhibit marking is covered in a procedural order, but if not, it is generally acceptable either to number exhibits accompanying a witness statement in a manner that ties them to the witness (e.g., Smith Ex. 5) or to reference a single set of exhibits (e.g., Claimant's Exhibit 22). In construction cases it will generally be more efficient and less confusing to use a single numbering system. Multiple witnesses may reference the same document, and a common numbering system means they always reference the same exhibit number. And if exhibits are later reorganized into hearing bundles (discussed next), a single numbering system significantly reduces confusion. A possible exception is the resume or CV of a witness. This can be referenced as "Smith Attachment A," since other witnesses will not be referencing it, and attached to the witness statement for ready reference.

European arbitrators in particular are fond of asking the parties to prepare and submit a series of bundles (sometimes "core bundles" or "hearing bundles") prior to the hearing. Bundles do not include anything that has not been previously prepared or produced but rather are compilations of documents related to the case that have been previously submitted and reorganized by type and, conceptually at least, are more convenient for the counsel and tribunal to utilize at the hearing and reference in briefs. So when you reference exhibits orally at the hearing or in your prehearing or posthearing brief, you include the exhibit number but also the bundle designation and page number. This effort may seem at the time like little more than a large make-work project for your paralegals, but if the task is handled properly, you will likely find the bundle system a quicker and easier way to access a document, whether electronically or in hard copy (both are often required).

An example list of bundles that may be called for in a prehearing procedural order is as follows:

Bundle A—Initial Pleadings and Memorials (without exhibits)

Bundle B—Witness Statements (without exhibits)

Bundle C—Key Fact Exhibits (as agreed by the parties)

Bundle D—Expert Reports (without exhibits)

Bundle E—Legal Authorities

Bundle F—Procedural Orders and Correspondence (to and from the tribunal)

Bundle G—All Fact Exhibits

Bundle H—Expert Reports (with exhibits)

Bundle I—Photographs

In this list, the intent of Bundles B, C, and D is to have reasonably sized and at hand at least 90 percent of what will be referred to at the hearing, with only occasional need to refer to the more complete document sets in Bundles G and H. It is also important to take the time to prepare an accurate and useful index to each bundle, so that a desired document can be quickly located.

Documents to be used solely for purposes of impeachment, and not previously submitted, present a particular problem (as they tend to do in many U.S. arbitrations). Many tribunals will expect such impeachment documents to be included in the hearing bundle (Bundle G), but some will allow their use even if not included in a hearing bundle. It is accordingly wise for counsel to discuss and agree in advance how impeachment exhibits will be handled at the hearing.

X. Expert Witnesses

There are several important differences in how expert witnesses are dealt with in international arbitration. To start, it has become common to require each expert to submit, in his or her written report, a certification attesting, among other points, that his or her stated opinions are "impartial, objective, [and] unbiased" and "ha[ve] not been influenced by the pressures of the dispute resolution process or by any party to the arbitration." The certification also confirms the expert's understanding that "my duty in giving evidence in this arbitration is to assist the arbitral tribunal [to] decide the issues," rather than to support or refute a particular party's claims.[24] It is an open question whether such certifications have had the intended effect of reducing the likelihood of

24. Chartered Inst. of Arbs., *Protocol for the Use of Party-Appointed Expert Witnesses in International Arbitration*, art. 8 (Sept. 2007), https://www.ciarb.org/media/6824/partyappointedexpertsinternationalarbitration.pdf.

experts acting as "hired guns" for the party who appointed them, and opinions of counsel on the practical effect of such certifications vary widely.

The most significant potential difference respecting experts in international arbitration, however, is the use of tribunal-appointed experts, either in supplementation to or in lieu of party-appointed experts. Most international arbitration rules expressly provide for such tribunal appointments to be made "after consultation with the parties," meaning the tribunal has the final say and the authority to disregard any objections from the parties.[25] Sometimes a tribunal expert is appointed where the tribunal desires expert input on a particular issue but the parties have not named experts on the subject. More commonly, the tribunal either believes (in advance of receiving the party-appointed expert reports) that it is not competent to rule on a technical issue even with the assistance of party-appointed experts or (after receiving those reports) remains uncomfortable with deciding between the opposing opinions that have been stated. Use of tribunal-appointed experts is not common, in part because of the added costs involved, but it is by no means rare either.

Article 6 of the IBA Rules sets out the procedure most often adopted when a tribunal expert is appointed. The tribunal establishes the scope of the expert's engagement, after consultation with the parties, and the parties have an opportunity to object to the proposed qualifications or independence of the proposed expert. After delivery of the expert's report to the tribunal and parties, the parties can respond via additional witness statements, expert reports, or other submissions. Then at the hearing, the tribunal and counsel (and sometimes even the party-appointed experts) all have the opportunity to question the tribunal-appointed expert. Tribunal-appointed experts are often also authorized to meet separately with the party-appointed experts before delivering their report, with the aim of identifying areas of common ground and areas of disagreement.

American counsel often are uncomfortable with the concept of a tribunal-appointed expert, whether due to unfamiliarity with the procedure, its added cost, or the loss of any semblance of control over what are likely to be quite influential expert opinions. Underlying this is often a fear that the tribunal may just adopt the opinions of its appointed expert without detailed consideration of the differing opinions of the party-appointed experts. But the reality is that if the tribunal expresses strong interest in a tribunal-appointed expert, it is quite likely to happen despite any objections, and you will need to adjust your perspective and make the best of it.

25. *E.g.*, ICC Rules of Arbitration, art. 25(4) (Jan. 1, 2021); UNCITRAL Arbitration Rules, *supra* note 9, art. 29.

Another common feature where there are only party-appointed experts on a topic is an added procedural step that takes place after all the expert reports are submitted. The competing experts on the particular subject (such as delay, damages, or a particular alleged defect in the work) are required to confer (usually in the absence of counsel) and agree on a list of points where they agree, along with those where they disagree. These lists are set out in an agreed joint report to the tribunal and parties. This report most often is quite brief, often only two to three pages, but in other cases the experts actually draft jointly a more extensive report.

The concept is that if the experts are truly independent and have their represented expertise, they should reach the same or almost the same conclusions on many matters, and the expert testimony and questioning at the hearing can then focus more efficiently on the areas of disagreement. Accounting/damages experts, for example, can frequently agree on issues such as the amount of costs actually incurred in various categories, while still disagreeing whether those costs are potentially recoverable as damages if the ruling on the merits is favorable. This practice works effectively enough that it is occasionally creeping into domestic U.S. arbitrations as well.

The final significant difference relates to when expert evidence is heard during the merits hearing. As stated in the IBA Rules (Article 8(3)), "ordinarily" all fact witnesses, from both sides, testify first, followed by all experts. This is so that the experts can incorporate any changes in their opinions that might be needed based on the oral testimony of the fact witnesses. It also helps the tribunal in that the contrasting expert opinions will be presented closer together in time than if all the claimant's witnesses testify before any of the respondent's witnesses. It similarly accommodates the trend to have opposing experts on the same issue testify jointly (as discussed further later).

XI. Additional Submissions

To a significantly greater degree than is the norm in U.S. arbitrations, tribunals in international construction arbitrations are not shy about requesting the parties to make additional submissions that will facilitate their task. These can take any number of forms, limited only by the tribunal's imagination. According to the recent ICC Arbitration and ADR Commission Report on Construction Industry Arbitrations (ICC Construction Arbitration Report),[26]

---

26. *ICC Arbitration and ADR Commission Report on Construction Industry Arbitrations: Recommended Tools and Techniques for Effective Management* (Feb. 18, 2019),

the recommended practice includes requesting early on (1) a list of the key persons involved ("dramatis personae" or "cast of characters"), (2) a chronology of relevant events, and (3) a glossary of case-specific terms. The procedure recommended is to have each party submit these and then require the parties to merge them into single documents, which can thereafter be supplemented as need be.

Where a list of issues to be determined has been submitted earlier in the process, it is fairly standard practice to request an updated list shortly before the hearing, which can then serve as a checklist for the tribunal in writing the award. If additional issues emerge during the hearing, the tribunal may ask yet again for a final list of issues after the hearing.

Substantial construction disputes often encompass a large number of discrete claims, such as a sizable list of disputed change proposals, disputed punchlist and warranty items, or alleged delaying events. How best to manage such cases and the likelihood of confusion they entail are challenging issues in domestic and international arbitrations alike. The answer in international arbitration practice is most frequently to require the parties to collaborate in preparing one or more schedules as a tool to present in streamlined form the essential elements of each party's case. These schedules take the form of a spreadsheet (often called a Scott schedule or alternatively another form of Redfern schedule). The ICC Construction Arbitration Report contains an extensive discussion of the use of such schedules, along with two illustrative examples. In the example of a Schedule for Additional Work and Disputed Valuation, the column headings suggested are:

Item number

Items of extra work claimed

Claimant's case, including by whom ordered and when

Claimant's valuation

Respondent's case

Price, if any, admitted by the respondent

A final column for use by arbitral tribunal

---

https://iccwbo.org/publication/construction-industry-arbitrations-report-icc-commission-arbitration-adr/.

When budgeting for an international arbitration, it is wise to allow for a significant amount of effort in preparing additional submissions such as these that may be requested by the tribunal but that are not usually a part of U.S. practice.

XII. Conduct of the Hearing

As noted previously, international arbitration rules (and even more specific guidance such as the IBA Rules) tend to be quite vague with respect to the specifics of how a hearing is to be conducted, leaving most matters to the discretion of the tribunal. If the tribunal, and most particularly the chair, has a common-law background, the hearing will in all likelihood proceed much in the manner that a domestic arbitration hearing would, with the usual sequence of direct (but done via the witness's written statements), cross, and redirect examination of each witness. If the tribunal's orientation is more to civil law, you may well find that the tribunal (starting with the chair and then moving to the wings) takes the lead in examining witnesses, with counsel able to ask questions of the witness only once the tribunal is done.

It is not uncommon for the tribunal simply to assume that counsel is already familiar with the details of how it will conduct the hearing, leading to a considerable potential for surprises when the day arrives. The best way for U.S.-trained counsel to anticipate the specific hearing procedure and avoid surprises is to assume nothing and ask a lot of questions in advance as to how the process will unfold. The risk of appearing naïve or uninformed usually pales compared to the challenges of dealing on the fly with surprises, and questions asked politely have little risk of offending the tribunal.

That said, there are a number of aspects of the hearing that you can reasonably anticipate. First, there will likely be an opportunity to submit a prehearing brief shortly before the hearing. Given the prior extensive filings in memorials covering the evidence, the tribunal may suggest that focusing on the legal issues and the context in which they will arise is desirable at this stage. Notwithstanding the prehearing brief, upon request there may additionally be an opportunity allowed for an opening statement. Second, the tribunal is likely to make an express allocation of the available hearing time between the parties in advance, to assure completion of the hearing within the agreed duration. This is specifically recommended in the ICC Construction Arbitration Report and is a common practice. The allocation need not be equal, depending on the number of witnesses each party asks to examine and how many of them will be testifying through interpreters.

Assuming the fact witnesses have all submitted witness statements, the tribunal will likely establish a deadline well before the hearing when each party needs to indicate which of the other party's witnesses it desires to cross-examine. Oftentimes there will be some minor witnesses for whom cross-examination is not really necessary (or at least not worth the time it will take), or alternatively the risk of highlighting the adverse testimony the witness has provided outweighs any damage likely to be accomplished on cross. Witnesses not requested to be present for cross-examination are excused, and their witness statement is simply admitted as is (although this is without any implication that the opposing party accepts or concedes its accuracy).

If a witness is requested to appear at the hearing but fails to do so, his or her witness statement will be either disregarded entirely or, alternatively, given little or no weight by the tribunal, in its discretion. While rarely encountered in practice, most international arbitration rules also allow the tribunal to insist that a witness appear, even when the parties do not propose to call or cross-examine that witness.

The testimony of fact witnesses at the hearing typically begins with a short period (five to ten minutes is generally allowed) where the party presenting the witness asks the witness to confirm his or her witness statement and to identify any errors and corrections that may be needed (the colloquial term for this short introductory examination is "seat warming"). Nothing new can be added in seat warming, unless the witness can rebut something that came up only after his or her final witness statement was submitted. The witness is then turned over for cross-examination (or examination by the tribunal in the civil law model) followed by redirect as needed. The scope of cross is generally not limited to the scope of the witness statements, and counsel will usually be allowed to explore any other material issue within the knowledge of the witness. Objections during cross, while not prohibited, are generally not welcomed, to an extent even greater than in U.S. arbitration practice.

After redirect, American lawyers might then expect an opportunity for further limited rounds of questioning (recross, re-redirect, etc.), but beware that this may not be automatically allowed. In some cases, the chair may permit only an added question or two in an unusual situation.

For those not used to cross-examining key witnesses without the benefit of a discovery deposition, you are likely to find that preparing for cross is in many ways easier under this system, since you have the precise testimony of the witness in hand, often for months in advance, and plenty of time to locate documents contradicting the witness statement and prepare other lines of questioning. Keep in mind also that the technique of bringing out the main points of your case on cross is doubly effective in this system, since in terms of the oral evidence you effectively get to go first with cross, as the direct is all in writing.

The use of joint testimony of experts with the same area of expertise (colloquially "hot-tubbing") and, to a lesser extent, fact witness panels is seen frequently in international arbitrations. Since there are many possible variations as to how to conduct such joint testimony, the tribunal will often suggest a protocol in advance, subject to comments from counsel. If they do not, it may be advisable to suggest this, so you can best prepare your witnesses for what to expect. Most often, joint testimony of experts will start by allowing each expert an agreed period to make a presentation in lieu of direct examination, generally accompanied by PowerPoint slides (preferably with hard copies of the slides provided to the tribunal for taking notes) covering the main opinions in his or her report, without adding anything new. This is then followed by questioning by the tribunal and counsel, although the order and manner vary. Such joint testimony, in combination with the joint expert report previously referenced, is quite effective at reducing the total hearing time needed for the experts and focusing quickly on the important issues in dispute.

Fact witness panels can also be an effective time saver and work best when you are presenting multiple witnesses who cover different aspects of the same issue. For example, if the contractor had three project managers over the course of the project and the relevant events spanned the tenures of all three, presenting them for cross-examination in panel format can aid considerably in having their testimony be presented clearly and coherently. A question directed at one panel witness that more relates to the tenure of another can be answered at one time by both witnesses involved. Apparent contradictions that may arise during cross can also be cleared up more easily on redirect when both of the people involved are on the panel. Similarly, a witness panel to address a particular group of related change orders can be very efficient in getting all relevant points regarding those change orders presented at once. The tribunal may inquire as to whether there are any combinations of witnesses best presented in panel format. Otherwise, counsel should suggest this well in advance of the hearing, when desirable.

Finally, closing arguments at the hearing are quite rare, and the norm is to submit posthearing briefs instead. The timing and format of the posthearing submissions are often left for discussion and direction by the tribunal at the hearing, however.

XIII. Translation and Interpretation Issues

As English is a predominant language in international business, it follows that the majority of international arbitrations are conducted in English, sometimes even when neither party is from an English-speaking country. In fact, the ICC reports that 80 percent of ICC awards are in English, presumably meaning that English was the language of the arbitration.[27] However, it is a very common occurrence that many of the witnesses for one or both parties are much more comfortable in their non-English native language or speak no English at all. Moreover, a party that is sending and receiving contract communications to the other party in English (as the language of the contract) may well be nevertheless using a different language for all its internal communications, as well as communications with outside consultants and subcontractors from its home country. Accordingly, there is a good chance that you will encounter a need for translation and interpretation services in the course of the proceeding.

The general rule (though it is generally not found in the institutional arbitration rules) is that all submissions to the tribunal need to be translated into the official language of the arbitration, either as specified in the arbitration provision or as determined by the tribunal. The original document should always be submitted with the translation. This applies equally to exhibits, witness statements, and expert reports.[28] The cost of translation is borne by the party submitting the document. Obtaining a good translation, particularly when numerous documents are involved, requires significant lead time, and accordingly you need to plan for this when preparing memorials or other evidentiary submissions. You always have the right to timely object to the other party's translation of any document, but of course that requires having someone available who speaks the foreign language fluently to review the original document and compare it to the proposed translation.

The situation in respect to disclosure is less clear. If you are representing the owner in a dispute with a Japanese contractor, you can reasonably expect that many, if not all, of the documents you receive in disclosure will be in Japanese. If you have a basis to assert that this imposes an unfair hardship on your client, via motion you can attempt to transfer the burden and cost of translating

---

27. *ICC 2020 Statistics*, *supra* note 6, at 19.

28. For documents mainly consisting of numbers using Arabic numerals, such as a cost report or other accounting record, it may well be sufficient to translate column headings and other notations in the form of a key or translation guide, rather than reproduce the entire document.

the Japanese documents to the Japanese party, but the outcome is not likely to be positive. Many tribunals are content to leave translation to you, since you asked for the documents.

At the hearing, a witness who does not speak the language of the arbitration with reasonable fluency will generally be allowed to testify in his or her native language, at the advance request of counsel. The party proffering the witness is responsible for providing the interpreter to accomplish this. If your level of trust of the other party or the skills of the interpreter is low, you may need to employ your own interpreter to follow the questions, the answers, and their interpretation and raise issues at the time. Counsel objections to the interpretation in real time are cumbersome and time consuming but may be necessary. Mistakes in interpretation are easy to make in a construction case involving a lot of technical terms, and the court reporter will be transcribing only in the official language. This means that only the erroneous interpretation of the answer by the witness (possibly to an erroneously interpreted question) will appear in the transcript, eliminating any ability to later object to the translation.

Questioning with reasonable efficiency a witness testifying in another language is a skill that may take some practice. The usual sequence is that your question will be translated, the witness will answer in his or her native language, and the answer will then be translated. The time lag involved is significant, a test of patience for everyone in attendance. If, for example, you tend to frequently strike your question and reframe it more clearly, you will likely find that the interpreter is already translating your question before you realize that it should be reframed, and you must wait for the cycle to complete before reasking your question. Similarly, an adverse witness is just as likely as elsewhere to ask for clarification of the question before answering, again requiring a separate interpretation cycle before any answer is obtained. All in all, you should figure that you will be fortunate if the time required to question a witness through an interpreter is only two or three times as long as the same examination conducted in one language.

Given the challenges of fully interpreted testimony, an alternative approach, which has been gaining traction in recent years when a witness is semifluent in the language of the arbitration, is to have an interpreter on standby who can consult with the witness if the witness does not understand a particular word or phrase. When this method is used, the examination proceeds in English until the witness has trouble understanding a particular question or phrase, at which point the witness asks the interpreter (in his or her native language) to clarify. The ensuing colloquy between the witness and the interpreter is not translated but rather is summarized by the interpreter for the benefit of the tribunal and the record. Then the witness proceeds to answer in English. It is an imperfect solution, to be sure, but it has the benefit of speeding up the proceeding considerably as compared to full interpretation.

XIV. Posthearing Submissions

The tribunal will generally provide instructions as to what it desires by way of posthearing submissions. The possibilities cover a wide range: from oral arguments presented at a later date (in lieu of or after posthearing briefing), to written responses to a list of specific questions provided by the tribunal, to a full posthearing brief with record references, to a complete draft award, similar to proposed findings of fact and conclusions of law. There may or may not be an opportunity for a reply submission; the availability of an opportunity to reply should not be assumed.

On request, the tribunal may well permit a few supplementary evidentiary submissions, responding to points that came up late in the hearing, before formally closing the record.

XV. The Award and Postaward Motions

International arbitration awards tend to be lengthy and detailed, frequently hundreds of pages in a complex construction dispute. The reasons for this go well beyond the inherent complexity of the disputes. The tribunal has no way of knowing in what country a reviewing court, asked to enforce the award, might be sitting. As mentioned later, enforcement proceedings are not limited to the country of the arbitral seat or the countries where the parties are headquartered. Since court rules and proceedings regarding enforcement differ significantly among countries, it is generally considered that the safest course for the tribunal is to include everything in the award itself that a reviewing court might need to know in determining whether to enforce the award.

This normally leads to the tribunal including in the award a detailed recitation of the procedural history of the arbitration proceeding, to make clear that both parties had an opportunity at every procedural and substantive step to express their views. Additionally, this consideration leads to the tribunal setting out in considerable detail the factual and legal basis and reasoning for its findings and conclusions, so that the tribunal's careful consideration and reasoning to reach its conclusions are apparent from the face of the award. The result is a quite lengthy and detailed award compared to what is generally seen in domestic arbitrations.

It follows that preparing the award often takes considerable time, and this can be the most frustrating aspect of international arbitration—the protracted wait for the result. It is unfortunately not uncommon for awards to be issued eight to 12 months after the posthearing submissions are completed, notwithstanding efforts by the arbitral institutions to encourage more prompt issuance.

Awards are not made public, although the ICC has instituted a transparency initiative providing that awards made in 2019 or later will be released two years after they are rendered, unless a party objects. Parties can also request the right to redact identifying information prior to release. It is too soon at this point to tell how many awards will actually be released and whether other arbitral institutions will follow ICC's lead. Awards can also become public via the confirmation process, when the confirming court does not consider the award to contain information requiring confidentiality protection.

International arbitration rules do not generally allow for requests for reconsideration as such but do typically allow for postaward changes if requested by a party within a short time, usually 30 days. The types of changes that the tribunal is authorized to make generally include (1) correcting errors in computation, clerical and typographic errors, and errors of a similar nature; (2) interpretations of the award, meaning clarification of some aspect that a party believes to be unclear; and (3) an additional or supplementary award on an issue in the case that a party points out was not decided in the primary award. Short periods are generally allowed for objections or responses to such requests and for the tribunal to issue its determination of the request and any appropriate change or supplement. The ICC 2020 Statistics indicate that a request for some type of postaward modification is made in about 28 percent of cases.[29]

XVI. Costs, Including Attorney's Fees

International arbitration rules generally include a broad provision authorizing the tribunal to fix the costs of the arbitration and decide which of the parties shall bear them and in what proportions. The definition of what is included in "costs" generally encompasses the administrative fees of the arbitral institution, the fees and expenses of the arbitrators, and the fees and expenses of any experts appointed by the tribunal and expressly also includes the legal fees and other costs incurred by the parties.

29. *ICC 2020 Statistics*, *supra* note 6, at 20 (109 requests and 383 final awards).

The general principle of "loser pays" is widely and regularly applied. That said, it is not generally applied in an all-or-nothing manner. The applicable rules generally permit the tribunal considerable discretion in the manner of awarding costs that are considered "reasonable" under the circumstances and often expressly permit an apportioning process. The ICC Rules make this broad discretion quite clear: "In making decisions as to costs, the arbitral tribunal may take into account such circumstances as it considers relevant, including the extent to which each party has conducted the arbitration in an expeditious and cost-effective manner."[30] The distinction is subtle but critical in construction cases, where substantial counterclaims are frequently asserted, and it is rare for either party to recover 100 percent of its claimed damages. All in all, you can reasonably expect that a significant sum, including at least some of the legal fees, will change hands by way of the award on costs, although it may well be considerably less than either side's total eligible costs.

Costs are generally handled in one of two ways. The first method, which has the advantage of shortening the total time needed to conclude the case, is to require both parties to submit their entire claimed costs as a posthearing submission, with substantiating records and invoices, often a short time after submission of the final posthearing briefs. The allocation of costs is then addressed and determined in the final award.

The second method is to issue an interim award on the merits first, along with directions as to whether one or both parties should submit their costs. The tribunal's direction may also include in some cases instructions as to segregating particular aspects of the costs, such as where the tribunal considers that one party has substantially complicated the proceeding and magnified costs by arguing an issue at length that the tribunal considers to have been particularly unsubstantiated or avoidable. The fixing of costs is then included in a revised final award. This method can have the benefit of reducing the burden on the parties, at least to the extent it does not require both parties to submit the entirety of their claimed costs, as well as allowing the tribunal to make cost allocations on a more granular basis.

Under either approach, the opposing party will generally have an opportunity to comment on the costs claimed by the other. However, decisions on costs

---

30. ICC Rules of Arbitration, *supra* note 25, art. 38(5). The ICDR Rules contain a similar provision: "The tribunal may allocate such costs among the parties if it determines that allocation is reasonable, taking into account the circumstances of the case." International Centre for Dispute Resolution, International Dispute Resolution Procedures (Mar. 2021), art. 37.

are normally made on the written submissions, without a hearing. Finally, some arbitration rules expressly permit interim awards of costs, such as where significant portions of the case are disposed of in advance of the primary merits hearing, but this is relatively rarely done.

XVII. Enforcing the Award

Enforcing an international arbitration award is a vast and complex subject in itself, but as stated at the outset, it is important for prospective claimants to give significant thought in advance of filing the Request for Arbitration to the possibilities for enforcing an eventual award, presuming success in the arbitration. As in domestic practice, if an award is not paid voluntarily, it must be enforced by a court having jurisdiction over the party against whom the award has been entered. In domestic practice, the basis for enforcement is provided by the Federal Arbitration Act or an individual state arbitration act, all of which provide for an expedited enforcement proceeding and quite limited circumstances when an arbitration award will *not* be enforced.

In international practice, the equivalent basis for enforcement is usually the New York Convention on the Recognition and Enforcement of Foreign Arbitration Awards (the NY Convention).[31] Signed in 1958, the NY Convention is not only critical to enforcing international arbitration awards but also considered a major milestone in the development of international trade generally.

It is not an overstatement to say that the NY Convention and its brethren make international commercial arbitration not only feasible but also the clearly preferred means of resolving international contract disputes. If you bring litigation against an opposing party in a country that has jurisdiction over that party and are lucky enough to obtain a judgment, enforcing that judicial judgment in another country is not governed by clear treaty terms like the NY Convention. It is instead a matter of the general principles of international comity, which are considerably more fluid. Accordingly, while invoking the NY Convention and obtaining an enforceable judgment in a foreign country is often not simple

31. There are other treaties on the subject, some predating the New York Convention and some postdating it, but the New York Convention is by far the most significant. The New York Convention applies only where the parties are from different countries, even if they have chosen a set of international arbitration rules to govern the proceeding. If the parties are from the same country, the arbitration law of the arbitral seat will govern enforcement instead, and enforcing the award in a country other than that of the seat is also likely dependent upon the law applicable in that jurisdiction.

or fast, it is considerably easier than is the case in international litigation, with only rare exceptions. Over 160 countries are signatories to the NY Convention, and the exceptions are a few countries that are not significantly involved in international commerce.[32]

Like the Federal Arbitration Act, the NY Convention mainly addresses two essential points. The first is that courts in signatory countries are required to "recognize" a written agreement to arbitrate and to refer the case to arbitration when it involves parties to such an agreement. The second is that courts in signatory countries are required to recognize international arbitration awards as binding and to enforce them, subject only to the limited grounds in Article V of the NY Convention for refusing to enforce an award. Those grounds are:

> 1(a) The parties to the [arbitration] agreement . . . were, under the law applicable to them, under some incapacity, or the said agreement is not valid under the law which the parties have subjected it . . . ;
>
> 1(b) The party against whom the award is invoked was not given proper notice of the appointment of the arbitrator or of the arbitration proceedings or was otherwise unable to present his case;
>
> 1(c) The award deals with a difference not contemplated by or not falling within the terms of the submission to arbitration, or it contains decisions on matters beyond the scope of the submission to arbitration [with a proviso allowing enforcement of matters that *were* submitted to arbitration if they can be segregated];
>
> 1(d) The composition of the arbitral authority or the arbitral procedure was not in accordance with the agreement of the parties, or, failing such agreement, was not in accordance with the law of the country where the arbitration took place;
>
> 1(e) The award has not yet become binding on the parties, or has been set aside or suspended by a competent authority of the country in which, or under the law of which, it was made.
>
> 2. Recognition and enforcement of an arbitral award may also be refused if the competent authority in the country where recognition and enforcement is sought finds that:

---

32. *Contracting States—List of Contracting States*, N.Y. ARB. CONVENTION, https://www.newyorkconvention.org/list+of+contracting+states (last visited Apr. 27, 2023).

(a) The subject matter of the difference is not capable of settlement by arbitration under the law of that country; or

(b) The recognition or enforcement of the award would be contrary to the public policy of that country.

What the NY Convention therefore permits is that you can take an international arbitration award and seek to enforce it in any signatory country, generally so long as the award was issued in a signatory country.[33] The main requirement is that the courts of the enforcing country must have jurisdiction over the party you want to enforce the award against. Of course, in order for you to collect the enforced award, that party must also have assets in the country (whether bank accounts or tangible assets like a factory or distribution center) that the court is able to reach via its attachment and collection powers. You are not limited to a single country, so where the availability of attachable assets in a given country is in question, you can seek enforcement in multiple countries in parallel.

It should be apparent that the drafters of the NY Convention did their best to make the exceptions to enforcement as clear and narrow as practicable. Nevertheless, enforcement disputes are not uncommon, especially with large awards, and seem only to be increasing in recent years. These disputes can be protracted and expensive, especially if enforcement actions are required in more than one country in the search for assets to satisfy the award.

Tribunals are usually well aware of the potential for challenges to enforcement of their Award and of the grounds for refusing enforcement under the NY Convention. They accordingly take care in conducting the arbitration to avoid any actions that might give rise to arguments under an enforcement exception. However, counsel are also well advised to keep the NY Convention exceptions in mind and be alert to any procedural missteps the tribunal may inadvertently make. Most commonly this can involve taking up for decision a matter arguably outside the scope of the arbitration agreement or varying the arbitration procedure in a manner inconsistent with the arbitration agreement or the specified arbitration rules. Even if the tribunal is taking an action favorable to your client, it is generally still wise to point out politely the potential problem rather than to jeopardize the award.

All in all, international commercial arbitration in the context of construction disputes offers several challenges and inefficiencies not often encountered

33. This reciprocity requirement is not stated in the NY Convention but is a qualification imposed by many signatory countries, including the United States.

in domestic arbitrations and involves substantial variations in the specific procedures utilized. But it is nevertheless a generally effective means of resolving disputes and shifting monetary losses to the responsible party. In any event, it is the best game in town when disputes cannot be otherwise settled.

XVIII. Resources for International Construction Arbitration

Locations of the various secondary guidelines, reports, and rules referenced in the text or footnotes, and a sampling of the many other readily available and useful online resources, are provided here.

1. New York Convention, including text, list of signatory countries, judicial decisions under the Convention, and more. https://www.newyorkconvention.org/
2. International Chamber of Commerce (ICC), International Court of Arbitration, including ICC Arbitration Rules and *Practice Notes, Forms & Checklists*. https://iccwbo.org/dispute-resolution-services/arbitration/
3. Published ICC arbitral awards. https://jusmundi.com/en/partnership/ICC
4. London Court of International Arbitration (LCIA), including LCIA Rules and *Guidance Notes*. https://www.lcia.org/Dispute_Resolution_Services/LCIA_Arbitration.aspx
5. Singapore International Arbitration Centre (SIAC), SIAC Rules. https://siac.org.sg/siac-rules
6. Hong Kong International Arbitration Centre (HKIAC), HKIAC Rules. https://www.hkiac.org/arbitration/rules-practice-notes
7. JAMS, including JAMS International Arbitration Rules and *JAMS Efficiency Guidelines for the Pre-Hearing Phase of International Arbitrations*. https://www.jamsadr.com/adr-rules-procedures/
8. International Center for Dispute Resolution (ICDR), AAA international rules. https://www.icdr.org/rules_forms_fees
9. International Institute for Conflict Prevention & Resolution. https://drs.cpradr.org/rules
10. United Nations Commission on International Trade Law (UNCITRAL), including UNCITRAL Arbitration Rules, Model Law on International Commercial Arbitration, and *Notes on Organizing Arbitral Proceedings*. https://uncitral.un.org/en/texts/arbitration

11. International Bar Association (IBA), including guidelines and rules. https://www.ibanet.org/resources. In addition to the IBA Evidence Rules, the *IBA Guidelines on Party Representation in International Arbitration* (2013) and the *IBA Guidelines on Conflicts of Interest in International Arbitration* (2014) are particularly significant.
12. Chartered Institute of Arbitrators (CIArb). CIArb's collection of guidelines currently includes 16 titles, covering numerous relevant subjects—among them jurisdictional challenges, interim relief, expert testimony, use of technology, and multiparty arbitrations. https://www.ciarb.org/resources/guidelines-ethics/international-arbitration/
13. *International Commercial Arbitration: A Guide for U.S. Judges* (S.I. Strong 2012). Directed at U.S. judges who may be presented with issues related to international commercial arbitrations. https://www.fjc.gov/content/international-commercial-arbitration-guide-us-judges-0
14. J. Hinchey & T. Harris, *International Construction Arbitration Handbook* (Thomson Reuters 2016). This is a very comprehensive two-volume treatise covering all aspects of both arbitration agreements and the arbitration itself.
15. University of London, Queen Mary School of International Arbitration, publishes research studies and annual surveys regarding aspects of international arbitration. https://arbitration.qmul.ac.uk/research/